FROM THE
BLOODY
HEART

The embalmed heart of Robert the Bruce,
which Lord James Douglas carried into battle
against the Moors in Spain,
became the badge of the Douglas family
and one of the inspirations
behind years of plotting
to undermine the kings of Scotland.

The Bloody Heart blaz'd in the van,
Announcing Douglas, dreaded name!

Walter Scott, *The Lay of the Last Minstrel*

Wine is strong, the king is stronger,
even stronger are women,
but the truth is strongest of all.

Inscription believed to have been requested
by Elizabeth Douglas for the crypt door
of Rosslyn Chapel

FROM THE BLOODY HEART

THE STEWARTS AND THE DOUGLASES

OLIVER THOMSON

SUTTON PUBLISHING

First published in 2003 by
Sutton Publishing Limited · Phoenix Mill
Thrupp · Stroud · Gloucestershire · GL5 2BU

British Library Cataloguing in Publication Data
A catalogue record for this book is available from the British Library.

ISBN 0-7509-3078-0

Typeset in 10/12 pt New Baskerville.
Typesetting and origination by
Sutton Publishing Limited.
Printed and bound in England by
J.H. Haynes & Co. Ltd, Sparkford.

Contents

List of Illustrations

PLATES

MAPS

Preface

This book is an examination of the 400-year rivalry between the Stewart and the Douglas families which had such an influence on the fortunes of Scotland. It deals with personalities, violence, inherited power, wealth and arrogance passed on from one generation to the next. It is a remarkable tale. In 1330 Sir James Douglas from Scotland joined a Spanish army near Granada to help drive out the Moors. He had taken with him the embalmed heart of Robert the Bruce, who had been too busy to fulfil his own vow to go to fight the infidels. At Teba de Ardales in Andalucia the Good Lord James went into battle against the Moors. Seeing his friends in trouble, he hurled the casket holding the heart into the midst of the fighting and rode after it to his death. From that moment his family had the bloody heart as their crest and from that moment they became involved in a centuries-long struggle with the Stewarts, who by a fluke of genetics both acquired and kept the prize which the Douglases thought should be theirs: the crown of Scotland.

For a dozen generations as the largest landowners in Scotland the Douglases bullied and intimidated, harassed and murdered, as they sought supreme power.

This epic rivalry between the Royal Stewarts and their most powerful subjects led to a number of extraordinary incidents: the murder of the Black Douglas under safe conduct by James II; the virtual dethronement of James III by the Red Douglas; the abdication of Mary Queen of Scots, enforced by another Red Douglas who had organized the murders both of her favourite and of her husband; the pushing-through of the Act of Union by yet another branch of the Douglases. In more recent years this amazing family provided the adulterous botanist of fir-tree fame and the man who designed the Dakota. Meanwhile, we also look at the superb heritage of buildings left behind by the Douglases, some of Scotland's largest castles, palaces and some fine churches.

My thanks go to the patient editors at Sutton Publishing and as usual to my long-suffering wife, Jean.

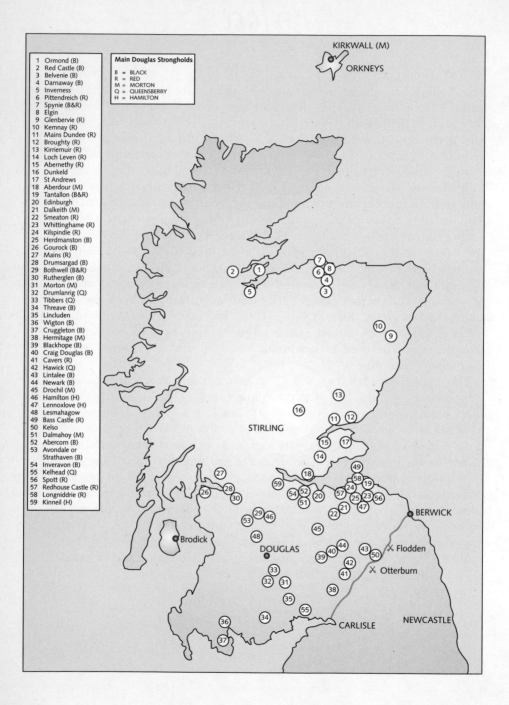

Main Douglas Strongholds

B = BLACK
R = RED
M = MORTON
Q = QUEENSBERRY
H = HAMILTON

KIRKWALL (M)

ORKNEYS

STIRLING

BERWICK

Brodick

DOUGLAS

× Flodden

× Otterburn

CARLISLE

NEWCASTLE

Main Douglas Strongholds

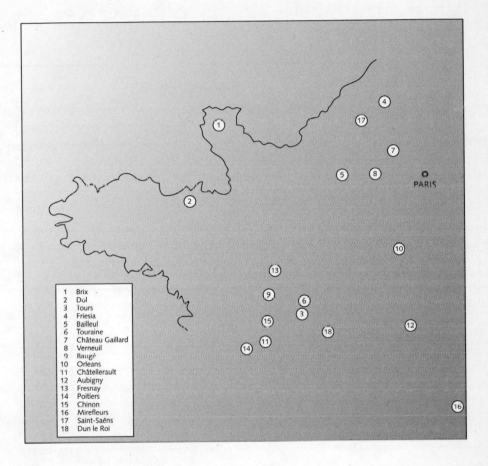

1	Brix
2	Dol
3	Tours
4	Friesia
5	Bailleul
6	Touraine
7	Château Gaillard
8	Verneuil
9	Baugé
10	Orleans
11	Châtellerault
12	Aubigny
13	Fresnay
14	Poitiers
15	Chinon
16	Mirefleurs
17	Saint-Saëns
18	Dun le Roi

PARIS

The French Connections

Genealogical Table

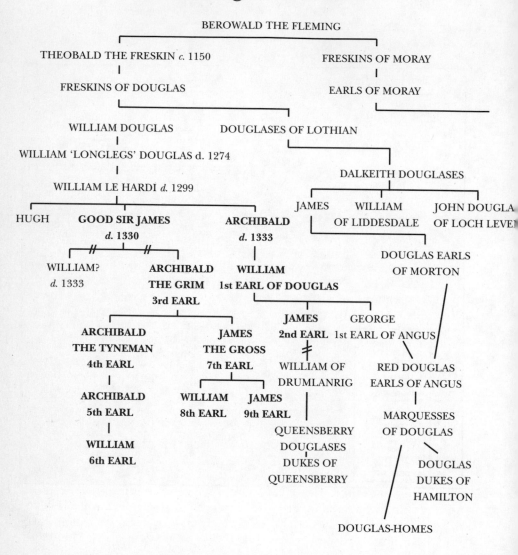

BEROWALD THE FLEMING

THEOBALD THE FRESKIN *c.* 1150

FRESKINS OF MORAY

FRESKINS OF DOUGLAS

EARLS OF MORAY

WILLIAM DOUGLAS

DOUGLASES OF LOTHIAN

WILLIAM 'LONGLEGS' DOUGLAS d. 1274

DALKEITH DOUGLASES

WILLIAM LE HARDI *d.* 1299

JAMES   WILLIAM   JOHN DOUGLA
          OF LIDDESDALE   OF LOCH LEVEN

HUGH   **GOOD SIR JAMES**   **ARCHIBALD**
         d. 1330   *d.* 1333

DOUGLAS EARLS
OF MORTON

WILLIAM?   **ARCHIBALD**   **WILLIAM**
d. 1333   **THE GRIM**   **1st EARL OF DOUGLAS**
             3rd EARL

ARCHIBALD   **JAMES**   **JAMES**   GEORGE
THE TYNEMAN   **THE GROSS** **2nd EARL** 1st EARL OF ANGUS
4th EARL   **7th EARL** WILLIAM OF   RED DOUGLAS
                                DRUMLANRIG   EARLS OF ANGUS

ARCHIBALD   **WILLIAM**   **JAMES**
5th EARL   **8th EARL** **9th EARL**
                                              MARQUESSES
                                QUEENSBERRY   OF DOUGLAS
WILLIAM   DOUGLASES
6th EARL   DUKES OF   DOUGLAS
                                QUEENSBERRY   DUKES OF
                                              HAMILTON

DOUGLAS-HOMES

BOLD TYPE signifies Black Douglases

Introduction

The Bloody Heart was in the field . . .
Sir Walter Scott, *Marmion*

In the 1130s, during the reign of King David I, forty or so immigrant families arrived in Scotland roughly at the same time, and four of these in particular were to achieve great power. All four had come originally from the west coast of France or the area that is now called Belgium. All four belonged to the lower fringes of Norman/French aristocracy, had trailed across to England during the Norman Conquest and had not quite fulfilled their desperate greed or ambition south of the border. All four had opted to look for their fortunes in Scotland instead, though they still also clung to properties that they had acquired in the south. None of the four had a surname in the modern sense but each quite soon acquired one. The first took its name from the village in Brittany from which it had first set out sixty years earlier, Brix, Brus or, in Scots, Bruce. The second, though also from a village in Brittany, took its name from the job-title given by the King of Scots: Steward or Stewart. The third, from the village of Bailleul in Normandy, kept that name in a new form, Balliol. The fourth, from Flanders, took its name from one of the rivers in Scotland by which they settled, Douglas Water. All these families were to win power, vast lands and influence. All four were to have members who married into the royal family of Scotland, but only three of the four were to win the Crown.

These Anglo-Norman families were to remain desperately ambitious. The Balliols won the Crown of Scotland first but kept it the shortest time, a little over three years in the case of John and in practice even less for his son Edward. The Bruces were to win it more spectacularly, but even they held it for little over sixty years. The Stewarts not only held the Crown of Scotland for 344 years, but also that of Great Britain and its empire for over a century. The fourth family, the Douglases, were to come extremely close to gaining the Crown on several occasions, but never quite made it.

It is the turbulent relationship of these families, particularly the last two, over some 400 years, the damage their violent rivalry caused to Scotland, and the personal miseries and joys brought to their many

xi

members that this book is designed to examine. In the course of our survey we must look at the bitter personal feuds which stood in the way of the development of sound kingship, at the dreadful crimes which the rival families committed against each other and the extraordinary deeds of bravery which they undertook in their quest to better each other. In the aftermath we see the scattering of the Douglases to all corners of the world as they found new outlets for their ambitions and energy.

The tour section at the end of the book reprises in a different form many of the incidents mentioned in the main narrative, so by consulting the index they can be read in parallel. Because the book essentially consists of a succession of short biographies, readers will, I hope, excuse the fact that the overall narrative occasionally backtracks where the generations overlap.

To avoid the distraction of footnotes, whenever another author is quoted the source can be found by referring to the bibliography. Please note that dates quoted beside the key figures in this narrative are for birth and death, not for the period as king, earl, etc. Particularly in the early period, many of these dates should be regarded as approximate.

PART I

The Black

I am the Douglas, fatal to all those
That wear those colours on them.
William Shakespeare, *1 Henry IV,* Act V, sc. iv

So many so good the Douglas have been
Of one surname in Scotland never yet were seen.
Saying quoted by Hume of Godscroft

CHAPTER ONE

Four Rival Families

Douglas a name through all the world renown'd,
A name that rouses like the trumpet sound.
John Home, Douglas

Of the four new immigrant families – the Balliols, the Bruces, the Stewarts and the Douglases – the first to achieve the throne of Scotland and the first to lose it were the Balliols. Of the four they were the most half-hearted in their transfer from England to Scotland. John Balliol senior (d. 1269) had married into the Scottish royal family yet made his main home most decidedly at Barnard Castle in Yorkshire. Previously the family had lived in a village called Bailleul, but there are several of these in France, the most likely being the one in L'Orne near Argentan, though one near Abbeville or one near Hazebruck are possibilities. John Balliol's marriage was to Devorguilla, a great-great-granddaughter of King David I (1080–1153) who not even the most calculating of bridegrooms could ever have guessed would provide a pathway for his family to the Scottish throne. The odds were far too great. But the Balliols were helped not only by the amazing lack of sons produced by the royal house of Alpin in its final years, but also by their Englishness, for when the old dynasty finally petered out the final choice between the competing applicants for the throne was passed over to the English King Edward I (1239–1307), and he naturally chose the most reliably pro-English of them.

The Bruce family served an apprenticeship of about 170 years before it gained the Crown of Scotland, and even then it was something of a fluke. King Robert the Bruce was in fact the eighth Robert de Brus to make his home in Britain. The first Robert (1040–95) had emigrated as a Norman knight from a village called Brix on the Saire district of the Cotentin peninsula near Cherbourg. He had been given lands in Yorkshire after the Conquest. His son, the second Robert, became friendly with Earl David (1080–1153), a Scottish prince living as an exile in England. David became heir to the throne of Scotland – a surprise in its own right, since he had three older brothers, none of whom produced an heir. Bruce accepted his offer of some extra land near Annan in return for military assistance from himself and his ten knights. But this did not mean another permanent migration for the Bruces. For some time they regarded their English baronies as just as important as – or possibly more important than – their Scottish ones. In fact, the second Robert de Brus was so cautious that when his master King David went to war with the English he first advised against it and then made sure he backed both horses by having one of his sons on each side, one with the Yorkshire holding fighting for England and the other with Annandale on the Scottish side. As it turned out, both sons survived, but even five generations later the Bruces still had their English territory: young King Robert had to make the painful choice between a secure, rich Yorkshire inheritance and a very insecure, rather poor Scottish throne. Meanwhile, the family built a castle near Annan and then one with walls up to 9 feet thick on land jutting into Lochmaben. Nearby at Buittle and Loch Doon Castle were the Scottish homes of that other Norman family – the Balliols – who were briefly to reach royal status a few years ahead of their neighbours.

In the meantime, two marriages had moved the Bruce family almost imperceptibly up the social scale. The first, and the one with the more far-reaching though unexpected results, took place when a spare, English-born granddaughter of King David, Isabel of Huntingdon, married the fifth Robert the Bruce (c. 1200–45?). No one can ever have expected all David's many other descendants to die without heirs, but they did, some eighty years later. So, despite this somewhat tenuous relationship, the sixth Robert Bruce (1210–95) spent a short time as heir to the throne, until King Alexander II (1198–1241) managed at last to produce a son of his own. Then in his old age the sixth Bruce again became a candidate, albeit unsuccessful, for the Crown: Edward I was called in as arbitrator and he preferred John Balliol (1250–1315), the son of John and Devorguilla. It was the sixth Bruce's grandson, the eighth and most famous Robert Bruce (1274–1329), who was to go one step further, but only after the dismal failure of Balliol, who briefly held the Scottish throne and is now better remembered for his mother's foundation of an Oxford college. The sixth Robert had anyway very much kept his options open and was a regular at the court of Edward I, who had supposedly been his father's companion during the crusades.

The other marriage was that of the seventh Robert Bruce (1253–1304) to Marjorie of Carrick. This aggressive lady was the widow of a crusader, Adam of Kilconquhar, and as Countess of Carrick in her own right she could turn any new bridegroom that she picked into an earl. She seems to have made all the running with the handsome, but for some reason initially reluctant, seventh Robert Bruce. She snared him in her castle at Turnberry until he succumbed to her advances. This increased the family's power base substantially, and potentially gave their eldest son both an earldom and wide extra tracts of land as a foundation for his own bid for the Crown thirty years later. It may be suspected that it also gave him an inheritance of iron will from his mother, something apparently lacking in his father.

Having become a potential king through a genealogical quirk, the eighth Robert Bruce had of course to overcome huge difficulties before his claim became a reality. Even to accept the challenge meant losing all his inheritance south of the border. It also meant the savage enmity of Edward I of England, who was determined that either he himself or one of his puppets should rule Scotland. William Wallace (1274–1305) had just been savagely executed and three of Robert's brothers were to suffer a similar fate. It is not within the scope of this book to retell the drama of Bruce's struggles to establish himself on the throne, but we may simply note that his only son, David II, died childless, so a dynasty which came to power through a genealogical quirk also in effect came to an end through one, and lasted just over sixty years.

The third family at this stage of our saga had a very similar background to the Bruces. Flaald was a Breton baron from the small cathedral town of Dol near Dinan. His family had been hereditary stewards – *dapiferi* (feast-bearers) – to the archbishops and counts of Dol. He came to England a few years after the Conquest, when Henry (1068–1135), ruler of Brittany and the Conqueror's youngest son, became King Henry I of England and Normandy. Flaald's son Alan (d. 1120) was rewarded with land on the Welsh border and built a castle at Oswestry, coincidentally not far from where that other subsequently royal family in Scotland, the Balliols, also had lands. Then this family too met up with Earl David of Scotland, perhaps when he joined King Henry in his attack on the Welsh, and two younger sons were recruited to go to Scotland. Like the Bruces, the family of Alan Fitzflaald, now sheriff of Shrewsbury, kept its eggs in two or three baskets. The eldest son, Jordan, went back to Dol to maintain the family's position in Brittany. Two other sons stayed in England, taking the name of Fitzalan, and eventually became earls of Arundel. The two youngest boys, Walter and Simon, moved to Scotland. Walter was given land round Renfrew, where he built a castle on an island in the Clyde. Whether King David knew the history of the family as hereditary stewards in Dol or whether it was pure coincidence, Walter was made Steward of Scotland, and from that was to come the family's new surname. The younger brother, Simon, who was given estates in Kilmarnock, was fair-haired, in Gaelic *buidhe*, which was anglicized into his new surname as Boyd.

The Stewarts were to serve a much longer apprenticeship than the Balliols or the Bruces before they achieved the Crown, and in their case too it was a bit of a genealogical long shot. For again no one can have seriously expected that the marriage of Bruce's daughter Marjorie to Walter the young steward would have such consequences sixty years later. Yet, despite two wives and some possible bastards, David II, the second Bruce king, had no legitimate children, and his aged uncle Robert the Steward became heir apparent. It was even more amazing because Robert's mother had fallen from a horse while riding from Renfrew to Paisley in an advanced state of pregnancy. She died by the River Cart near Knockhill, and her baby survived only thanks to an intelligent forester who had a knife handy. But this was nearly a quarter of a millennium and eight generations after the Stewarts had first arrived in Scotland. Meanwhile, they too had built fine stone castles at Renfrew, Paisley and Dundonald. They had added to their landholdings in East Lothian and the Borders as well as Renfrew and Ayrshire. They had founded a monastery in Paisley dedicated to three saints: St James, their patron back in Dol; St Milburg, their patron in Shropshire; and St Mirren, the local saint of their new home. They had visited the English court as honoured barons, Walter the Steward, for example, going with King Malcolm IV (1141–65) of Scotland to meet Henry II (1133–89) of England at Toulouse. There the Scottish king received the accolade of knighthood, which could only be awarded to a king by another king.

The Stewarts had also participated in at least two significant battles, though it is hard to estimate just how strenuous their participation in them was. The first was at Knockhill, where the islanders' rebellion under Somerled was defeated near the Clyde in 1164; the second at Largs, when the Vikings were driven back into the sea in 1263. They had also either been, or claimed to have been, on crusades, like the Bruces and indeed the Douglases. Alan may have been on the third crusade; his son Walter Stewart was killed at Damietta in 1249, and certainly they gave an endowment in Ayrshire to send funds to Acre in the Holy Land. They also had a dozen or so knights and their support troops, some of them Flemings in origin like the Douglases. Sir Tancred left his name in Thankerton, Sir Ralph in Ralston, Sir Simon in two Symingtons, Sir Robert de Croc in Crookston, and so on. So they were a significant part of the infrastructure of the Scottish monarchy. What is more, a sister of Alan had married Duncan, the Earl of Carrick, who by another coincidence was to be a grandfather of Robert the Bruce. So there was a precedent for marriage alliances between the two families.

The fourth of our families was the most obscure in origin. Perhaps its founder in Scotland was Berowald the Fleming, who gave his name to Bo'ness, or Erkenbald of Flanders. A number of Flemings had come across from the Ypres area to England as mercenaries during the civil war of Stephen and Matilda. One family from this group known as Freskin (a corruption of Friesian) was given land in Moray round about 1130, and in due course about 1190 William Fitzfreskin changed his name to Moray. Another branch, headed by his brother or cousin Theobald the Fleming (Theobaldo Flammatico), was given land at Poniel on the Douglas Water by the Abbot of Kelso in 1150, probably in return for acting as protectors for the abbey's outpost at Lesmahagow Priory. In 1202 a Freskin was appointed priest at Douglas, and about this time the family adopted their new surname from their local river, the Douglas Water. At Douglas, Theobald and his son William (1174–1214) built a motte, a large mound of earth with a wooden castle on top surrounded on three sides by the Douglas Water, which several centuries later was diverted into the ornamental lakes that now dominate the landscape.

Of William's five sons three or four seem to have moved up to Moray among the other Flemish immigrants, their relations, now called Moray. Their joint origin is corroborated by the three silver stars which both families have on their coats of arms. Brice or Brixius Douglas (d. 1222), who had begun his career as prior of the family abbey at Lesmahagow, went on to become the Bishop of Moray, where he first established a new cathedral at Spynie, north of Elgin, but then, after a visit to the Pope in Rome, changed his mind and set in motion the building of Elgin Cathedral. Shortly after his death he was canonized, without question the only Douglas to qualify for sainthood.

Within a couple of generations one of the family, William Longlegs Douglas (*c.* 1220–74), was appointed by King William I the Lion (1143–1214) to lead a raid into Northumberland, where, as it happened, the Douglases now also held land. Later he was appointed one of the guardians for the young Alexander III. Gradually the Douglas family were to achieve vast landholdings and huge power. The men's fighting prowess meant that they made reliable husbands for wealthy heiresses, and in 1259 William's son Hugh married Marjorie of Abernethy, which brought that prestigious little town into the Douglas domain. They often provided regents or guardians of Scotland and intermarried with the royal family, but despite great endeavour and ruthless plotting they never actually seized the Crown. The conflict and violence, however, which their desire for it engendered had a devastating effect on the growth of monarchy in Scotland and on the development of Scotland as a nation.

Our four families were part of a group of at least forty such brought into Scotland at this time, and with them came about another 200 or so Anglo-Norman knights as their liegemen. What they all had in common, apart from chain mail and fighting skills, was a disciplined approach to colonization.

They almost immediately had earthen mottes thrown up, on top of which they built strong wooden castles, replaced soon afterwards by even stronger stone ones. They mostly married local heiresses, which helped them to legitimize and extend their landholdings as they displaced the old Scots baronage. They were also accustomed to working closely with the Church and were followed into Scotland by a wave of Cluniac monks who provided a useful, literate infrastructure. The reign of King David I therefore saw Scotland acquiring large numbers of new castles and a significant number of new monasteries, particularly in the Borders. And three of the families had married members of the royal house of Alpin, Scotland's dynasty dating back to Kenneth MacAlpin in the ninth century, which now seemed to find it increasingly hard to produce healthy heirs.

Thus Scotland enjoyed – or suffered – a Norman conquest by stealth. There was remarkably little resistance from the old baronage. And the royal dynasty of Scotland which had invited in the Trojan horse allowed intermarriage to such an extent that, when the house of Alpin ran out of male heirs, it was followed by three successive dynasties descended from these Anglo-Norman immigrants. Yet all three were to be faced in turn by a very much stronger dynasty, also of Norman origin, the Plantagenets from Anjou. And they were also to be faced by a very strong dynasty within their own midst, one which deeply resented being so close to the Crown yet never quite able to snatch it – the Douglases.

CHAPTER TWO

A Very Savage Douglas

And in general the account of many deaths
Whose portents which should have undone the sky
Had never come – is now received casually
You and I are careless of these millions of wraiths.
Keith Douglas, 'Negative Information'

As we have seen, when the Scottish magnates could not agree among one another as to who should be the new king after all the grandchildren of Alexander III (1241–86) had died, they asked Edward I to make the choice for them. So the Anglophile John Balliol was chosen and crowned in 1292. Within three years the magnates very much regretted this, both because John was ineffectual and because Edward I, partly encouraged by his role as mediator, was becoming ever more arrogant in his demands. Balliol was known as Toom Tabard, the Empty Jacket. Naturally he never had the support of the Bruces since they regarded themselves as having a better right to the position than he had, but in the time of the cautious seventh Robert Bruce they had not rebelled against him. Balliol did have general support from the Stewarts so long as the English kept backing him, and from the Douglases even after that had stopped. This was mainly because William Douglas le Hardi (1248–98) had behaved so outrageously that Edward deprived him of all his estates, both north and south of the border. Nothing, however, could save John Balliol once he took his first trembling step towards resisting the will of his master Edward I. In 1296, after a half-hearted attempt at battle at Spott near Dunbar, he was stripped of his crown by the man who had given it to him.

When the Scottish Wars of Independence began in 1296 the heads of our three remaining rival families were men of very different temperament: the seventh Robert Bruce, the crusader and reluctant bridegroom, with his principal bases at Lochmaben and Turnberry; James, the fifth Steward (c. 1250–1309), with his main castles at Renfrew on the River Clyde and Dundonald in Ayrshire; and the troublemaker William le Hardi of Douglas, with his family seat at Douglas. He had fewer lands than the other two, and had no official titles or position, but had been expanding them with rugged ruthlessness. After the death of his first wife, the Steward's sister Elizabeth, he had abducted a rich English widow while she was on a visit to Scotland, thus acquiring at least her Scottish estates. But the main leader of the opposition to the English under Edward I was none of these three. William Wallace, a man of lower rank and lesser wealth than any of them, had appeared almost from nowhere as a talented and inspiring guerrilla leader.

The seventh Bruce, who was still concerned with his family landholdings in Yorkshire and whose Scottish estates were too close to the border for comfort, was officially Sheriff of Cumberland for Edward I and Governor of Carlisle. He had bitterly resented the elevation of John Balliol and spent some time in voluntary exile in Norway to avoid doing homage to him, marrying his daughter Isabel off to the King of Norway in the process. His heir, the eighth Robert, was ambivalent and was to change allegiance several times before finally committing himself after Wallace's death in 1305. He had also been influenced by the fact that Wallace supported John Balliol as King of Scotland, a role to which Bruce had some claims himself. Thus in 1296 he was fighting for Edward I and stood in for his father commanding the defence of Carlisle against the Scots. Yet soon afterwards he went over to Wallace's side, and it was he who dubbed William Wallace a knight in Selkirk forest in 1298, not long before Wallace's last disastrous battle at Falkirk. Bruce was then appointed joint guardian with John Comyn of Badenoch, but changed sides again back to Edward I in 1302. Edward, however, not surprisingly, still did not trust him. He was reluctant even to give him back all his estates, let alone to support the idea of his becoming King of Scotland. So in the end Bruce had little choice but to try his luck again as a rebel. He changed sides for the last time and claimed the Crown of Scotland himself, soon afterwards murdering his main rival, John Comyn, in a fit of temper at Dumfries.

James the Steward was the local magnate in Wallace's area – the Wallaces had probably come from the Welsh border (hence the surname) to Scotland at the same time as the Stewarts – but he too vacillated in his support for the self-made leader. He had been one of six regents after the death of Alexander III in 1286, and he was given charge of the vital castle at Roxburgh near the border in 1296. He was now elderly by the standards of his time, an establishment figure. Like Bruce he had a lot of territory to lose, including some in England, and had a track record of backing down realistically when he saw the odds against him were too heavy. The most humiliating example of this he shared with Bruce at Irvine in 1297, after which, like Bruce, he provided the English with a hostage, his eldest son, Andrew, who died in captivity. His brother Sir John Stewart of Bunkle, however, was a Wallace supporter to the last and died fighting at Falkirk.

Of our three family heads William le Hardi of Douglas was the only one who gave himself wholeheartedly to the cause of Wallace and ultimately paid for it with his life. He seems to have had an elder brother Hugh, who was killed or died, for a story survived in a traditional ballad (quoted by Fraser) that he was ambushed by a neighbour but won the contest:

> Patton Purdie brach a chaise [ambush]
> Upon the Lord Douglas
> Hugh Lord Douglas turned again
> And there was Patton Purdie slane.

It is certain that by now Douglas was a proper stone-built castle, for a Hugh Abernethy (perhaps a relation) was in its dungeon in 1288, charged with the murder of the Earl of Fife. William himself was an experienced border fighter who also may have been on a crusade, though this was possibly make-believe. Certainly he had been severely wounded when his father's castle at Fawdon in Northumberland was attacked by a neighbour in 1267 and barely survived. His mother was a Carrick, so his family was later able to argue that they had Bruce or Balliol blood and therefore some entitlement to the throne themselves. Meanwhile, William was far from scrupulous in his methods of increasing the family estates, and among others harried the monks of Melrose. The most notorious example of his brigandry was when he caused scandal by abducting a wealthy English widow who had several useful estates in Scotland as well as England. He could not hope to win approval for absorbing his wife's English properties, but he did assert his right to the Scottish lands. The lady was apparently most reluctant to marry him and according to Blind Harry's *Wallace*:

> His wyff was wraith bot it sche shawit nocht
> Under cover hyr malice hid perfyt
> As a serpent wates hyr tym to byt.

She bore him two sons and after his death went back with them to her estates in England.

As Balliol's governor of Berwick Castle, William le Hardi put up a stalwart defence against a large English force. He was lucky not to be among the several thousand defenders of Berwick town who were butchered when it was at last captured by trickery, the English marching up to the gate carrying Scottish banners instead of their own. He was taken prisoner and briefly, like so many, changed sides, but was later released. Wallace appointed him as Constable of all castles in the south-west of Scotland. He attacked Sanquhar Castle, later a Douglas seat, and captured it using a trick later copied by his son. He used the services of a local friend to disguise himself as the firewood deliveryman and slipped through the door when it was opened, then held it open long enough for a few of his followers to get in too. However, he soon suffered an English counter-attack until he was rescued by Wallace himself.

In 1297 William le Hardi burned Turnberry Castle, the seat of the Bruces. Young Robert Bruce, whose father had been ordered by Edward I to get rid of Douglas, took his revenge by ravaging Douglasdale and seizing Douglas's wife and children. But at this point Bruce, who was still not even the head of his own family – for his father did not die until 1304 – came over to the side of Balliol and Wallace, James the Steward following in his wake. So for a brief period three of our families were on the so-called patriotic side. However, this did not last long. At Irvine the army of Scottish nobles, not at this point led by Wallace nor including Douglas, who was elsewhere, met a large English army, could not decide on strategy or choose a leader, and surrendered. Young Bruce agreed to change sides as usual, and allowed his daughter Marjorie to go south as a hostage for his good behaviour. James the Steward also changed sides, yet apparently soon afterwards was fighting in support of Wallace at Stirling Bridge. William Douglas also later surrendered or was recaptured but would not provide his children as hostages, so was sent first to Berwick, where he was reported as 'very savage and very abusive'. Edward anyway regarded him as beyond redemption since he had broken his vows to him once too often. He was kept in irons and then transferred to the Tower of London, where he died in 1298, presumably executed on the orders of the English king. David Hume of Godscroft, the somewhat biased chronicler of this family, described him as 'a paterne of true vertue'. He seems to have had four sons, two from each marriage. The eldest, Hugh, died before him; the second was the famous Good Sir James; the third was another Hugh, known as Hugh the Dull, who was brought up in England and became a priest; the fourth was Archibald, who was to die leading the Scottish army at the disastrous battle of Halidon Hill.

After three years in English dungeons John Balliol was released and allowed by Edward I to retire from political life in 1302. He went to live on the family estates back in Normandy, and died thirteen years later at Château Gaillard. The seventh Robert Bruce died after a relatively undistinguished career in 1304, though with his vivacious wife he had fathered the Queen of Norway and two future kings, Robert of Scotland and Edward of Ireland. James, the fifth Steward, had been slightly more distinguished, but played it very safe and died of old age in 1309. William Douglas le Hardi had died in 1298 in the Tower of London. It was now time for a new cast of players.

CHAPTER THREE

The Bloody Heart

The ostrich fortified by common sense
And strong in every tactical resource
When he perceived the enemy in force
Concealed his head behind a bush or fence.

Lord Alfred Douglas, 'The Ostrich'

Of the three family heads in this generation, Robert the Bruce, the eighth of that name and the first to be king, was the senior in every sense. Sir James Douglas (1286–1330) was just twenty when he first came to support the newly crowned Robert I, himself just thirty-two. Walter Stewart (1293–1326) succeeded his father as Steward in 1309, aged only sixteen. The prospective head of our fourth family, Edward Balliol (1283–1364), was the oldest of the four but was to play no serious part in the events of Robert's reign. In this generation, apart from the Balliols sulking in exile, there does not seem to have been the jealousy and plotting between the families which were to become such a feature later.

There is no need here to retell the struggles of Bruce to establish a meaningful kingship in the face of his many opponents, both Scottish and English. Our concern is with the relationship and character of Robert, James and Walter in so far as these factors laid the foundations of future tensions.

Having vacillated between the pro-Scottish and pro-English factions while his father was still alive, and to some extent afterwards, Bruce thought his moment had come. After the humiliation of Balliol in 1302, he had expected Edward I to turn to the Bruces as a safe choice for the Crown of Scotland, but Edward snubbed them, preferring to conquer Scotland for himself rather than risk appointing another puppet king. He knew from bitter experience that he simply could not trust the Bruces. So, realizing that he would never be given the Crown by Edward, Bruce eventually burnt his boats in 1306. The stabbing to death of his rival John Comyn, a nephew of Balliol's and another strong claimant for the vacant throne, made turning back impossible. The Comyns were yet another Anglo-Norman family, originally from Comines near Lille, who had won English lands after the Conquest and then been given even more in

Scotland. In fact at one point they had four Scottish earls and thirty-two knights in the family. Two months after Comyn's murder, the worse for being committed in a church, Bruce underwent a makeshift coronation at Scone, and thereafter suffered a succession of reverses. Two of his brothers were caught and executed by Edward I, Thomas being first dragged round Carlisle tied to a horse's tail. Badly beaten by the English at Methven and then by the Comyn and Argyll faction at Dalry near Tyndrum, Bruce had to make an undignified escape to Ireland, and it was some months before he had the resources to land again at Turnberry. He then scored his first victory against the English at Loudon in May 1307. He was perhaps helped by the death of his old enemy Edward I, whose successor, Edward II (1284–1327), was not quite so well disciplined, but whose forces nevertheless should not be underrated. From this point onwards Bruce proved his capacity to be an effective guerrilla leader like Wallace, and studiously avoided major pitched battles until his brother Edward made one inevitable by challenging the English to rescue their garrison in Stirling.

Yet, however much it was against Bruce's policy to risk a major battle with the full English army, the one occasion he had to do so he managed it at Bannockburn with magnificent aplomb. His exhibition of single combat at the outset of the battle when he killed de Bohun was the stuff of legends. The remaining fourteen years of his reign he avoided unnecessary risks and showed substantial maturity in consolidating the fruits of his victory. Military action was confined to carefully targeted border raids to try to extract a long-term settlement from the English. The only risk-taker was again his brother Edward, who had made himself King of Ireland in 1317 and was killed defending his new kingdom at Dundalk a year later.

Little is known about the personality of Walter, the sixth of his family to be hereditary Steward of Scotland. He fought at Bannockburn with nominal command of one of the three schiltrons – huge hedgehogs of pike-carrying infantry which goaded their way into the English cavalry – but as a 21-year-old he had the much more experienced James Douglas as his second in command and the real person in charge. He took part also in the defence of Berwick, and joined Bruce in his naval expedition to the Western Isles when they stopped at Tarbert to supervise the building of a new castle there. In 1316 he was appointed alongside Douglas as joint deputy for the King when Bruce went to help his brother in Ireland. There were few other notable events in his relatively short life – he was only thirty-three when he died – except for the one which turned out in the end to have the greatest effect on his family and nation's history: his marriage to Marjorie, Bruce's daughter. As with the similar, rather off-hand royal wedding of the fifth Robert Bruce, there can have been no serious expectation at the time that it would lead to a change of royal dynasty. Bruce had fathered several bastards and, though much of his early married life with his second wife, Elizabeth of Ulster, had been spent away from her, she could still be expected to produce an heir. In fact their son David was not born until 1324, eight years after Walter and Marjorie had produced their son Robert. So the uncle was eight years younger than the nephew, but that was of little consequence. David Bruce was now the heir to the throne and would himself be expected in due course to father his own heirs. Yet, just as the surprising failure of all three brothers to produce heirs had unexpectedly brought David I to the throne in 1124, then the death of all Alexander III's children and grandchildren had created the vacancy which brought in first Balliol and then Bruce, amazingly it was to happen a third time in 1370 when the Bruce dynasty also ran out of male heirs.

Sadly Walter's marriage to Marjorie Bruce lasted only a very short time – in fact it was remarkable that it produced any offspring, for in an advanced state of pregnancy Marjorie fell from her horse while riding from Blackhall Castle to King's Inch (it must have had a different name then). She broke her neck and only the prompt action of a passer-by, reputedly a forester, saved the life of the unborn future King Robert II. Walter remarried but died a few years later.

Sir James Douglas, known later as the Good Lord James, was truly a legend in his own lifetime. He had a lisp, apparently, and was so dark-featured that he was given the nickname 'Black', which was applied to his family for the next eight generations. In Barbour's words:

> His visage was he sumdele grey
> And had blak har as I herd say
> But of limmis he was wel mad
> With banis grat and schaldris brad.

He was a teenager learning his trade in France when his father died in captivity, but when he returned to Scotland Edward I totally refused to restore to him any of the forfeited Douglas estates. So, penniless, he had to look elsewhere. By now in his twenties he met Bruce and offered his services at Ericstane, near the Devil's Beeftub, at the disastrous start of the new reign. The two defeats he shared in at Methven and Dalry were two of the thirteen defeats in his career out a total of seventy battles in which he was believed to have taken part. During Bruce's flight westward after Methven, Douglas made his reputation with the royal ladies as the best procurer of fish and game for their supper. As Barbour puts it:

> For quhile he veneson them brocht
> And with his handys quhile he wrocht
> Gynnis [traps] to tak geddis [pike] and salmonis
> Troutis, elis [eels] and als menounis [minnows].

He stayed with Bruce then through the hair-raising escape down Loch Lomond, where he got the credit for finding a waterlogged boat, then over in an oared galley to Dunaverty Castle, near the Mull of Kintyre, before heading for safety to Rathlin Island off the Irish coast.

James Douglas then commanded the small raid on Arran which gained a foothold back in Scotland and joined in the first Bruce counter-attack on Turnberry. Thereafter he showed himself a brilliant guerrilla fighter, picking off English troops in isolated areas with minimal losses to his own men. Famously he three times attacked his own castle at Douglas and its English garrisons. The first time his men joined in a Palm Sunday church parade and captured the English garrison in the church, killing them all later, for squeamishness in the slaughter of prisoners was not a feature of this war. He then piled the bodies, dead horses and all the stores into the castle cellar and set it alight, the famous Douglas Larder. Then, in Barbour's words:

> That he tumil down the wall
> And destroyit the housis all.

The second attack did not result in retaking the newly repaired castle, but he did kill the new governor. Now that two English garrison commanders had been killed in quick succession Douglas became known as Perilous Castle (Castle Dangerous for Sir Walter Scott's last novel) and a severe test of a knight's courage to accept its command, for despite its lootings the English kept repairing it. One English knight, Sir John Walton, was egged on by a lady friend to prove his bravery and thus became the third commander to die. This time Douglas had disguised his men as cattle drovers heading for Lanark market and lulled the English into a false sense of security. Having killed poor Walton, the commander, and again destroyed the castle, he for once spared the rest of the garrison, acknowledging their gallantry.

Douglas also played a key role in the battle at the Pass of Brander in 1309 when Bruce got his revenge against the Comyn Argyll faction, the McDougalls of Lorne. It was Douglas who led a group of light archers up the hillside round the flank of the McDougall army, blocking the gorge, so that they could be attacked from two sides at once. The battle was also important in that it secured the future support for Bruce of Angus Og and the Islay MacDonalds.

Three years later Douglas accomplished the daring capture of Roxburgh Castle, the massive English-held fortress a few miles from the border. It was Shrove Tuesday and the garrison had been celebrating. This time Douglas had his men hooded in black so that from the battlements above they would supposedly look like cattle. They brought ladders specially made with hooks by Sym of Ledehouse to push up onto the walls. By this time James Douglas had acquired the image of an ogre among the English, and the story of Roxburgh Castle was embroidered to include a young mother who was soothing her child with the lullaby:

> Hush ye, hush ye little pettie
> The Black Douglas shall not get ye.

Then the man himself sprang over the wall beside her with the words 'You are not so sure of that.' He spared her life, but the rest of the garrison were executed. Stories like this were doubtless embellished by men like Barbour, who wrote his *Bruce* in 1370 to eulogize the Bruce–Douglas partnership. For Douglas was certainly not always totally chivalrous or even loyal, and he routinely mutilated captured bowmen before letting them return to their own country.

Thomas Randolph, Bruce's nephew, who had come over from the English side after being captured by Douglas near Peebles, had by this time become the Good Lord James's most serious rival. He was inspired by the Roxburgh success to mount an attack on Edinburgh Castle, leaving Stirling Castle as the only major outpost still in English hands. This gave rise to Edward Bruce's rash challenge to the English which forced Edward II to come to the rescue and Robert Bruce into full-scale battle with the English, something he had so far wanted to avoid. Douglas played a key role in the battle of Bannockburn which followed, as effective commander of the schiltron nominally led by Walter the Steward. Both James Douglas and Walter Stewart were dubbed knights by the King before the battle. Afterwards it was Douglas who led the party in pursuit of Edward II as he raced back to the border at Berwick.

In the subsequent period Douglas was rewarded by the King with large further tracts of land, with five extra baronies in the Borders, Jedburgh Forest and the stewardship of the royal Forest of Selkirk. These gifts were granted by King Robert with an emerald ring to symbolize their permanence, hence the concept of the Emerald Charter. Lord James built himself a hunting lodge at Lintalee on the Jed and there were other meeting points at Tinnis and Erncleugh in Ettrick Forest, as well as Craig Douglas in Yarrow and Eddybredshiels by Selkirk. Using tough local men with Jethart axes and Ettrick bows, he continued to take charge of deliberately provocative raids into England to demonstrate to Edward II that he must make peace with the Scots. These also had the advantage of bringing booty, ransom money and blackmail. In 1318 he burnt Scarborough and Skipton, and won a battle against the English at Mitton by burning haystacks to blind them. In 1321 he went with Walter the Steward to maraud round Hartlepool and Durham, partly in support of the rebel Earl of Lancaster, whom they chose to recognize as King Arthur of England, in retaliation for the fact that Edward would not refer to the Bruce as the King of Scotland. In 1325 Douglas burnt Preston and scores of northern villages. On one occasion he came close to capturing Edward II and his queen, Isabella. In these expeditions Froissart tells us that the Scottish troops could march or ride 24 miles without a rest and carried no food but a small bag of oatmeal, simply picking off cattle for meat as they went. This enabled Douglas to have great mobility and speed for his hit-and-run raids over the border. In one of his raids he was challenged by Sir Robert de Nevill, known as the Peacock of the North, but was again successful in an ambush, this time using the small birch trees of the forest plaited together to hem the English into his trap.

Meanwhile, Douglas, among other senior barons, had signed the Declaration of Arbroath which Bruce sent to the Pope in his long-drawn-out effort to obtain official forgiveness for the murder of John Comyn and recognition of himself as king. One of James Douglas's most daring later raids was the surprise attack near Durham on a much larger English force led by sixteen-year-old King Edward III (1312–77), whose father had just been murdered, impaled on a red-hot poker at Berkeley Castle. Cheekily, according to the chroniclers, Sir James crossed the Wear, rode right into the English camp and, assuming a southern accent, told off the sentries for keeping such a poor watch. Douglas and his troops then cut the guy ropes of the English tents and would have captured young Edward if he had not crawled out through the back. The Scots, however, were still at risk and still had to avoid a pitched battle against heavy odds. Douglas disguised their retreat by leaving large campfires burning. He then led his men back north over a temporary wooden causeway previously laid over an intervening marsh and lifted up again after they had passed. Hence the name of this battle – Shorn Moss. Douglas is quoted by Barbour in his *Bruce* as justifying the retreat to his colleague Randolph, saying that where the numbers were so disproportionate it was no dishonour to the weaker party to use every advantage they might chance to obtain, and he also quoted the story of the fox trapped by a fisherman who pulled the man's cloak into the fire and ran away with the fish while the fisherman went to save his cloak.

Douglas, who had by this time acquired the equivalent of superstar status in the world of European chivalry, was also sent by Bruce to France to persuade old John Balliol formally to renounce his family's claim to the throne, so soon afterwards a treaty with England was at long last signed.

Of James Douglas's private life very little is known, except that he had an illegitimate son, Archibald, very shortly before he died and may also have had a legitimate son, William, who was killed at Halidon Hill soon after his own death. He also had two surviving half-brothers: Hugh the Dull, a priest, and young Archibald, who also died at Halidon Hill. There is no mention of his wife or mistress.

When King Robert, who had been suffering from leprosy for some years, was dying in his favourite mansion at Cardross, Douglas was one of those who specially went to say farewell, yet, despite his reputation as the dying king's favourite general, he was not asked to become a regent or guardian for the prospective child King David II. Earlier he had been joint deputy with Randolph and before that with the Steward, so it has been suggested that the dying Bruce foresaw trouble if the two of them shared power; so he asked Douglas to go to the Holy Land for him, perhaps as a tactful way out of the dilemma. Froissart gives an emotional description of the final conversation: 'Because I know not in all my realm a knight more valiant than you, I require you my dear special friend for your love of me that you undertake this journey.'

So Douglas headed off with a group of knights towards Jerusalem with the embalmed heart of Robert Bruce, stopping off at Sluys, where he entertained lavishly. French knights who had heard of his deeds were amazed that he had no scars on his face. Then it was on to Spain, where he died fighting for King Alphonso of Castille against the infidel Moors at Teba in Andalucia. There he uttered the immortal words 'Jamais arrière' (Never behind) as he flung Bruce's heart forward into the mêlée. A small monument now marks the spot. The legend runs:

> Have down, have down my merry men all
> Have down into the plain
> We'll let the Scottish lion loose
> Within the fields of Spain.

Remarkably in this period the rivalry of our four families had been thrust into the background. The Balliols were almost penniless and powerless exiles. Robert Bruce had acquired a natural authority, an image of competence and indestructibility which deterred likely contenders during his lifetime. Walter Stewart and James Douglas were both loyal adherents who gained immensely from their contact with Bruce, the first in particular a royal princess as wife, the second his tracts of land and castles, plus the opportunity to indulge his favourite pastime, fighting. As Godscroft put it, 'Seldome it is found that these vertues concur in one persone, habilitie to governe and willingness to be governed.'

Unfortunately for Scotland, the Bruce, Douglas and Stewart all died relatively young. The one to survive into the next generation and a malign old age was the Balliol.

It is tempting to be cynical about calling these events a war of independence. It was really just the rivalry of various groups of Norman barons, some of whom happened to have a stake in Scotland. It was all perhaps made worse by the fact that the so-called feudal system was most effective when the barons' lands were well scattered, so many therefore had estates on both sides of what we now know as the border but which then was not quite set in stone. Talk of treason in terms of national allegiance at this time is anachronistic, and in terms of personal loyalty most of these men made and broke vows without a second thought. Similarly, any moral line between cross-border thieving as part of a war effort and the same for personal gain was to become almost indistinguishable.

What the Good Lord James had shown was that a successful warrior could hugely enhance his inheritance by his own efforts and this was to be a consistent characteristic of his successors. But he had also set an example of cross-border raiding for profit which became an appealing source of adventure for many Scottish knights, yet wreaked huge destruction and presented major consequential problems for their kings. It inevitably provoked retaliation, so that the end result was nearly three centuries of mutual devastation on both sides of the Anglo-Scottish border, causing huge misery for ordinary people and considerable economic degradation.

CHAPTER FOUR

The Flower of Chivalry

The stars, dead heroes in the sky
May well approve the way you die.
                    Keith Douglas, 'The Offensive'

Edward Balliol, son of King John Balliol, was only nine years younger than Robert the Bruce, but during the Bruce's lifetime he figured hardly at all since he had neither the resources nor the backing even to dream of regaining his father's lost Crown. He was thus about fifty, old in those days for a fighting man, when the new English king, Edward III (1312–77), decided that he might be useful as a rallying point for disaffected Scots. But Bruce had left only a five-year-old son, David II (1324–71), to take over from him, and despite his excellent work as king Scotland was to prove a distressingly easy target for potential invaders.

It started to go wrong when Thomas Randolph, Bruce's own choice as guardian or regent, died a mere two years into the new reign. His replacement, chosen by the magnates, was a nephew of Bruce's, Donald of Mar. Meanwhile, Balliol landed on the Fife coast with an army of around 1,500 men, and faced a much larger Scottish army at Dupplin Moor near Perth. But the Scots under Mar were over-confident, rashly celebrating their victory before the battle, and at a crucial moment Sir Robert Bruce, a bastard son of King Robert, accused his cousin Mar of consorting with the enemy. The large but thus demoralized Scottish army suffered badly from the Anglo-Scots archers, got in the way of one another and gave Balliol an unexpected victory. They also gave Balliol the chance to be crowned King Edward I of Scotland at Scone, though naturally he did so as a vassal of Edward III of England, who had paid for his army.

The Scots now chose their third new guardian in two years, and, when he was captured almost immediately by Balliol's men, their fourth. This was Sir Archibald Douglas (1296–1333), the younger half-brother of the Good Lord James. He must have been a reasonably experienced commander, for he had led at least one successful raiding party into England under his brother, but as in effect a fourth choice, he was perhaps not a military high flier. He had also attempted to ambush

Balliol on his way north past Jedburgh and failed dismally. Embarrassingly there were now two kings of Scotland at the same time, nine-year-old David II, Douglas's nominal suzerain, and Edward Balliol, recently crowned at Scone, who had the support of England and some dispossessed Scottish barons. To complicate things King David had been married by proxy to Edward III's sister Joanna.

Douglas made a somewhat inauspicious start to his guardianship by calling a truce with Balliol and then cancelling it unilaterally to make a surprise attack on him at Annan. He caught the force off guard and very nearly captured Balliol, who had to head for the border half-dressed: as a chronicler put it, 'with one limb dressed and one naked'.

Unfortunately this was Douglas's only success. King Edward III came to his namesake's rescue and attacked Berwick, still at this time held by the Scots. Douglas retaliated rather too slowly by harrying Northumberland, burning Tweedmouth and attacking Bamburgh Castle, where the English Queen Philippa was in residence. But Edward III would not give up his siege of Berwick and started hanging hostages two a day. Douglas was morally obliged to go to the rescue of Berwick, just as Edward II had had to try to save Stirling before Bannockburn. It was the classic situation where Bruce and James Douglas had always advised the avoidance of pitched battles against superior English armies, but the appeals of the suffering people of Berwick were too hard for Archibald to resist and he felt emotionally bound to go to their rescue whatever the risk. It is easy enough to condemn him in hindsight.

Edward III had the better choice of ground at Halidon Hill, outside the town. The Scots had to cross ground too boggy for their cavalry and then climb a steep hill which left them breathless. Once again a Scottish army suffered badly from the English bowmen. As Sir Walter Scott put it in 'Halidon Hill':

> The clothyard shafts shall fall like death's own darts
> And though blind men discharge them find a mark
> Thus shall we die the death of slaughtered deer.

Sir Archibald Douglas was killed, along with six other Scottish earls and most of the survivors of the battle, including Sir Robert Bruce, bastard son of the old king, who had given him Hermitage Castle as his base, and William Douglas, the supposed legitimate son of the Good Lord James. It was a disaster which meant that a defenceless Scotland could be totally overrun by Balliol, who proceeded to cede half the border country to his master, Edward III. Archibald's own widow took refuge in the large castle at Cumbernauld, but it was burnt from beneath her. Young King David had first to be taken for safety to Dumbarton Castle, prior to being shipped off to France. At Dumbarton he was joined by his uncle Robert the Steward (1316–90), who was one of those who managed to escape from Halidon Hill. He was just nineteen, heir to the Stewarts, a grandson of Bruce, yet at this point with no serious expectation of the Crown. He had had to escape across the Clyde from his castle at Rothesay in a rowing boat, as Balliol's disinherited supporters, such as the Comyns, swarmed back over Scotland under the protection of their English patron. And the Scottish magnates were about to recruit their fifth guardian in three years.

One of the new joint guardians was in fact Robert the Steward, now aged twenty, and with his colleague young Randolph, son of Bruce's nephew, he organized a not unsuccessful attack on the Scottish border counties which Balliol had handed over to England. Edward retaliated with a full-scale invasion of Scotland in 1336, which was met by the Scots with a scorched-earth and guerrilla-war tactic reminiscent of the early days of Bruce. Even English armies relied on picking up some of their food in the country through which they travelled and the Scots left them none, though at some serious discomfort for their own people .

There now appeared on the scene a new Douglas, William of Liddesdale (1300–53), one of five sons of a Sir John Douglas of Lothian (de Laudonia) based at Blackness and Herdmanston. Known later as the Knight of Liddesdale and later still as the Flower of Chivalry, William Douglas proved himself one of the most gifted if ruthless commanders of his generation: as Jonathan Sumption puts it, he was 'a guerrilla leader of genius'. He was also referred to as 'a notable instigator of feud'. The chronicler Froissart commented, after spending two weeks with William, Earl of Douglas, at Dalkeith Castle a few years later: 'in a castle five miles from Haindeburg [Edinburgh] which is known as Dalquest [Dalkeith] I have seen five brothers who bore the name Douglas, all of them esquires in the household of King David'. Meanwhile, young King David was still spending seven years in exile in France, much of it with an entourage of Scottish courtiers at the magnificent Château Gaillard on the Seine.

William Douglas spent 1334 in irons in Carlisle Castle after being captured in a raid on Lochmaben Castle. He missed the fiasco of Halidon Hill, but managed to scrape together his ransom. Then together with the Earl of Moray he led a new guerrilla campaign which took advantage of every occasion when Edward III's main army was otherwise occupied. In 1335 he helped defeat Balliol's ally and the official replacement as royal steward, the Earl of Strathbogie, at Culblean (or Kilblain) on Deeside, then captured Kildrummy Castle with typical Douglas trickery. In 1336 he conducted numerous raids against English stragglers or relief parties, and when Edward was having Bothwell Castle repaired he harried his supply lines. In fact he seems to have spent a number of years based in the depths of Jedburgh Forest, from where he made English control of the border counties a farce. Using the same tactics as the Good Lord James, he built up a devoted following of hardened warriors who lived in the discomfort of Jed and Ettrick Forests. Two of his brothers and five of his nephews were killed.

In 1337 Edward III became frustrated with Scotland, and more ambitiously claimed the throne of France. He declared the war that was to last for a hundred years. For the next century and beyond this was to offer the Scots both some useful opportunities and some dangerous temptations to attack the English when otherwise occupied. William Douglas of Liddesdale and Moray seized the chance to invade English-held Fife. They captured St Andrews. The next year Douglas visited the now fourteen-year-old King David at Château Gaillard, presumably to ask for money, and he recruited some crossbowmen. On his way back he hired some French privateers, led by a Hugh Hautpool, who helped him blockade the Tay so that the Scots were able to capture English-held Perth and Cupar, though Douglas himself was wounded in the thigh by a crossbow at Perth.

The climax of the campaign came in 1341 when William Douglas and the anti-Balliol party captured Edinburgh Castle. He used the ingenious trick of sending a fake wine and provisions merchant up to visit the hungry English garrison. Their commander naively decided to place an order with him, and Douglas's men got into the castle dressed as draymen. He also defeated the English at Crichton or Boroughmuir, swooping down to the rescue from the Pentlands to attack a heavily armed troop of Gascon mercenaries employed by Edward III. Laurieston, Kinclave and Dunottar Castles were captured, and it was at last possible for David II to come home in safety from France. Douglas deserved a lot of the credit for driving the English out of most of Scotland, but of course at the same time he had been building up his own estates in the newly liberated countryside. His brother had Dalkeith Castle and William was now made warden of the middle march. He was officially given Liddesdale, previously held by the absentee Lord of Douglas, and was generally known as the Knight of Liddesdale, embellished by admirers as the Flower of Chivalry. This image was enhanced if not created by his prowess in jousting tournaments, particularly his combat with the English Henry, Earl of Derby, in 1341. His virtual usurpation of leadership of the Douglas family and estates was also helped by the fact that the only surviving brother of Good Lord James, Hugh Douglas the Dull, was a priest at Glasgow Cathedral. This Hugh had inherited some of the estates and had no use for them, particularly since many of them were then inside the current English border and he had no inclination to fight for them. The heir of Sir Archibald Douglas, the guardian, killed at Halidon Hill, was another William Douglas (1330–84), who also had a serious claim to this recently worthless inheritance. He was at this time in France, probably at the Château Gaillard, still too young to do much about it. At least William of Liddesdale had made a practical effort to make the area uninhabitable for Englishmen. Among other rewards he acquired Hermitage Castle in Liddesdale for himself by right of occupation, marriage and the consent of a reluctant steward, who only agreed to part with his rights to it after getting Atholl in exchange.

Unfortunately it was at this time that the Flower of Chivalry somewhat overreached himself by kidnapping a neighbouring baron, Sir Alexander Ramsay, from Hawick Church. He seems to have coveted Ramsay's lands or posts as Sheriff of Roxburgh and Constable of the Castle, which he had captured recently from the English with panache worthy of a Douglas. Ramsay died of unknown causes in the dungeons of Hermitage, but legend had it that he lay starving in the dungeon called Massie More for seventeen days, nibbling the odd grain of corn that fell down from the granary above. In Sir Walter Scott's time some bones were uncovered in the vaults of Hermitage which seemed to confirm the story. William Douglas of Liddesdale never quite recovered his reputation, though he still had much useful work to do. As Abbot Bower sadly commented, 'O exterminabilis invidia Diaboli' (Misleading is the devil's hatred).'

The young Bruce King David II returned to Scotland still aged only about seventeen, so comparisons with his father were odious if inevitable. He was still only twenty-two when in 1346 he led his first major invasion of England. The battle of Neville's Cross, near Durham, was, like Halidon Hill, another example of risking almost the entire available army of Scotland against an English force which if beaten could be quite easily replaced, but which if victorious could overrun Scotland almost at will. The reason for even thinking of it was that Edward III was otherwise engaged with most of his troops in the Crécy campaign against the French. It must be said that the 'auld alliance', the idea of helping the French by diversions whenever they were attacked by the English, was one of the most pernicious in Scottish history.

At his age David can hardly be blamed for the lack of strategy and the rashness of accepting battle. Robert the Steward was senior commander and should have known better. King David himself fought bravely, knocking out the teeth of one opponent, but was hit near his eye by an arrow and captured. He spent the next eleven years in detention in

England, much of it in the Tower of London. This removed any chance of his rebuilding a solid monarchy and left Scotland once more in chaos and vulnerable to attack. Even when he was at last ransomed it was to have a crippling effect on Scotland's finances.

Apart from leaving Scotland open again to invasion, Neville's Cross was also significant for one other notable prisoner and one notable escapee. The captive was William Douglas of Liddesdale who was to spend six years in English prisons, though he was sometimes allowed out on parole to act as a negotiator. The escapee was Robert the Steward, who at Halidon Hill had already shown his ability to get away from disastrous battles. He repeated this feat at Neville's Cross to the subsequent disgust of his kingly nephew, who might be forgiven for thinking that Robert now saw himself seriously as heir to the throne, for David's Queen Joanna had as yet shown no sign of producing an heir. As Andrew of Wyntown put it in the *Orygenale Cronykil*, the Steward 'left David to caper as he wished'.

Robert the Steward was now in his early thirties, not yet at the middle of what was to be a very long career. In effect he was to be steward for forty years, twelve of which included periods as sole or joint regent, and king for another twenty after that. He had at this point demonstrated the knack of surviving serious battles without either being killed or caught, and of being a reasonably competent if unexciting guardian. According to Fordun, he was 'a comely youth, tall, robust, worthy, liberal and with an innate sweetness'. Twenty years later he was described by Abbot Bower as 'impressive, humble, mild, affable, cheerful and honourable'. Only his bloodshot eye, a relic of his remarkable birth, marred an otherwise commanding appearance. Yet perhaps he lacked some aspects of drive and energy. His military ambitions were modest, which accounted for his survival, and even the temptation of the throne seems to have excited him only occasionally.

Robert's main concern was perhaps his massive family – he had twenty legitimate children and a few bastards – whom he used when he could throughout his life to patch up alliances and buy off enemies. His period as guardian, therefore, throughout most of King David's absence as a prisoner, was not notable for much action, nor for a great deal of effort or money collected to secure the release of the prisoner. In 1347 he could not prevent Edward Balliol from once again ravaging the Borders, and he had difficulty with many of his own barons, especially those in the outer isles. He could not, however, be blamed for the onset of the Black Death, which arrived in Scotland in 1349, a year later than in England, causing huge misery and many deaths, especially among the poorer members of the population.

Meanwhile, William Douglas of Liddesdale, with his customary ability to improvise, was making his own efforts to get out of prison. Even when he was in captivity he still managed with his mafia-like tentacles to ensure the murder of Barclay of Brechin in Aberdeen, in revenge for helping to murder his brother John. Much of this activity centred on William's capacity to act as a go-between negotiating the ransom for his king and other affairs. This resulted in his being reinstated to Hermitage by Edward III. He made various vows of service to the English which he doubtless simply regarded as a means to an end but which led to some accusations of treachery later. His return to Scotland in 1350 was made the more uncomfortable by the fact that the genuine senior baron of the Douglas dynasty had meanwhile himself reappeared in Scotland from France, and was realizing how much of his patrimony had been purloined by the Flower of Chivalry, his namesake and godfather.

William, the rightful new Lord of Douglas, had been only three when his father, Sir Archibald, died at Halidon Hill. He had been brought up in France, like young King David, and was now in his early twenties. The fact that the Flower of Chivalry was suspected as a traitor and known to have been the murderer of Ramsay made it seem all the more understandable that his injured godson might quarrel with him. Godscroft adds the suggestion that Liddesdale was involved with his godson's wife, but that is a little unlikely. Moreover, the younger William Douglas had taken over some of the role previously fulfilled by his namesake, operating small guerrilla attacks against the English or Balliol supporters from a lair in Jedburgh Forest. He had a notable success luring the English commander of Roxburgh Castle into an ambush in Teviotdale. According to Bower, in a skirmish with Laurens de Abernethy he was beaten back seven times, but fought back so doggedly that he won in the end.

No one is sure how it happened, but in 1353 William Douglas, Lord of Douglas, came across William Douglas, Lord of Liddesdale, hunting in Ettrick Forest, and killed him. The murder took place at Galswood in Minchmuir, near Traquair, and the spot was later marked by William's Cross. The younger Douglas was perhaps on his way back from a raid against Edward Balliol's lands in Galloway. He had plenty of reason to resent the success of his godfather, besides the story that the older man was having an affair with the younger's wife. As the ballad put it,

> The countess out of the bower she came
> And loudly there that she did call
> It is for the Lord of Liddesdale
> That I let all these tears down fall.

The Flower of Chivalry had only a daughter, who died soon afterwards, so it was not all that hard for his godson to start reacquiring the missing parts of his estate. Bower referred to Liddesdale as 'brave in battle', Fordun as 'a wise and very prudent man', but the apologists of the main Douglas line saw him perhaps more as a traitor and the black sheep of the family. The old rascal had refounded a small chapel at Crookboat where the Douglas Water joined the Clyde, and after he was buried at Melrose his relations arranged for annual masses at the altar of St Bride or Bridget, the family patron. His career illustrated yet again what could be achieved by a self-made man who had the military panache to attract a competent group of knights, who in turn expected to be led to regain their own forfeited estates. His brother Sir John founded the Douglases of Lochleven and his nephew on that side took over Aberdour and Dalkeith Castles, which were to become the power base of the Morton branch of the Douglases.

Whatever the moral judgements that might be made, in Liddesdale's death a genuinely successful guerrilla leader against Balliol and the English had been killed: in the words of the Scotichronicon, 'Flagellus Anglorum et Scotorum murus' (Scourge of the English and rampart of the Scots). The man responsible for his death took up the challenge of both replacing him in that role and maintaining the Douglas name at the forefront of Scottish politics.

It is possible that either of these two Williams may have been the historical basis for the Lord William featured in the ballad known as 'The Douglas Tragedy'. This was alleged to have taken place at the small Douglas Castle of Blackhouse or Blackhope, 'of an aspect stern and savage', built by the Good Lord James or his father, which stood on another stream called Douglas which flows down into St Mary's Loch in Yarrow. The story went that Lord Douglas's daughter fell in love with a Lord William of whom the family disapproved and who killed her father and seven brothers as they tried to prevent the elopement:

> She held his steed with her milk white hand
> And never shed one tear
> Until that she saw her seven brothers fa'
> And her father hard fighting that loved her so dear.

The two lovers also died and all were buried in St Mary's Chapel. Seven stones at Rispdyke are said traditionally to mark the site of the tragedy.

Meanwhile, the Scots were again beginning to get the upper hand against the English garrisons in the border counties. The effort was helped by the supply of men, arms and money by the French, who were still grateful for any diversion to distract Edward III. There were the so-called golden arguments from the French to encourage the Stewart guardian to take more action. William Douglas used the baited trap and ambush technique so beloved of his family to defeat an English force near Norham. He also attacked Caerlaverock Castle, a Balliol stronghold. The Steward himself undertook a siege of Berwick and organized scorched-earth tactics to starve the English soldiery when Edward III once more led an army back into Scotland. Robert Stewart's eldest son, John of Carrick, later King Robert III (1340–1406), led a raid into Annandale. Edward III retaliated by killing indiscriminately and burning everywhere in southern Scotland which had not already been burnt, an event known as the Burnt Candlemas, but his men had no food and he had to retreat. Douglas managed another ambush near Melrose and regained Hermitage Castle.

The English really needed some peace in the north so that they could concentrate on their war in France which was again coming to a head. So at long last Edward Balliol, now bankrupt, admitted defeat and in 1356 resigned the Crown of Scotland, which he had never really been properly able to wear. He spent the rest of his life hunting, and died in Yorkshire some years later. Edward III called a halt – the English were to keep out of Scotland for the next thirty years – and serious negotiations started for the ransoming of David II. William Douglas with other Scottish barons took a fighting holiday, joining King John of France's army against the Black Prince at Poitiers in 1356. It was a serious French defeat, but it was not of much consequence to the Scots, except for those, like the Lord of the Isles, who were captured. Douglas nearly was, but his friends dragged him away, badly wounded, just in time. As Michael Brown points out, the Poitiers expedition was conceived as a kind of crusade to replicate the prestige achieved by the Good Lord James at Teba and as a team-building exercise for the new Douglas retinue of knights. And William liked the sound of having a barony at St Saens in Normandy, even if in reality it was still in English hands.

Thus in 1357 David II, now in his early thirties, returned a second time to Scotland, having so far been absent from his country for sixteen of the twenty-six years that he had officially reigned. Naturally the Steward was uncomfortable at losing both the regency and possibly his position as heir to the throne once David returned to his wife. He must also have been uncomfortable, having arranged the promotion of so many of his children to earldoms and other positions of power. For the last fourteen years of David's reign he was to be as often out of favour as in it, the lowest ebb being when he was locked up in Lochleven Castle for nearly a year. But he was always a great survivor, and for the most part he kept a low profile waiting to see what happened.

Douglas, on the other hand, initially fared quite well after David's return. As a guarantor of the king's ransom he had to visit the English court regularly as a kind of hostage, and he seems to have enjoyed meeting other knights in England just as he had in France. For his work on the ransom negotiations he was made 1st Earl of Douglas in 1358. But within three years he was finding himself excluded from power and irritated by David's behaviour. There is no doubt that David had been affected by his stay in England, observing at first hand the charismatic professionalism of a king like Edward III, and no doubt impressed by the relative munificence of his court. In attempting to match some of that professionalism back in Scotland David perhaps did not have quite the personality to carry it off – it would have been far from easy. With senior barons used to having their own way in his absence, it was extremely difficult to bring them to heel without offending them. And he had the added difficulty of having to collect the vast ransom of 100,000 merks which was due to be paid to the English in instalments. Since this was largely his own fault, the barons perhaps expected him to curb his own personal expenditure, rather than having to pay up for him themselves. But that was not David's style. Having had an unsatisfactory, childless marriage with Edward III's sister, who no doubt rubbed in his inadequacies and who returned to England for good the year he came back from captivity, he needed money to impress a series of mistresses, one of whom later became his second wife.

Thus David's apparent extravagance riled his barons, and a group of them, apparently led by Thomas Stewart, Earl of Angus, arranged for one of the mistresses, Katherine Mortimer, to be murdered on a journey near Soutra Hospital. In reaction the King seized Kildrummy Castle from the Earl of Mar. In kingship at this time there was a very fine line between effective disciplining of rebellious barons and treatment of them which could be represented by others as unjust. David II did not quite get it right, just like James I sixty years later, who had also spent many years in English detention, copying a style of kingship which only the very ablest and most charismatic could carry off. Robert the Steward could see that David was about to marry his new mistress, Margaret Drummond, who had already proven her capacity to have children, and he dreaded the possibility of losing the expectation of the Crown which he had perhaps begun to take for granted. When David gave the old Bruce lands of Annandale to his new stepson, John of Logie, it was bad enough, but when the still childless king suggested in 1364 that the English Prince Lionel should be declared the official heir instead of the Steward it was the last straw, and showed rather poor judgement, perhaps even spite.

The Earl of Douglas was also perhaps acquiring delusions of grandeur, rating his own personality as stronger than the Steward's, and playing with his genealogy to prove some far-fetched descent from the Comyns or Balliols. But for the time being in 1362 the Steward and Douglas joined forces and began an armed rebellion. Perhaps it was a surprise for them, but David acted with speed, efficiency and ruthlessness, characteristics of which he was quite capable. Douglas had successfully seized Dirleton Castle for the rebels, then moved to Lanark, without posting adequate scouts to warn him of any attack. David attacked and Douglas soon had to surrender, as did Robert the Steward and his two eldest sons. The rebellion was a total failure.

David's last few years were, however, far from satisfactory. Ordinary people had been suffering from another epidemic of the Black Death, not improved by the disordered condition of the countryside. The kingdom was in upheaval and the Steward took the blame, being locked up at Lochleven at the request of the new queen. But, like her predecessor, she failed to have children and, like her, she was divorced, as David considered taking a third queen, Agnes Dunbar. Robert was released and partially rehabilitated, as was the Earl of Douglas, who went with David on his naval expedition to suppress the McDonalds. In 1369 David achieved the remarkable feat of gaining submission from both the Campbells and McDonalds. He did in his final two years also achieve considerable gains in the Borders area from Edward III, so his reign was far from ineffective. The Earl of Mar for his disobedience was severely disciplined with a spell on the Bass Rock. Perhaps because David was still having to pay off the instalments of his ransom, he had perforce to improve the finances of the Scottish exchequer, and he had to instil some discipline among his barons. As Ranald Nicholson puts it: 'It is doubtful if any medieval Scottish king . . . was in so strong a financial position.'

But then quite suddenly, at the age of forty-seven, David died, in February 1371.

Of the four families that we have looked at from the beginning of this book, two had achieved royalty and both had lost it. The Balliols had bowed to pressure in 1356 and never appeared again in Scottish history. The male line of the Royal Bruces died out in 1371 and they did not feature in mainstream politics again. It was now at last the time for the Stewarts, but the Douglases were also now panting in the wings and acquiring an international image. Writers such as Barbour and Froissart publicized their tales of exotic chivalry, utilizing the romanticized memories of Jean le Bel of Hainault, who had been a mercenary on the losing side against Lord James Douglas in 1327. Significantly too the junior branches of the Douglas dynasty were also expanding, for it was in 1369 that James Douglas of Dalkeith, son of the Flower of Chivalry's younger brother, acquired Morton Castle in Nithsdale, a name (in fact they took the title of Earls of Morton officially from a much more obscure Morton in West Lothian) that was later to be associated with the best and worst of Douglas ambitions.

CHAPTER FIVE

The Stewarts Win

He is thy ancyent enymy werst of ane
A thousand wylis he hes and many a trane.

Gavin Douglas, *Eneados*

Robert II, the seventh hereditary steward and the first of the Stewart family to become royal, was in his mid-fifties by the time he at last reached the throne in 1371, an old man by the standards of that era and nearly a decade older than the king who had just died. He had proved himself a survivor rather than an energetic or proactive ruler when he had been regent for his nephew, and now nothing much was to change. But then it could be argued if he did not do a great deal of good he did not either do any serious harm or take foolish risks with other people's lives. As Michael Brown describes him, he was 'the arch political realist'.

William, Earl of Douglas, who was about ten years Robert's junior, now made his move. He came to the castle at Linlithgow and put himself forward as an alternative choice for the throne. His genealogical evidence of entitlement was pretty poor, but doubtless he hoped that his personality and greater reputation as an English-baiter might compare favourably with the rather more unassuming attitude of the new king. He was wrong. Even his own nearest relatives persuaded him that he should desist from his claim and, as eight years previously in his confrontation with David II, he backed down without much apparent loss of face. As the Douglas tradition in war had always been to order a strategic retreat when faced with overwhelming odds, so in politics it was to back down and wait for another opportunity. What might seem remarkable was that he could do so with impunity, but Robert realized, as David had, that if he tried to punish Douglas too severely then his back would be to the wall, his numerous relations would rally round and the King might be faced with a long campaign of guerrilla tactics, expensive sieges and the probability that he could not rely on enough of his other barons to join in punishing one of their own number, however much a traitor. It was a game of chess with knights, castles and pawns, and not easy for a king to win unless he was very strong or wily.

So instead of punishment Douglas received rewards. He was bought off with two important posts, the Justiciarship of the South and the Wardenship of the East March, together with a straightforward bribe and a royal marriage to the Princess Isabella for his fifteen-year-old son James (1358–88). He soon afterwards also acquired the land of North Berwick and its castle at Tantallon – which he rebuilt as one of the most massive and strongly fortified in Scotland – possibly from King Robert's second son, the Earl of Fife. Then to his vast collection of estates in 1374 he added the earldom of Mar and its huge castle at Kildrummy from his wife's brother – the Earl had died in suspicious circumstances with no children, so his sister, Douglas's wife, inherited the earldom and automatically passed it to her husband.

To add insult to injury, a few years later Douglas, now in his fifties, had a torrid affair with the dead earl's widow, Margaret Stewart, a relationship which in the law of that period was regarded as incestuous. As it happened Margaret had herself inherited the earldom of Angus, and when in due course the affair, conducted under the nose of Douglas's wife at Tantallon, produced an illegitimate son, the couple organized a bending of the law to let the boy George (1380–1403) become the first Douglas Earl of Angus. He was thus founder of the Red Douglases, a dynasty whose erratic fortunes will occupy several chapters later in this book. Thus William Douglas's late-middle-age fling led to a division of the now vast Douglas empire. It was big enough for that not to matter too much, but it meant that future Stewart kings would have greater opportunities to divide and rule, playing off the Red against the Black.

For the time being Douglas was immensely wealthy, as is shown by the frequent spending sprees which he and his wife indulged in south of the border, though some of this was to buy food for his people who were suffering from famine after the long-term devastation of so much of their lands by both sides, English and Scots. He had to keep the loyalty and foster the morale of the numerous families who made up his power base, such as the Kerrs, Rutherfords, Turnbulls, Pringles, Glendinnings and Colvilles. He had to keep impressing everyone with the size of his retinue and the opulence of his lifestyle.

In 1376 the first of two very important deaths occurred south of the border, that of the Prince of Wales, Edward, the Black Prince, an able and ruthless general who if he had lived to take over the Crown of England might have made life very difficult in Scotland. The second, less than a year later, was that of his father, Edward III, who had beaten Scottish armies and invaded Scotland so often, yet never, because of his other ambitions, had the patience to consolidate his conquests. His final years had been marred by family bickering and an affair with a greedy lady-in-waiting, so there had been no invasions for some years, but the English did still hold a number of Scottish castles and border counties. Now that the new king, Richard II (1367–1402), was only ten years old, life might be even easier for the Scots. The regent John of Gaunt, Duke of Lancaster, was still pursuing the very expensive war with France and his poll tax provoked a massive uprising in England in 1380. Thus, as the English looked more vulnerable, so the Scots' confidence revived.

The Earl of Douglas, although old for soldiering, was tempted to indulge in a few more years of border raiding, assisted by his heir, James, who was now about twenty. In 1378 they raided Berwick and captured it briefly, but did not have the resources to keep it, so they made a tactical withdrawal. Two years later they organized a major attack on the Percy estates in Northumberland, burnt Penrith, threatened Carlisle and brought back 40,000 head of livestock with other booty. Unfortunately they brought back something else as well. As Abbot Bower put it: 'While the Scots thirsted for booty they came to unconsolable grief because from their spoil arose a pestilence in the kingdom by which almost a third of the population died in the same year.' This was Scotland's third experience of the bubonic plague or Black Death – it would probably have come anyway, but was perhaps expedited by the raid down south.

Douglas's final expedition was in 1384. By this time he was in his fifties, so the real leaders on the field were his son James and his cousin Archibald Douglas (1328–1400), known as the Grim, Lord of Galloway. This attack, funded partly by the French and provoked by a cross-border raid led by the Duke of Lancaster, resulted in the retaking from the English at long last of Lochmaben Castle and the expulsion of the English from Teviotdale. Soon afterwards Douglas died, and was buried at Melrose.

His successor, James, the 2nd Earl, was of course the son-in-law of King Robert II. He was in his mid-twenties, and, while his ten-year marriage to Princess Isabella had produced no offspring, he had sired a couple of bastards. His brief but exciting occupation of the earldom was to be noted for his total disregard for the wishes and policies of his father-in-law. Robert II, whose reign Ranald Nicholson perhaps a little unkindly refers to as 'futile and aimless', was now in his seventieth year and almost senile. He needed all such faculties as he still retained to try to manage his own twenty children, among whom Alexander, the Wolf of Badenoch (1344–1405), was simply the most notorious of his greedy progeny. What is more his heir, John, Earl of Carrick, now in his forties, was regarded by his peers as potentially no great improvement. He had taken part in a few military actions without great distinction, but his fighting career was finished ironically at about this time by a kick from a Douglas horse. The horse belonged to Sir James Douglas of Dalkeith and the injury left John an almost permanent invalid, so that when a few years later the family decided to put aside the senile father it was his next brother, Robert, Earl of Fife (1340–1420), who was made regent.

In this undisciplined atmosphere James, 2nd Earl of Douglas, appointed himself chief enemy of the English. This was helped by the fact that he had the dashing image that was then required in the international chivalry circuit and hit it off very well with the French knights who came or were sent across to Scotland in search of adventure and to help divert the English from their conquest of France. So in 1384 Douglas mounted his first attack on the Percy territory of Northumberland, taking with him the French knights who thoroughly enjoyed the sport. As Bower put it, they went 'To brinne, to robbe and to steale', and came back with plunder and minimal loss of life to their own troops.

In 1385 Douglas repeated the venture, leaving Roxburgh still in English hands as too tough a target, but he laid waste Northumberland, captured Wark Castle and then retreated as usual. This time, however, the consequences were dire, for Richard II, who was still only eighteen, put together a large army and retaliated with a full-scale invasion of Scotland which Douglas could not do, or chose not to do, anything to halt. The English burnt most of the border abbeys and Edinburgh itself, but achieved little positive, as once again the Scots had removed all livestock and grain, leaving no food for the English soldiers or horses. As Froissart describes it, the English 'saw not even a bird, owls alone excepted'.

Douglas retaliated with a raid on Carlisle and Cockermouth from which he brought back plenty of livestock, but not enough to make a serious difference to the famine throughout Scotland which his policy had provoked. As Boece puts it, they 'cam sa warly throw the watters of Sulway that they came to Cokirmouth in Ingland and abod there thre days invading the country with great cruelties and returning with great prey of guddies in Scotland'. The Scots even had the effrontery to demand extra payment from the French for the damages done to their estates by the English retaliating against the Scottish raids which had included a few French knights.

After this there was a lull for a couple of years, but in 1388 Douglas again called together his friends and, in defiance of the known wishes of Robert II, organized another raid on Northumberland. The target looked vulnerable, for Henry Percy, known as Harry Hotspur (1364–1402), the Lord of Northumberland, was quarrelling with his own neighbours, and King Richard II, now of age, was falling out with his bossy uncles. In addition, splendid new armour for the Scottish knights had been sent across by the French, and the Scots were desperate to try it out. The King's second son, Robert, now about to become regent, was to take a larger army down the west coast accompanied by Archibald Douglas, the Grim, Lord of Galloway, and they were to create the diversion; James Douglas was to go down the east coast with a smaller force and attack Hotspur. Douglas gathered first at Eddybredshiels, his house near the border where the Ettrick joined the Yarrow (near where Bowhill now stands), then went on to Southdean Church in Ettrick Forest where his force came together. As the old 'Ballad of Otterburn' said:

> It fell about the Lammas tide
> When the muir-men win their hay
> The doughty Douglas bound him to ride
> Into England to drive a prey.

Then it was on south to Durham and back to Newcastle, which they tried to besiege. Sadly their ladders were too short and, according to a chronicler, the defendants in the spirit of chivalry let down a pipe of wine (two hogsheads) as consolation. By this time most of the major castles had artillery, but besiegers found it difficult to move heavy cannon around the countryside, so they still relied mainly on old-fashioned, pre-gunpowder missile projectors, such as trebuckets and mangonels.

According to legend, at this point Hotspur offered to settle the issue by single combat and Douglas accepted. They rode at each other with unprotected lances, and as the ballad tells us:

> But O how pale his lady looked
> Frae aff the castle wa,
> When down before the Scottish spear
> She saw proud Percy fa.

One version of the legend has Douglas unhorsing Hotspur and getting away with his pennon. Hotspur was determined to recover this before Douglas could get back to Scotland. However, his pursuit of the Scots was at first half-hearted because he thought the force of the regent, Robert Stewart, was there too and he would be outnumbered. In fact, he soon saw that this was not the case, and as he chased Douglas up to Otterburn he could see that the Scottish force was only half the size of his own. Thus in the end the English attacked the Scots late in the evening when they were eating or sleeping and very nearly surprised them. The poet says of Douglas:

But I have dreamd a dreary dream,
Beyond the Isle of Sky;
I saw a dead man win a fight,
And I think that man was I.

Barry, the writer of this hagiographic poem, was the Douglas-appointed clergyman at one of their pet foundations, Bothwell.

Douglas was in fact seriously wounded early in the battle, and as he lay dying was asked how he felt. According to Froissart the reply was: 'Right evil; yet thank God but few of my ancestors have died in their beds. . . . I pray you revenge me. . . . Rayse my banner which lyeth near me on the ground; shew my state neither to friend or foe, lest mine enemies rejoice and my friends be discomfited.' As the minstrel put it:

Hosts have been known at that dread sound to yield
And Douglas dead his name hath won the field.

So in the end the Scots won, with only a few hundred casualties, the English losing several thousand. The battle of Otterburn or Chevy Chase was of course wonderful material for chroniclers and minstrels, but, while all this tit-for-tat cross-border raiding was excellent sport for the knights in shining armour, it was desperately damaging to the economies and to the lives of ordinary people over a wide area between north Yorkshire and the central belt of Scotland. It also led to the destruction of many fine buildings. The adulation which the dead Douglas received was perhaps more than he deserved:

O bury me by the bracken-bush
Beneath the blooming brier
Let never living mortal ken
That ere a kindly Scot lies here.

In fact the young earl's body was taken back for burial at Melrose. He left a widow and no legitimate children to succeed him. Two years later, in 1390, the aged King Robert II at last died, at Dundonald Castle, so in some respects it was the end of an era.

One other remarkable Douglas died at this time. Sir William Douglas of Nithsdale (*c.* 1350–92) was a bastard son of Archibald the Grim (see next chapter) who made his name by holding a bridge near Carlisle with a mere 800 Scots faced by 3,000 English. He fell in love with and married young Princess Egidia Stewart, one of Robert II's numerous daughters. She was known as the Lady Gellis and was reputed to be a woman of exceptional beauty; as Boece puts it 'Gels excellit all othir wemen in beaute.'

Then, while his illustrious cousin the 2nd Earl was at Otterburn, he staged a raid on the English in Ireland which led to the capture of fifteen ships, the burning of Carlingford and 'sa mervellus slauchter'. He harried the Isle of Man on the way home and was still in time to join the main army under his father as it raided Cumberland. So this had in fact been a three-pronged attack on the English: in Northumberland, Cumberland and Ulster. The next year we hear of William joining one of the north German crusades and being appointed an admiral in Danzig ready to take 100 German ships to fight the heathen. At this moment he was murdered, apparently by an English knight called Clifford, with whom he had a long-standing feud rising from a challenge to single combat which never took place.

CHAPTER SIX

Dukes and Drakes

For my brothers and sisters were black as the gate
Whereby I shall pass tomorrow
But I was white and delicate
And born to splendour and sorrow.

Lord Alfred Douglas, 'Perkin Warbeck'

John, Earl of Carrick, inherited the Scottish Crown in 1390, as the eldest legitimate son of Robert II. In fact he was only legitimate because of the power and influence of his family, for Robert's first marriage to a cousin was technically incestuous and was legitimized by the Church only when, many years later and after another ten children, Robert at last had the muscle as Guardian to extract permission from the Pope. At the time of his accession John was already past fifty, and not even in his youth had he been regarded as very effective or energetic. He had been theoretically in charge of justice during the early part of his father's reign and achieved little in that role, not even the curbing of his avaricious and ill-behaved brothers. Then as his father became senile he had been passed over for the regency in favour of his younger brother Robert, Earl of Fife.

The lack of general respect for John's abilities was perhaps eventually shared by the man himself and was exacerbated by the crippling kick from a Douglas horse which had left him in almost permanent pain. In the first months of his reign his credibility was further damaged when his maverick brother, Alexander Stewart, known as the Wolf of Badenoch, burnt the cathedral and town of Elgin just because the bishop was refusing any longer to pay him protection money. Now the new king decided to discard at least one symbol of his bad luck, the name John which had been borne by three unfortunate kings over recent years: John Balliol of Scotland, King John of England and King John II of France, who had died a prisoner in the Tower of London. So John of Carrick became King Robert III of Scotland. For many of his subjects, however, he retained the nickname 'John Faranyear' (for one year).

Remarkably the man whose horse kicked the future king so badly became his son-in-law. This Sir James Douglas of Dalkeith and Morton was one of the richest, most cultured men in Scotland of his time, organizing his numerous estates with great efficiency and paying more attention to peace than war. His extensive library contained books on law, logic and grammar. In due course his family was to produce the third major branch of the Douglases, the earls of Morton.

Because of Robert III's perceived lack of competence in a demanding age, his brother Robert, Earl of Fife, acted as his lieutenant and de facto head of government for most of his reign, a position he was already used to from the period when their father had been declared unfit to rule. Certainly he was more competent than either father or brother, and was a reasonable if unexciting leader in war, but his rule at this time and later was characterized by deviousness as he sought to grasp the Crown to which he was so very close. But he never quite went through with usurpation, and amazingly, despite the number of weak or juvenile incumbents of the Stewart monarchy, the line was to remain unbroken during a period when usurpation by stronger relatives happened quite frequently among the English kings. The Regent Robert paid far less attention to the dull detail of government than had David II, especially to finance. In fact, like his nephew later, he tended to blur any distinction between the cash in his own pocket and the government exchequer, so that in particular he failed to pay off the remaining instalments of King David's ransom to the English, always an excuse for another row.

The new Earl of Douglas, Archibald the Grim or 'Blac Archibalde', was even more of a veteran, twelve years older than the king. Nor in the normal course of events would he ever have expected to inherit the title, but for the premature death of his distant cousin James, the victor of Otterburn. He had been born the illegitimate child of an unknown mother and the Good Lord James two years before the hero's death in Spain, so he had to claw his way up the baronial chain by sheer ability. Like the Good Lord James and the first Black Douglas earl, he had spent some of his early years in France, probably at the Chateau Gailllard, sharing the exile of David II and his courtiers. Unlike his legitimate relations, he had everything to gain by giving wholehearted support to the Bruce dynasty while it lasted and then to the Stewarts, for he could never see himself as their rival, and in fact needed their help to attain any standing he could acquire. Thus in 1342, when David II returned from France, he made himself useful to the inexperienced king. He was rewarded by being given entitlement to some of the Douglas estates from Hugh Douglas, the Glasgow priest, who had reluctantly inherited them after the debacle of Halidon Hill and who had also given some of his share to the Knight of Liddesdale. Most of these estates were in English hands at the time so the award of them was rather a challenge than a prize. No other record of Archibald's career before 1356 survives, but it can be assumed from the results that he gained ample military experience in the numerous attacks on English garrisons and supply wagons north of the border at that time.

In 1356 Blac Archibald, as he was then known, fought for the French army against the Black Prince and was captured at the battle of Poitiers alongside some of his more illustrious relations. According to legend he managed to escape by the double bluff of pretending to be a serving man dressed up as his own master. He arranged for a friend to accuse him loudly of stealing his master's armour, easy enough for apparently 'he looked more like a coco [cookboy] than a noble', and was thus able to ransom himself for forty shillings – it was not unusual for important barons in that period of big ransom money to have lookalike decoys so that they could distract the enemy. In 1361 David II made him constable of Edinburgh Castle, a position of very great trust and one which he used to organize much needed repairs of the castle, including what is now known as David's Tower. In this role and later as Sheriff of Edinburgh he opposed the rebellion led by Robert the Steward and the then Earl of Douglas in 1363. Then, using his role as Warden of the Western Marches, he began to carve an empire for himself in enemy-held Galloway. According to one chronicler, his sword was two ells in length, too big for a normal knight to use, and he was an impressive warrior: in Godscroft's words, 'A most worthie captane, being as terrible in countenance with horrible luikes, as austeir in maners and lyfe be the whilk he was callit the Grim Douglas.' He was recorded as having a famous victory over the Englishman Thomas Musgrave near Melrose. According to Godscroft again, 'He tuke grit trawell to purge the country of English blude', and his reward in 1369 was to be recognized as Lord of Galloway. At the same time he was supporting his distant cousin James Douglas of Dalkeith, who wanted back Liddesdale, against the might of his nearer cousin the first Black Douglas earl. As Michael Brown points out, this ganging together of the two junior Douglas branches against the senior helped both of them.

Archibald even had time to go on pilgrimage to Saint-Denis, outside Paris, though doubtless there was a diplomatic by-product, quite possibly the stirring-up of the French against the English. He was in fact to take one more delicate mission for David II to France when he was sent to the Pope's palace at Avignon to procure the King's divorce from his second wife, Margaret, as David II proposed to make one final effort to produce an heir to his throne. But that was not to be. As we have seen, David died childless and the Stewarts succeeded the Bruces as the ruling dynasty.

Also about this time Archibald the Grim, now approaching forty, acquired a wife. According to legend he had to challenge five Englishmen to duels before he won the hand of Joanna of Moray. But once he had won the lady he acquired as her dowry significant additional lands in Moray and the magnificent castle at Bothwell, which had been rebuilt by Edward III himself, together with Drumsargad outside Glasgow and Carmunnock. He was now rich enough to buy himself the county of Wigtown from its former earl in 1372, doubtless at a knock-down price since he had already terrorized most of the local barons into submission. During this period he was building for himself a new castle at Threave, the new headquarters for his lordship of Galloway, living meanwhile on Brent Isle, a crannog (artificial island) on Loch Ken. One version of the story claimed that the castle was built in a single night with a huge army of workers acting as a human chain 15 miles long from the quarry. This building was the start of a new architectural fashion and was to set new standards for the era. He pioneered the concept of the large fortified tower house with access only up a single turnpike stair which could be defended by a very small number of men. In addition he was responsible for the founding of two collegiate churches which still stand, Lincluden, outside Dumfries, and Bothwell, as well as being a patron of the Holywood monastic hospital founded by Edward or Sir Robert Bruce north of Dumfries. At Lincluden he first had to shut down the nunnery, but seems to have excused this on the basis of the irregularity of the nuns who lived there. In several of his buildings he seems to have employed the French master-builder John Morrow, as the quality of workmanship is very high.

Despite his age, Archibald took part with his senior Douglas cousins and the new king's second son, Regent Robert, in the invasion of England during part of which his cousin was killed at Otterburn, and in the raid on Annandale which led to the capture of Lochmaben Castle from the English. Again in 1389 he joined Regent Robert in an invasion of England, ravaging huge swathes of the north, and it was said that the two of them offered to settle the issue by single combat with the English Earl Marshal, an offer which was rejected. It was said by Richard Maitland that the Regent Robert Stewart 'luifit this erle sa weill that thai never syuerit cumpanye fra other during the time of his government'. It was Archibald who repelled the English retaliation which followed.

Thus, when the second Black Douglas earl died leaving only two illegitimate sons, Archibald the Grim, now aged sixty and also illegitimate, but acknowledged as a self-made senior baron, suddenly saw a chance to inherit the earldom of Douglas. There was already a legally valid claimant, Malcolm Drummond, one of the old earl's sons-in-law, but with his ally James Douglas of Dalkeith, Archibald set about nobbling all the minor barons in the earldom, so that Drummond soon found his position untenable. Not that the extra earldom (he was already Earl of

Wigtown) made a vast difference to Archibald. In fact he was to get the reputation of being unimpressed by titles, for when the new king, Robert III, gave his own brother Robert and his son David dukedoms, the first ever such in Scotland, Archibald is believed to have turned down a similar offer – as Godscroft put it, 'He despisit the title of Duk', and he is recorded as commenting 'Sir Duke, Sir Drake'. But with the earldom he did gain Douglas itself, Buittle and Selkirk, while James of Dalkeith got Liddesdale, and the Red Douglases hung onto Tantallon and Cavers. By uniting the old Black Douglas lands with his own acquisition of Galloway he created the larger power base for the next few generations. In fact Michael Brown comments: 'It was Archibald the Grim who would be the real founder of the Black Douglas dynasty.'

Despite a level of service to the monarchy during three reigns which was more consistent than most of his predecessors, one of old Archibald's last acts was perhaps one of vanity, and was to have unforeseen and very damaging effects after his death. This was the arrangement of his daughter's wedding to David, Duke of Rothesay, the King's eldest son, with the prospect that she would soon be queen. The reason that it was a potential disaster was not so much the probable weakness of David's character, though that was a factor, but that David's marriage to another woman, Elizabeth of March, had already been ratified and indeed paid for in gold by her father. It is possible that Douglas used his influence and his cash with his old friend the King's brother Robert, now known as the Duke of Albany. But perhaps not, for a few months earlier Archibald seems to have sided with the delightful Queen Annabella against Albany in a small palace coup, which resulted in his prospective son-in-law replacing Albany as the King's lieutenant. Frustrated by her husband's incompetence and infidelity, the saintly queen at least wanted to assert the rights of her son against her crafty brother-in-law. The royal government under Albany had not unfairly been accused of general 'mysgovernance', and while the gentle Robert III took the blame himself, the real target was Albany, whose extravagances had made him unpopular. At about the same time Richard II of England was removed from the throne and murdered by his family for similar reasons.

So in a short period David of Rothesay, who was only twenty-one, was promoted far beyond his abilities and allowed enough rope to make plenty of mistakes. He was also seen to have jilted his fiancée, for although both marriages were doubtless arranged for him it is hard to believe that such a headstrong young man did not have quite a say in giving up Elizabeth March in favour of Marjorie Douglas. The outcome was very serious. Elizabeth's father, the Earl of March, was so outraged by the royal breach of promise that he went over to the English and his knowledge of Scottish tactics was such that he made a major contribution to English successes over Scotland during the next ten or so years. And the promotion of his son-in-law, which Douglas had helped to arrange, was to leave the royal heir's extravagance and incompetence so open to public view that he could be destroyed. These two disasters, caused indirectly by Archibald the Grim's action in his old age, were to occur after his death. He died in his new castle at Threave on Christmas Eve 1400, and was buried at Bothwell. According to Bower, 'in worldly prudence, bravery, boldness, wealth and possessions he surpassed other Scots of his time'. At least, unlike some, whenever he stopped for the night at a monastery, he always left a donation.

CHAPTER SEVEN

The Magnificent Loser

For as often as not we meet
In dreams our own dishevelled ghosts
And opposite the modest hosts
Of our ambition stare them out.
                    Keith Douglas, 'Negative Information'

Robert III's last couple of years were a personal tragedy and a public disaster. The north of Scotland was being ravaged by the Lord of the Isles, the son of Robert's own sister, who burnt Elgin and created general havoc. His beloved eldest son, David, Duke of Rothesay, was arrested for incompetence as the Lieutenant and died mysteriously at Falkland Palace. Then his only surviving son, young Prince James (1394–1437), was kidnapped by the English in 1406 while *en route* to safety in France. It was recorded by Bower that when Robert heard the news, while eating his supper at Rothesay Castle, the old man – he was approaching seventy – was so overcome with grief that he never ate again, and died soon afterwards. His own suggestion for an epitaph, according to Bower, was: 'I would prefer to be buried deep in a midden, providing my soul be safe in the day of the Lord. Wherefore bury me, I pray, in a midden and write for my epitaph "Here lies the worst of kings and the most wretched of men in the whole realm."'

Meanwhile, the new 4th Earl of Douglas, Archibald (1369–1424), sometimes unkindly known as Tyneman, or the Loser, had taken over leadership of his aggressive family from his father, Archibald the Grim. His relationship with the Stewarts was to be as tortuous as any. His wife was the old King's daughter, and his sister was married to the King's eldest son, the Duke of Rothesay, so the relationship should have been close. In 1400 Tyneman and Rothesay together held Edinburgh Castle in face of a determined attack by Henry IV of England (1367–1422). But for most of his active life Tyneman seems to have been a supporter of Robert, Duke of Albany, the King's younger brother and long-term Regent. In a short period of four years, when these two were leading figures in the country, it was deprived of the King and both his male heirs: David of Rothesay died in very suspicious circumstances while in the custody of

Albany and Douglas; the young Prince James was captured by an English ship, when his voyage was supposed to be top secret, and Douglas's brother James was in the neighbourhood as he was being trans-shipped. This, combined with the effect that both Albany and Tyneman were at best lethargic if not deliberately evasive in any efforts to ransom the kidnapped prince, suggests that both men preferred to have their legitimate king shut up in the Tower of London than back home consolidating the monarchy. It was reminiscent of the period when Robert the Steward for similar reasons was so slow to get David II back from English captivity.

Looking at the two incidents in more detail it is easy to see what Albany's motivation was in stopping the advance of Rothesay towards the throne. He had lost his job to him in the palace coup organized by Queen Annabella and supported by Tyneman's father three years before. But Tyneman's motivation in aiding the arrest of his brother-in-law (twice over, since Tyneman was married to Rothesay's sister, and he was married to Tyneman's sister) is less clear, unless he simply could not stand Rothesay's extravagance or arrogance, or had knowledge that the fickle Rothesay was being unfaithful to his sister. Or it may be that Tyneman simply saw Albany as a better potential ally in pursuing his main interest – war against the English. What is known is that Albany and Douglas met at Culross to discuss their handling of the Rothesay problem, both of them greatly angered that he had claimed the earldom of March. Rothesay was arrested *en route* to St Andrews, where he had hoped to take over the archbishop's treasure chest, was locked up in Falkland and died of unknown causes soon afterwards. Albany and Tyneman were both exonerated by the aged Robert III and parliament, but that did not mean they were innocent.

In the second incident, the capture by English privateers of Prince James, there is no evidence of involvement by either Albany or Tyneman. Yet Albany certainly had a strong motive again, for as a result of this kidnap he was to remain Regent of Scotland for the rest of his life, and his son was to inherit the same position. Tyneman had nothing at all to gain from it and was probably in England when it actually happened, yet afterwards he made no real effort for nearly twenty years to put it right, and he remained a staunch ally of Albany more or less until his death. Yet it was a strange coincidence that Tyneman's brother James Douglas of Balvenie (1371–1443) happened to be leading an ambush on the escort party which had just seen the young prince off on his boat to the Bass Rock pick-up point; he killed all the party, including a disobedient baron of his own, at Herdmanston Moor. Apparently he had just saved Tantallon from being snatched from the Douglases in a Stewart plot.

Perhaps Tyneman had aspirations to the Crown himself – the French certainly at one point thought he was a possibility – and if two royal Stewarts could be got rid of perhaps so could the rest. It was not until he saw that Albany was passing over the reins to his own son, the impossible Murdoch, that Tyneman made a real effort to get back James.

Meanwhile, there were other considerations. Tyneman had taken over the estates of the Earl of March, who had reacted so badly to the jilting of his daughter by Rothesay and was now advising Henry IV how best to attack the Scots. The attack on Edinburgh in 1400 had been devastating but had to be aborted by the English for the usual reason: a scorched-earth policy from the Scots meant that the English army was starving. The bitter Earl of March then organized Harry Hotspur into some devastating border raids to which Tyneman successfully led the retaliation. For a couple of years there were typical tit-for-tat raids in both directions, the Scots usually returning with more booty than the English. But naturally the tempo intensified, and one raid under Hepburn was badly mauled. In 1402 Tyneman with Regent Albany's son Murdoch led a bigger force of 10,000 men towards Newcastle but they were caught by Hotspur on the return leg, laden with booty. Hotspur, advised by March, was waiting in a good position with his archers near Homildon Hill.

Archibald Douglas, the Tyneman, was wearing elaborate new armour that had taken three years' work to finish, and perhaps he thought himself invincible. The fashion was for plate armour with heraldic jupon or surcoat and hinged helmet, while his foot soldiers wore a brigandine or jacket and a salade helmet, and carried a Jedburgh stave. He underestimated his opponents and should have attacked the Northumbrian archers sooner. As usual the Scots took heavy casualties in such a situation, and as they fled 500 were drowned in the River Tweed. Douglas and Murdoch, the two leaders, were both captured, Douglas sustaining five wounds through his new armour and losing an eye. It was a devastating defeat, and Harry Hotspur, only five years after being defeated by the 2nd Earl of Douglas, was rewarded by the English King with all the 4th Earl's lands, if he could control them. Tyneman was imprisoned and it was six years before he ransomed himself. His cousin George Douglas, first of the Red Douglas earls, was also captured and died of the plague before he could be ransomed.

Despite all his successes Harry Percy, known as 'Hotspur', Earl of Northumberland, was not happy; he wanted more. He thought Henry IV, a self-made king, could be replaced and he resented being asked to hand over most of the huge ransoms he had earned at Homildon Hill. So he recruited his now recuperating captive, Archibald the Tyneman, into his rebel army, pretended to stage an invasion of Scotland, but actually headed south to join up with the Welsh. At Shrewsbury in 1403 there was a battle between the Northumbrian rebels and the English royal army led by Henry IV, but also including the future Henry V (1387–1422). Percy and Tyneman fought well and might have won. Tyneman concentrated on trying to kill or capture Henry IV himself, but the latter had sent three lookalikes wearing regal armour onto the field: Tyneman surprised at the quantity of royals shouted, 'Where the devil do all these kings come from?' He killed all three of them and was wounded in the process, but despite all his valiant fighting the real king was saved by the alertness of his own son, Prince Harry. Tyneman's efforts were anyway all in vain since the would-be replacement king Harry Hotspur had opened his visor for a breather and took an arrow in the head. Then Tyneman's horse fell and he was captured. Having already lost an eye at Homildon, he had also now lost a testicle at Shrewsbury.

So Tyneman was a prisoner again albeit his reputation as a knight errant had increased, despite two defeats. During the winter of 1405 there was a series of tournaments held in London – 'great joustings and tiltings', as Maxwell puts it – where the sons of Tyneman, Archibald and James, took part, as well as William Douglas of Drumlanrig, the second earl's bastard, William Douglas of Nithsdale, son of Tyneman's illegitimate half-brother, James Douglas of Dalkeith, and James Douglas of Balvenie, Tyneman's younger brother; most of them were in London to act as hostages. Two years later Tyneman was released on parole to negotiate his own ransom and obtain a cross-border truce. This time he kept his vow and returned to imprisonment, but the next time, in 1409, he did not; however, he did eventually pay the ransom money. Significantly he had made no serious attempt at this point to assist in the ransoming of young James I, who had become a prisoner in England three years after Shrewsbury. James was now fifteen and was to stay in England for a further fifteen years. Nor did the King's uncle the Regent Albany make much effort for the release, being more concerned with his own son Murdoch. Even he had to wait eleven years before being swapped for Hotspur's son and £10,000. As Godscroft put it, James was left for eighteen years 'in captivitie which they cared not how long it was'.

The remaining fifteen years of Tyneman's career were mostly spent fighting, sometimes in the Borders, sometimes in France. As Alastair Macdonald says, 'Archibald . . . enjoyed fighting the English and did so with a ferocity beyond the dictates of "rational" policy.' As Constable of Edinburgh Castle he could use it as an impressive and secure base, at the same time extracting for his own benefit most of the Edinburgh custom payments to help fund his large and ostentatious retinue. In addition to knights he employed a group of priestly assistants, most of them graduates of the Sorbonne, to help with his correspondence. He was busy having Bothwell Castle remodelled with a splendid entertainment hall to impress his followers, and was expanding Threave. He was also giving patronage to Melrose, Sweetheart and Glenluce Abbeys, as well as his father's favourites of Lincluden, Bothwell and Holywood, all of which effort added to his prestige; he was even writing to the Pope about the state of leper hospitals.

Tyneman is not mentioned as being at the battle of Harlaw in 1411, when royal troops were led by Alexander Stewart of Buchan, one of the Wolf of Badenoch's cubs who had gained useful experience leading the Burgundian army against the English. This battle prevented Scotland from imploding from the north under McDonald pressure. Tyneman's interests were more in the south and abroad. In 1412 he signed an agreement in Paris with Jean sans Peur, Duke of Burgundy. This provided 4,000 men as mercenaries to fight for France against the English, and Tyneman seems to have done some fighting there himself in 1413, shortly before Henry V renewed the Hundred Years War in earnest. Young James I, still a prisoner, gained useful military experience accompanying Henry on the Agincourt campaign. In fact he was knighted by Henry, as one king by another.

In 1415 Tyneman was back burning Penrith while Henry V was still away in France. This became known as the 'Foul Raid', because Douglas and Albany retreated to Scotland from what they thought was a much larger English force, but found out they had been mistaken. They were punished by the usual English retaliations which they could do nothing to stop. Despite this, Tyneman claimed substantial expenses for his work, as he did when a year later he was sent to besiege Roxburgh Castle.

Not long afterwards Tyneman began some serious efforts for the release of James I, his young brother-in-law. Perhaps the fact that Regent Albany was now in his seventies made him at last realize that, unless he did something, Murdoch, now back from captivity, would inherit the regency and pass it on to his own unruly brood. In such a situation any alternative – even if it had to be a Stewart – was preferable, and James I must have seemed a fairly innocuous candidate. Tyneman's cousin Sir William Douglas of Drumlanrig, an illegitimate son of the famous second earl, had been sent to Croydon in 1412 to conduct initial negotations. He had made a name for himself in an action on Roxburgh Bridge and was given a barony in Hawick, where he built a second Drumlanrig Tower. The family he founded became the most prominent of the Douglases two centuries later when they took the title Queensberry. He himself was killed fighting for the French at Fresnay-le-Compte or Orleans.

Following up the Drumlanrig visit, Tyneman at last went to London to see King Henry, taking with him an impressive retinue of forty squires, even offering to fight for the English in France if James were released. But the negotiations came to no conclusion. More effective was his intervention to undermine the Regent Albany's adherence to the Avignon papacy. It was Tyneman who won all the glory for bringing Scotland back into the fold of Rome, which led to Pope Martin V referring to him as 'the eldest son of the Pope'. As Michael Brown argues, this was all part of Tyneman's aim 'to become the founder of a European princely dynasty'.

In 1419 it was Tyneman's son-in-law John Stewart, Earl of Buchan, the Regent's second son, and Tyneman's own eldest son, Archibald, who led a force of 6,000 Scots to Burgundy to fight against the English, but the Burgundians changed sides when their own duke was murdered by a rival French faction and peace was declared. Then followed the marriage of the French Princess Katherine to Henry V, where James I of Scotland was a captive guest. The Scottish force came back to France, however, in 1421, and scored a small but significant – and for the French hugely morale boosting – victory at Baugé. Specifically they managed to kill Henry V's brother, at that time heir to the throne of England. Buchan was made Constable of France and Tyneman's son Archibald (1391–1439), Earl of Wigtown, was made Count of Longueville with a castle at Dun le Roi.

Henry V was away in England at the time. His troops had previously been invincible, and this battle which caused the death of his brother undoubtedly angered him greatly in this last year of his life.

Meanwhile, the Regent Albany had at last died in 1420 and been succeeded by his less talented son Murdoch, now 2nd Duke of Albany. This was far from acceptable to Tyneman; even less was the idea of Murdoch, who was now over fifty, being succeeded by his even more thuggish sons. So Tyneman's efforts to secure the release of James I were intensified and were helped by the early death of Henry V, which left easier negotiators to deal with on the English side. Much more remarkably Murdoch too seemed to come round to the idea of ransoming the King, as if after a few months at the job he could not stand the pressures of being Regent and wanted rid of it, even if it cost him his head, which turned out to be the case.

Apart from the fact that the Scottish government was almost bankrupt because of a mixture of incompetence and corruption in the Albany household, Murdoch's life seems to have been made a misery by his own wayward sons. Godscroft, for instance, records how the eldest son, Walter, was seen 'reaving of a faulcon af his hand and thrawing the neck of her asunder in despyte of him'. Thus perhaps to spite his uncontrollable son and finding his regency hard to sustain, Duke Murdoch took the naive or apparently suicidal step of encouraging the ransom talks, which at last bore fruit in 1424.

Despite the fact that, as Ranald Nicholson puts it, 'Since 1421 it was Archibald the Tyneman who had shown most interest in obtaining the king's release' the Earl of Douglas does not seem to have been as confident of his relationship with James I as (with much less reason) was Duke Murdoch. As the day approached, after eighteen years of captivity, for the King's return, accompanied by his new wife, the royally born Joan Beaufort of Somerset, Tyneman decided to keep well out of the way and to concentrate on developing his role as a French grandee. He collected an army of 10,000 men at the expense of King Charles VII of France and took ship to La Rochelle before James's return. Perhaps, of course, there was the ulterior motive that if he had a trained army of 10,000 men on his return to Scotland he would be almost invincible and certainly untouchable.

Before leaving for France, Tyneman made various arrangements in case he never came back. He made generous donations to Whithorn Priory and Melrose Abbey, left his son the Earl of Wigtown to greet the returning King, and left his wife, Margaret, King James's elder sister, in charge of some of his estates. He tried to make sure that enemies rather than friends of his family were sent to London as hostages for the King's ransom. After a stormy voyage during which six of his ships were sunk, Tyneman – accompanied by John Stewart, his son-in-law, the Constable of France – met the French king at Chatillon-sur-Indre, where he was shortly appointed a lieutenant-general in the French army, Duke of Touraine and master of the castles of Chinon and Loches. On his triumphal entry to the capital of his duchy, Tours, his cousin Adam Douglas was installed as constable. Tyneman received twelve hogsheads of wine and was made an honorary canon of the cathedral. He was a European celebrity and spent vast sums accordingly, mainly on credit – as a Frenchman put it, 'Il vit sans comter.'

After that things did not go so well. In his final battle, in 1424, Tyneman was caught in the same dilemma as his long-dead ancestor Archibald the Guardian before Halidon Hill and Edward II before Bannockburn. He was deputed to save the castle at Ivry whose garrison had agreed to surrender by a certain date unless relieved. But instead, faced with difficult odds, he retreated to the pro-English town of Verneuil in Perche, which he captured by a ruse. He disguised some of his men as English corpses, tied them to the tails of horses, and dragged them up to the town, the rest of his men pretending to be English, shouting they had suffered a terrible defeat. The garrison at Verneuil took them at face value and opened the gates, but this was Tyneman's last success. He now had to fight a pitched battle against the English. The Duke of Bedford, his English opposite number, known as John with the Leaden Sword, invited him for a pre-battle drink, but he refused. No quarter was to be expected in the battle that followed.

On the morning of the battle of Verneuil, Tyneman knighted his second son, James, in the field. He had a good defensive position and might have won, but one of his French subordinates, the Viscount of Narbonne, thought it was cowardly to stay in a safe position and took his men into the attack, against Tyneman's orders. Once this happened Tyneman had no choice but to follow, as Narbonne's troop was being slaughtered. It had been fatal to abandon a good defensive position and the Scots paid for it. While the fire of their archers was extremely effective they were let down by the Italian mercenaries. No quarter was asked for or given. Tyneman, his son and his son-in-law were all killed, as were most of their several thousand followers. The Pluscarden chronicler commented: 'It was a frightful spectacle to behold the piles of slain heaped up on the field of battle, especially where the strife had been with the Scots, for not one of them received quarter. The cause of this implacable slaughter was the pride of the Scots.'

The two senior Douglases were buried in the choir of St Gatien's Cathedral in Tours. Tyneman's widow, Margaret Stewart, lived on for many years in Galloway, surviving both her eldest son and the tragic end of her two grandsons. Another survivor was Christian Ramsay, the daughter of one of Tyneman's grooms, who had been his mistress and borne at least one son to him.

Tyneman was referred to as 'a renouned giant of a fighting man' and he had most of the qualities of a great man, except luck. Ironically, as soon as he was dead the French king gave his dukedom to one of his own princes. Though the Douglases continued to pretend that it was hereditary and called themselves Dukes of Touraine, this was never acknowledged in France. Two Douglases who did apparently survive Verneuil stayed on in France to continue the war. These were William Douglas of Drumlanrig and William Douglas of Kinross, both of whom were killed four years later at Fresnay or in the famous defence of Orleans where Joan of Arc first began to make her name. They were buried in the Cathedral of Sainte Croix.

Duke Murdoch and his sons did not outlast Tyneman by long. They were arrested within a year of James I's return to Scotland, tried and executed.

CHAPTER EIGHT

So Near Yet So Far

For I was a king when they cut the corn
And they strangle me tomorrow.
Lord Alfred Douglas, 'Perkin Warbeck'

James I was thirty when he took over control of Scotland in April 1424. He was four years younger than his nephew Archibald soon to be the 5th Earl of Douglas, self-styled 2nd Duke of Touraine and victor of Baugé, who succeeded the dead Tyneman four months later when his father and brother were both killed in France. For the next thirteen years the two were to have a very uneasy, volatile relationship.

When Archibald, still just the Earl of Wigtown, went down to Durham to act in his father's place during the welcome ceremonies for the returning king, he may have been apprehensive. His father had preferred to be elsewhere, and though he had latterly made considerable efforts for the King's release there had been long periods when he had other priorities. He had acted as a hostage for the release of his own father from English captivity, acquiring something of an English education, but not done the same for the King. While James was in detention, young Archibald had carved out a career for himself as a mercenary commander in France alongside his brother-in-law John Stewart of Buchan, the king's cousin. Together in 1419 they had done useful work for the French in the Touraine at Chatillon, fighting for the Dauphin in Toulouse and Carcassone. Then they had won the remarkable victory at Baugé in 1421, which had overnight changed the reputation of Scottish mercenaries in France from drunken layabouts – 'drinkers of wine and eaters of sheep', the French said – to successful fighters. Their action there was reminiscent of Wallace's at Stirling Bridge, where a small force defeated a larger one by holding a narrow bridge. Buchan was made Constable of France for his efforts and Archibald Count of Longueville in Normandy with a castle at Dun le Roy (now Dun sur Auron) in Berry. The fact that the French king had made someone else Count of Longueville at the same time, and that after Baugé the Scots had lost all their pay –12,000 crowns – in a battle lost to the English at Fresnay-le-Comte, might not have been obvious. While James I was a captive onlooker with the English troops at Agincourt and attending Henry V's wedding, Archibald was paying more attention to the Dauphin at Le Mans, Tours and Angers. It was not necessarily the ideal foundation for a relationship between Archibald and his newly restored king, particularly as it was hard for young James I not to have admired the charismatic Henry V, and hard for him with his background not to think of the French as the enemy.

Even after the death of the superhuman Henry V, the Scots in France did not repeat their success at Baugé. They were badly beaten by the English at Cravant in 1422, losing as many as 3,000 men. The Dauphin, who was now King Charles VII, had asked for Scottish reinforcements and for Archibald's father, the Tyneman, to lead them. Thus it had been the father not the son who went to Verneuil to his death, and the son not the father who went to Durham to meet the king.

James I's eighteen-year compulsory stay in England had meant that he was brought up in a much sterner school of kingship than that favoured by his Stewart predecessors. He came back to a country where fraud and corruption at the highest levels were common, and the regency of the two Albany Stewarts had set a poor example. The famous saying is attributed to him by Abbot Bower: 'If God grant me life and aid, even the life of a dog, throughout all the realm I will make the key keep the castle and the bracken bush the cow.' He was able and on the whole well intentioned, but perhaps a little short on patience and tolerance, wanting to sweep away the corrupt baronial superstructure without quite appreciating his need to acquire its cooperation.

At least for his first clash with the Albany Stewarts he had the support of most of his nobles. The two senior members of the Douglas dynasty, Archibald, Earl of Douglas, and William, Earl of Angus (1398–1437), leader of the Red Douglases, were both knighted by the King after his Scone coronation and both seemed to get on well enough with him. But then Douglas was arrested at James's second parliament, along with twenty-five other magnates. Perhaps this was just a warning or a hint of intimidation if they did not cooperate, for Douglas and Angus were both on the jury panel of twenty-one which condemned to death Duke Murdoch Stewart, his two sons and his father-in-law a few months later. All four were executed immediately, a Stewart purge of the junior branch of their own dynasty.

Archibald kept a low profile for the next four years, consolidating the estates of his new earldom, but he did join the King's birthday celebrations at St Andrews in 1425. In 1429 he took part in the King's expedition against Alexander McDonald, the Lord of the Isles, which ended in the victory against the McDonald chief at Lochaber.

Significantly the Lord of the Isles was then incarcerated in the castle at Tantallon of William Douglas, Earl of Angus, the first signs of divide and rule between the Black and Red Douglases. Of the two Douglas earls Angus perhaps indulged in the more overt grovelling to the slightly paranoid King James than did his cousin. Archibald shuttled between his main home at Bothwell Castle and Edinburgh, where he attended parliaments. He was even employed as an ambassador to arrange a truce with the English. But eighteen months later the rift was much more severe: Archibald Douglas was arrested again for an unknown reason, possibly his efforts to help his brother-in-law Malise Graham, another hostage trapped in England, and was himself put into Tantallon, a grave humiliation, then moved to the island prison of Loch Leven, also a Red Douglas stronghold. He was released soon afterwards, apparently at the request of Queen Joan, but clearly James suspected him and did not like his attitude. For a while he retired again from public life, spending his time mostly at Bothwell, Eddybredshiels or Newark Castle, in the border forest, which he had just had built to replace an older castle, the Auld Wark. Walter Scott described it romantically in the *Lay of the Last Minstrel*:

> Whose ponderous gates and mossy bar
> Had oft rolled back the tide of war
> But never closed the iron door
> Against the desolate and poor.

And William Wordsworth wrote in 'Yarrow Revisited':

> Once more by Newark's Castle gate
> Long left without a warder,
> I stood, looked, listened and with thee
> Great Minstrel of the Border.

Meanwhile, Archibald's cousin William Douglas, 2nd Earl of Angus, who had made himself useful to the King as a gaoler, was appointed an ambassador to arrange a truce with England in 1430. Then in 1435 he enhanced the already growing prestige of the Red Douglases by winning a difficult battle, despite heavy losses, against some English raiders at Piperdean near Cockburnspath. He grovelled still further by arranging a marriage for his eldest son, James, with the King's dumb daughter, known as Dumb Janet.

By this time it was becoming clear that James I had overdone the disciplinarian act with his magnates. In his favour Nicholson says 'none of James's predecessors or successors was so committed as he was persistently, determinedly and emotionally to pursuing the common weal'. He was ahead of his time in highly intelligent legislation for turning Scotland into a more effective kingdom with a prosperous town life, but he could not continue without the support of the barons who still took most of the executive duties, particularly in war. It was war, as with so many Scottish kings and regents, that proved James I's downfall. He had snubbed Douglas and other senior nobles by giving command of his army to his young cousin Robert Stewart of Atholl and in retaliation the barons with their armed retinues failed to support his campaign to capture Roxburgh Castle from the English, which was meant to be the symbolic climax of his reign to date. Sadly for a medieval king this was the ultimate loss of face and similar occurrences were later to cause the downfall of two of his successors, James III and James V. It showed for the first time that James I had a weak spot. It seemed to remove the inhibitions of the group that were plotting to get rid of him.

Wisely Archibald, 5th Earl of Douglas, did not, so far as we know, take part in the plan to murder James I, though he had a motive and ended up as one of the chief beneficiaries. The chief instigator was one of the King's own dynasty, his uncle Walter, Earl of Atholl. Atholl had watched with some glee the destruction of the Albany section of his family. He could also see that James had only a five-year-old son to succeed him if he died. What is more, he had a case for putting himself forward as the legitimate heir to the throne since he was the eldest surviving son of Robert II's second marriage, and the first, technically incestuous marriage had only been legitimized by high-level manipulation of the rules. So in his old age he was overcome with delusions of grandeur. Most of the conspirators were Stewarts or Atholl Stewart retainers, but one was Robert Graham; Archibald Douglas was married to a Graham and had already been suspected of treasonable activity in trying to obtain the release of Malise Graham from English captivity.

Ironically, according to one chronicle, James I's life was nearly saved by Lady Elizabeth Douglas, sister of Sir James Douglas of Lugton and Lochleven, later one of the knights in the famous tournament at Stirling. She used her own arm as a bolt in the door against his attackers, but in vain. James was stabbed to death in the blocked sewer beneath the Dominican Friary at Perth. Walter Stewart of Atholl, the man who had hoped to become king through this crime, was pursued and captured by William Douglas, Earl of Angus, who had recently beaten the English raiding party at Piperdean. Walter Stewart had a red-hot crown placed on his head by the orders of Queen Joan. Archibald, Earl of Douglas, was made lieutenant-general, in other words effective ruler of Scotland and, if he were ruthless enough, in a good position to found a new dynasty.

But sadly the executive was in chaos. There was a serious outbreak of the plague, a severe shortage of food and frequent outbreaks of lawlessness. As Godscroft put it, 'Great enormities committit and not repressit.'

Now in his late forties and in a position of great power it is likely that Douglas did not have the strength or ability to tackle an extremely difficult situation. Two rival Edinburgh factions, the Crichtons and Livingstons, were fighting for power and for control of the young King James II (1430–60), who was in the custody of his mother, Queen Joan. She took him by stealth out of Edinburgh – hidden in her baggage, according to Pitscottie – to Stirling. Douglas seems to have been repairing Rothesay Castle as a place of refuge for the boy king and his mother, far away from the Crichtons, and perhaps there was a plot organized by Douglas and Queen Joan to regain control of the King. But in 1439 within eighteen months of his most important promotion, Douglas died of a fever at Restalrig. The Queen, looking for an alternative protector against the Edinburgh factions, hastily remarried, choosing a Stewart, the Black Knight of Lorne, and this gave the Crichtons their excuse to take over control of the King's upbringing. The Black Knight was suspected of being part of the Douglas plot to seize the King and was arrested.

Archibald Douglas's epitaph on his elaborate tomb at St Bride's Church, Douglas, shows a little sadly that his pretensions were perhaps greater than his abilities and perhaps that his greatest days had been those long since at Baugé when he had shared in a victory and won glory:

> Hic jacet Dominus Archibaldus Douglas, Dux
> Turoniae, Comes de Douglas et Longueville
> Dominus Gallovidiae et Wigtoun et Annandiae
> Locum tenens Regis Scotiae.
>
> Here lies Lord Archibald Douglas, Duke
> of Touraine, Count of Douglas and Longueville
> Lord of Galloway and Wigtown and Annandale
> Lieutenant of the King of Scotland.

CHAPTER NINE

The Black Dinner

Come back, come back with pity in your eyes
The night is dark, the sea is fierce and wide
There is no room for pity in my heart for pride
Though I become the scion of the wine.

> Lord Alfred Douglas, 'Plainte Éternelle'

James II (1430–60) was six years old when he was crowned at Holyrood, the fourth member of his dynasty to rule Scotland. Having lost his father at six, he effectively also lost his mother at eight, for after her second marriage she was deprived of control over him, and he became a pawn of the Crichton and Livingston factions. This was not a healthy background for the upbringing of a young boy who at least theoretically had great wealth and power. And of all the Stewarts he was to have the most bizarre relationship with his Douglas counterparts.

Two years after James's coronation he was still a child of eight when Archibald Douglas, the Lieutenant-General of the kingdom, died. His fifteen-year-old son William (1425–40) took over the earldom but not of course the lieutenancy, though perhaps he had been brought up to expect it. According to Godscroft he called himself a duke anyway, had a retinue of 1,000–2,000 horsemen and was already at this age extravagant. He was 'of a heigh and rare spirite and natural sweit, traitable and douce'. The youthful swagger could be put down to teenage immaturity and certainly did not justify the actions taken against him. But he was already married to a Lady Janet of the Crawford family, so it made some sense to deal with him before they had time to produce an heir.

A year or so after the previous earl's death, when the new one was barely sixteen, Sir William Crichton, the Chancellor, and Sir Alexander Livingston, the King's Governor, the two faction leaders, patched up their differences and made a plan to eliminate the influence of the Douglases. They saw the Earl's minority as an opportunity to reduce the excessive power wielded by one family and perhaps to pick off some of the non-entailed properties, such as Annandale, for themselves or their friends. They did not want the Queen or her new husband to gain strength from the Douglas retainers. They were also perhaps looking for a scapegoat for numerous acts of violence and disorder which had occurred over recent months, most specifically the massacre of Colqhouns near Luss by the Islesmen, and it was easy to blame the Douglases. So Livingston invited the Douglas boys to attend parliament in Edinburgh on the pretext of improving law and order. Then at Crichton's instigation, and presumably with the full collusion of James Douglas of Balvenie, now also Earl of Avondale, the young Earl William and his brother David were invited to dine with the King in Edinburgh Castle. Advisers warned the teenagers that it might be a trap, but they ignored this and went all the same. According to Godscroft, Crichton made the whole episode more bizarre by meeting the intended victims *en route* to Edinburgh and inviting them in to spend a couple of days in his own Crichton Castle. There Crichton 'interteinis him [Douglas] freindlie, cheirfullie and magnifiklie; and not ane day bot twa days kyndlie and amiablie'. Thus lulled into a false sense of security the two Douglases went on their way to Edinburgh Castle.

There we have the extraordinary spectacle of a ten-year-old king acting as host at the head of a banqueting table. Livingston the Governor welcomed the boys and the banquet proceeded. In Godscroft's words again, Livingston 'bankets him royallie, intertenis him cheirfullie and a long tyme; at last about the end of the denner they compas him about with armed men and presents a Bul head before him on the boarde; the Bul head was in these days a taiken of death'. So ended the charade known subsequently as the Black Dinner. After that the young earl and his brother were taken to a different room in the castle where they were tried for treason and condemned to death by a secret court. Within hours they were beheaded in the castle yard. As Michael Brown put it, 'The Black Dinner was carried out to save and extend the power of Avondale and Crichton . . . he was at least guilty by association in the violent death of his great nephews.'

Potentially the crime should have helped to stabilize the power of the Scottish monarchy which was always under threat from a rival dynasty which had acquired such a massive power base. In the words of Pitscottie, 'This realme sould be at greattar tranquilitie if the Earle of Douglas and his brother had been cutted off sudenlie.'

From this event derived the ballad preserved by Hume of Godscroft:

> Edinburgh Castle, toune and tower
> God grant thou sink for sinne
> And that even for the black dinoir
> Erl Douglas gat therein.

But as it turned out it was not to be the Stewart monarchy that benefited so much as a new branch of the Black Douglases, the family of Balvenie.

CHAPTER TEN

Four Stones of Tallow

You were a brute and more than half a knave,
Your mind was seamed with labyrinthine tracks
Wherein walked crazy moods bending their backs.
Lord Alfred Douglas, 'The Unspeakable Englishman'

Now that all Tyneman's sons and grandsons had been killed or died, about half the Douglas estates went to his granddaughter Margaret, thereafter known as the Fair Maid of Galloway. Another near half went to Tyneman's younger brother, James Douglas of Balvenie, who as the eldest male heir became the 7th Earl of Douglas. The one remaining portion, Annandale, went to the Crown. So Crichton had succeeded in splitting the Douglas empire and gaining at least one serious piece of property for the state.

The new earl was totally different from his predecessor. He was already close to seventy and overweight, hence his nickname 'The Gross'. Godscroft says 'His corpulence causit a dulness', yet he was far from stupid. As a younger son of Archibald the Grim he had largely had to make his own way in the world. He had thus been involved in a number of violent incidents on either side of the law. In 1405 he had burnt the town of Berwick when he was Lord of the East March. Then a year later, as we have already seen, he committed murder in the oddest of circumstances. The young Prince James had been waiting first at North Berwick, then on the Bass Rock, for the ship that was supposed to take him to safety in France. Douglas's baillie Sir David Fleming was involved in this exercise, as perhaps was James Douglas himself. But as he returned from North Berwick, Fleming was ambushed and killed by Douglas for reasons of revenge in a skirmish at Long Herdmanston Moor. Yet given the importance of the mission and the disaster that befell it soon afterwards, it was a very inopportune time for Douglas to settle some personal vendetta. At worst it suggests he had something to hide. At best he was looking after the interests of his captured brother and distant cousin, the earls of Douglas and Angus, both recently captured by the English at Homildon Hill.

Over the next eighteen years James the Gross had carved out an empire for himself. Balvenie, near Dufftown, he had acquired from his mother, and he hardly visited it; Abercorn came from his brother and was his reward for looking after Tyneman's interests while he was a prisoner of war. When not paid by the government for his efforts as Warden of the East March, James simply took his expenses by force and lived off the customs dues of Linlithgow as his elder brother Tyneman had done off those of Edinburgh. In 1409 he supervised the official demolition of Jedburgh Castle, which in his expenses claim he said had very tough cement, so the job took a long time. He was regularly accused of depredations against his neighbours, and regularly shut up tradesmen and officials in his dungeons at Abercorn Castle if they gave him any trouble, releasing them only when they handed over cash. Under the Regent Albany this was the kind of behaviour that went unchecked.

As well as the 'many towered castle' of Abercorn on the Forth and Avondale (Strathaven) Castle in Lanarkshire, which he inherited from his father, James the Gross was also given Aberdour, Rattray, Avoch and Strathearn in return for his continued support for his brother the Tyneman. He seems to have played some role in the negotiations between the Albany and Douglas families about plans to obtain the release of James I. After one last spell of banditry in West Lothian he was certainly present with his nephews, the earls of Douglas and Angus, at the welcoming of James I at Durham in 1424, and perhaps, like his Red Douglas cousin, found more favour with the new king than the head of the over-powerful Black Douglas dynasty. He involved himself with the then politically correct task of collecting ransom money for the King, and with his two cousins was a juror at the trial which condemned Murdoch, Duke of Albany. At about this time, now past fifty and childless, he married his own niece, Beatrix Sinclair, and they produced ten children in about as many years, five of them boys, including a pair of twins for whom in his old age he now became motivated to find titles and estates.

James the Gross is not recorded as having been in any further trouble during the active reign of James I, and seems to have turned respectable once he had created his little empire. Thus when the King was murdered in 1437, he was promoted to the unlikely role of justiciar-general for Scotland, serving under his cousin the new lieutenant-general. At the same time he was made Earl of Avondale in his own right. Three years later, now an old man, he received a second earldom after the double execution of his grand-nephews William and David at the Black Dinner. Naturally he has been suspected of some complicity in this act of judicial murder, specially considering his position, but his motivation cannot have been overwhelming unless it was sheer jealousy. After all, he had enough money and estates by this time to meet his own needs and those of his sons, so the addition of the prestigious earldom of Douglas and a few extra estates in Douglasdale should not have made a huge difference. But maybe we should not forget that he must have been a hugely ambitious and greedy man. Three of his sons did acquire earldoms (one had a bishopric first, just in case), and the fourth a lordship. Certainly neither as justiciar nor as a fellow Douglas did he make any effort whatsoever to wreak revenge on Livingston or Crichton for their cruel treatment of his grand-nephews, which perhaps confirms the suspicion that he was as guilty as they were.

James the Gross was Earl of Douglas for only three years and by this time too old to take much part in public life, but he does at least seem to have set in motion the arrangements for a marriage which undid any good to the Scottish monarchy that might have been argued to have accrued from the infamous Black Dinner. This was the wedding which took place soon after his death between his eldest son, William, and Margaret, the Fair Maid of Galloway, sister of the victims of the Black Dinner and heir to the other half of the Douglas estates. That this marriage was allowed to take place can only be explained by the efforts of both James the Gross and his son to undermine the influence of Chancellor Crichton with the young king. But if the King was party to the blame for allowing this, it was something that he was later very much to regret.

When James the Gross died in 1443, the Auchinleck Chronicle recorded 'Thai said he had in him four staine of talch [tallow] and mair', enough to make a large number of candles. Another legend, no doubt apocryphal, suggested that one of his pall-bearers suffered a broken arm when they carried his huge coffin to be buried at Douglas Church, where his effigy, suitably slim as he was when a young knight, still lies beside that of his wife.

CHAPTER ELEVEN

Murder under Trust

More easily you believe me a pioneer
And a murdering villain without fear.
                    Keith Douglas, 'Landscape with Figures'

The relationship between William, the new 8th Earl of Douglas (1425–52), who was eighteen when he took over the earldom in 1443, and King James II, five years his junior, was among the most complex and volatile in the history of the two rival families. Both were knighted together, James as an infant, William as a five-year-old, by the previous king in 1430, so they had this in common. At first William went out of his way to charm the boy king and succeeded brilliantly. James looked up to the dashing Douglas and began to listen to his undermining of Chancellor Crichton, the man who had murdered the two Douglas brothers after the Black Dinner.

Gradually the power balance shifted. Douglas was made the King's lieutenant-general and was allowed to besiege Crichton at his castle in Barnton. Crichton retaliated by burning two of the Douglas castles, Abercorn and Strabrock. But Douglas, meanwhile, at last got papal dispensation to marry his cousin, the Fair Maid of Galloway, who was by all accounts spectacularly beautiful albeit not quite in her teens, so he was able to reunite the huge Black Douglas portfolio of properties. He also got the confirmation of two of his brothers as earls, of Moray and Ormond, and of the third as Lord of Balvenie. Between the five brothers they now had massive wealth and manpower at their disposal and were, as Crichton had long realized, just as serious a threat to the country's stability as their cousins had been before the Black Dinner. The only Douglas not doing well was James, 3rd Earl of Angus (d. 1446), who was a Crichton supporter and had temporarily forfeited all his lands for rebellion.

Looking at the map of Scotland at this time anyone would have been impressed by the huge swathe of territory owned by the one family. William of Douglas had the biggest area, including Douglasdale itself. Its main castle was protected by three smaller outlying forts, including Parisholm, up in the Cairntable, where he could hide from any army. He also had his border estates round Liddesdale, Ettrick across to Selkirk and

Jedburgh. His favourite residences seem to have been Douglas itself, Craig Douglas in Yarrow and Newark Castle, newly built with the latest ideas in fortification, by the Tweed. William's second brother, James, was made Bishop of Aberdeen at the age of sixteen. Of his three other brothers, Hugh had Ormond Castle and his estates on the Black Isle, while Archibald, Earl of Moray, had the island fortress of Lochindorb, which he had refortified, and magnificent Darnaway Castle, south of Forres, which he was rebuilding; while their youngest brother John had Balvenie Castle, beside Dufftown, which had also been recently rebuilt. All told, between them they held twenty or so major castles and many more minor ones, spread across the Borders and up the east coast, and could easily muster a private army of several thousand men. Meanwhile, the Red Douglases had been briefly subject to forfeiture at the behest of their Black Douglas cousins but were restored soon afterwards, and harried Abercorn in revenge. They had Dalkeith and Tantallon Castles as well as Abernethy and their Angus bases, such as Mains by Dundee and Kirriemuir, further north. James, Earl of Angus, was engaged to but never married Janet, the King's deaf and dumb sister, for he died while she was across visiting her sister, the Queen of France. The reward for marrying Janet went to Sir James Douglas of Dalkeith (*c.* 1430–93), who thus became the first Earl of Morton. So now there were five Douglas eardoms.

Angus's brother George Douglas (1412–62) succeeded him and joined the Black Douglases under Hugh Douglas, Earl of Ormond, to help repel the English in 1448; when Edward IV burnt Dumfries he burnt Alnwick in return. He was to give moral support to James II during the crisis after his murder of the Black Douglas at Stirling (see below), and was given favours in return: money, permission to build a new castle at Broughty to replace his older one at Mains or Strathdichty in Dundee, and the hint of a dukedom.

For a five-year period (1445–50) William Douglas patched up his quarrel and shared power reasonably amicably with the Chancellor Crichton and the King's cousin, Bishop Kennedy. Nobody at or near the top, it seemed, could afford to fall out permanently with anyone else, so that even the most serious attacks could be forgotten when it suited them, but perhaps recalled later when the time was ripe. The two families of lesser rank who held executive appointments, the Crichtons and Livingstons, had an amazing capacity to fall out, make it up and survive, but in 1449 Douglas chose to side with his main enemies, the Crichtons, to get rid of the Livingstons. The King's basic strategy should have been to back the people who held office only through his own goodwill, as opposed to the big landowners, like the Douglases, who expected it by right. They had inherited power by the same code as himself, and he could not deprive them of it without huge general offence to a nobility which corporately had more power than he did himself. The Livingstons between them were governors of five major castles including Stirling. But they had bullied James II in his youth and he was perhaps easily persuaded by Douglas and the Crichtons that they had become too greedy. Besides, the young king was now desperately in need of money. His cash income from customs duty was almost negligible and his new queen, Mary of Guelders in Burgundy, had rashly been promised an income of 10,000 *écus* a year. There had also been big expenditure on the King's sisters, as one after another they had been given dowries to help them marry important foreigners: Margaret, the Dauphin; Isabelle, the Duke of Brittany; Mary, the Lord of Campvere; Annabelle, the Count of Geneva. So, just as the Livingstons were trying to extend their power by arranging a marriage between Elizabeth Livingston and the new Lord of the Isles, John McDonald, four of them were arrested for treason and two hanged soon afterwards. Ironically this marriage, which proved neither happy nor fruitful, was nevertheless later to push the Lord of the Isles into an unlikely alliance with Douglas against the King.

Meanwhile, in 1448 William, Earl of Douglas, had been involved in border warfare, like his ancestors before him. Dunbar and Dumfries had both been burnt by separate English armies, so Douglas, with his brothers Balvenie and the Earl of Ormond, supposedly with 40,000 men, led a retaliatory raid into England, causing damage as far south as Alnwick and Warkworth. William himself defeated Percy in a skirmish, while Ormond, with William Douglas of Drumlanrig, helped Angus at the River Sark or Lochmabenstane, near Gretna, in 1449, when they lost 600 men, compared with the 2,000 lost by the English, and collected a huge amount of gold and silver booty. James II was delighted with them.

Then in 1449 came the amazing tournament when Douglas power reached the ultimate in ostentation. Three Burgundian knights, high-fliers in the tournament circuit of European chivalry, challenged the three best knights in Scotland to meet them in the lists below Stirling Castle. It was to be a fight to the death. Of the three Scots selected to take part two were Douglases: James, the Earl's second brother, and John of Lochleven, a fringe member of the Red Douglas family. To emphasize their status the Douglases kept the Burgundians waiting three hours, and then made an entrance with a retinue of 5,000 men before a grandstand hung with velvet beneath the castle rock. The six knights tilted at one another with varying fortunes, none of them fatal, though James Douglas seems to have been unhorsed by the Burgundian Herve Meriadec, despite a little cheating. It would have gone to the death had not the King, doubtless hugely enjoying being the centre of such a spectacle, said enough was enough. So all six knights were allowed to depart with honour satisfied.

Early in 1450, soon after helping to eliminate the Livingstons and thus enhancing his own political stature, William Earl of Douglas decided, or was persuaded, to go on an embassy to Rome. Why he chose to leave Scotland for nearly a year is hard to understand and it was to prove disastrous. Perhaps he simply wanted to show off in England and on the bigger stage of Europe, or perhaps he was flattered to be asked to represent Scotland for such a glamorous event. Perhaps the Chancellor Crichton had persuaded the King to lure him abroad so that they could start to attack his power base while he was out of the way. The pilgrimage to Rome in the Pope's jubilee year may have been the real reason, or it may have been the excuse for getting a safe conduct – as pilgrimages so often were – in his case, to make a public relations tour of the courts of Europe: Burgundy, France, the Pope and England. Certainly he made a fine impression at the papal jubilee with a princely entourage, and when introduced to Pope Nicholas V he was treated with great honour and allowed to take home the charter for a new university at Glasgow. Similarly when he arrived back in the south of England on his way home he was welcomed by the Garter king of arms and escorted with great pomp to the court of King Henry VI. But Douglas was leaving behind a young king still not twenty, still easily impressed by whoever had spoken to him most recently and who must have been beginning to feel real resentment of a subject who could spend more lavishly that he could himself. He was also leaving behind the deviously clever Crichton, who still had the ambition of reducing any baronial power which challenged that of the king. It was put about, rightly or wrongly, but certainly quite plausibly, that, as Boece put it, Douglas 'was very oppressive and extorted by cruelty'.

Thus while Douglas was away in Rome and making his leisurely return through England, James II, now aged twenty, was incited by the Chancellor Crichton, and also perhaps Bishop Turnbull of Glasgow, to make an attack on the Douglas patrimony. William had left his youngest brother, John, Lord of Balvenie (d. 1462), in charge while he was away, and he was caught out by Crichton in some probably minor infringements of the law, enough to give Crichton and the King the excuse to pounce. He had failed to hand over some rents to the Crown, and there was also the siege of Ochiltree to be blamed on Douglas, and the murder of Richard Colvin, with several others. As Crichton said, according to Godscroft, 'The kingdom of Scotland wald never be at rest so long as the house of Douglas was on earth.' Perhaps also, as Ranald Nicholson points out, money was the main motive for the King, as it had been with his agreement to attack the Livingstons. And there was the additional excuse that Margaret Stewart, widow of Tyneman, 4th Earl of Douglas, had just died, and that created an opportunity for some of her properties to come back to the Crown instead of going to Douglas.

So in a rather sly but deliberate effort to intimidate the absent Douglas, James II besieged Lochmaben Castle, then Craig Douglas in Yarrow, which he destroyed. Black Douglas lands were harried. John Douglas of Balvenie must have put up some kind of resistance, for numbers of supporters were killed in the fighting or forced to swear loyalty to the King instead of the Earl. According to the Exchequer Rolls, the King 'slew many free tenants of the said earl'. Then the absent William was formally deprived of his title to Wigtown and some of his other estates.

As soon as he returned from England in 1451, Douglas gathered his own forces and threatened the royal army. Even more significantly he used his recent contact with the English court to suggest that if attacked by James II he could summon English help. James II backed down and returned Wigtown, Strathaven and Dunlop to him. There appeared to be a reconciliation, encouraged for some reason by the new queen, though perhaps it was just to save the King's face, leaving any image of leniency firmly on the female side of the monarchy. According to Auchinleck, 'the king resavit him till his grace'.

But clearly Douglas was not content, and though apparently restored to favour he began plotting a much bigger retaliation. At some point this involved a secret pact with his neighbour the Earl of Crawford and the hugely powerful chief of the McDonalds, John, Earl of Ross. Even at this stage the plot may have involved the English, for the brothers had of course quite recently met Henry VI. There was also perhaps an attempt to kidnap the Chancellor Crichton, but if so it failed. And out of the triumvirate of earls who made the secret pact, Crawford may have jumped the gun with an actual rebellion. Neither Boece nor Pitscottie has much sympathy with Douglas, whom they accuse of rebellion and cruelty.

At the same time Douglas, according at least to those who wanted to damn his reputation and excuse the King's later behaviour, became involved in a number of violent crimes. Pitscottie, for example, has the story of him beheading McLellan of Bombie at Threave, with the famous request of Sir Patrick Gray for the return of his nephew and the answer from Douglas – 'zonder is zour sister's son lying, bot he wantis the heid' – but this story is not corroborated by other near contemporary historians. James Douglas of Drumlanrig, an inveterate gambler, was also probably involved in the death of McLellan. Patrick Thornton, an associate of the Earl, murdered Sir John Sandilands of Calder, a relation of the King, and for flouting the Black Douglas authority he hanged John Herries of Terregles, against the King's specific orders. The problem with Herries was that he refused to pay the blackmail which Douglas expected from his neighbouring minor barons, and he was captured at a place later called Herries Slaughter, near Kirkcudbright, on the road to Dumfries. At least some of these stories were probably true, and as Sir Walter Scott put it of the Douglases: 'it was unfortunate for the country that their ambition and insubordination were at least equal to their courage'. Their power base depended on reward or intimidation of the retinue of lairds who held their subsidiary estates, and Douglas probably had to set a firm example with McLellan and Herries, albeit such acts gave the King an excuse to attack him.

It must have been exasperating for the 21-year-old James II, brought up to expect virtual omnipotence, to realize that he had several subjects who could flaunt his will and apparently get away with it. With their reputation for skill and gallantry in the tournaments and some glamorous success in border warfare, the Douglases must also have seemed psychologically intimidating. James had certainly hero-worshipped Douglas for a while when he was younger, and perhaps felt inadequate. His own good looks were somewhat marred by a birthmark, hence his nickname 'James of the Fiery Face'. Apart from attacking the castles of the absent Douglas he had not yet shown himself as a warrior. Nor had he the experience of a trip round Europe to Rome as Douglas and his brother had had. Dominated by Crichton or the Livingstons in turn, he hardly had the same freedom to spend money or extend his retinue the way Douglas did. So, when James summoned William to a meeting at Stirling, he is unlikely to have been mentally well prepared for a successful dressing-down of the older and more experienced man.

At least there is no argument that James did issue a safe conduct to Douglas for their meeting at Stirling, and that Douglas accepted the offer in good faith. Nor is there any argument that at the end of their meeting James lost his temper and stabbed him. What happened in between is inevitably less certain, as any witnesses were friends of the King's. The most likely versions are that James entertained Douglas initially, they drank together – no doubt a mistake, in the light of what happened soon afterwards – as a preliminary to their talk, and then the King told Douglas that he had found out about the three-earl plot. He asked Douglas to break the pact and Douglas refused. According to Godscroft, the King said, "'If ze will not break it I sall break it" and with these words strikes him on the breist with ane whinger [dagger]'. The King's fatal flash of temper was amazingly reminiscent of the similar act by Robert the Bruce in the church at Dumfries. Both of course at the time they committed their murders were just beginning to flex their muscles as kings, just beginning to feel the intense annoyance of being taunted by men they thought of as their subjects and inferiors.

Sir Patrick Gray, the man whose nephew, McLellan of Bombie, had been beheaded by Douglas at Threave, was one of several who joined in finishing Douglas off with pole-axes and knives, partly perhaps to help reduce the King's personal culpability but also no doubt out of genuine hatred and jealousy. Then they tossed his body out of the castle window. When found it had more than twenty wounds.

CHAPTER TWELVE

The Fall of the Black Douglases

I think with their famous unconcern
It is not gunfire I hear but a hunting horn.
Keith Douglas, 'Aristocrats'

The murder of William Douglas, 8th Earl, by James II and his friends achieved nothing. One slightly vain, impetuous and aggressive earl was replaced by another who had the same weaknesses in a perhaps more exaggerated form. The murdered Earl William and his wife, the Fair Maid of Galloway, had produced no children – she was still only about twenty when he was killed – so the earldom went to his next brother, James, who at the age of sixteen had been bishop of Aberdeen; even now he was still just a truculent twenty-six.

James Douglas (1426–88 or 91) was a twin with Archibald, Earl of Moray (1426–55), and it had been a toss-up which was the elder, decided by their father once he had seen how they began to grow up. He had apparently studied at Cologne University to help justify his outrageously young appointment as bishop of Aberdeen. Then he shared in the border raids of 1448 and organized the burning of Alnwick, so he had some military experience, and certainly he was recognized as one of the premier knightly performers in the tournament circuit, despite his gallant but slightly embarrassing loss to the Burgundian champion at Stirling Castle. He had also been trying to build an unofficial fort on the island of Fidra in the Firth of Forth as a means of controlling the sea passage into Edinburgh.

A month after the murder James stormed into Stirling, bristling with righteous anger. With him were his brother Hugh, Earl of Ormond, and 600 armed retainers. With a blast of twenty-four horns they formally denounced the King and his council for perjury. The safe conduct supposedly provided to his dead brother was nailed to a board at the mercat cross, then towed through the streets at the tail of a horse. According to Pitscottie, he 'gaif the king uncomlie words', then, announcing that he would be 'revengit upon his cruell tyrannie', he sacked and burnt the town, hardly an act likely to endear him to the populace.

James II, whose queen had just produced a son, the future James III, retaliated by turning out one of his new great bombards (possibly Mons Meg) to pound the castle of a Douglas supporter at Hatton, near Edinburgh. Among the few major barons still supporting him were George Douglas, 4th Earl of Angus (1412–62), leader of the Reds, and the Earl of Huntly. This latter was having a violent feud with Archibald Douglas, Earl of Moray, who had beaten him in a battle at the Bog of Dunkinty by Pittendreich outside Elgin, and driven him into the bog:

> Where left thou thy men thou Gordon so gay
> In the bog of Dunkinty mowing the hay.

John McDonald, Lord of the Isles, still angered at the hanging of his wife's Livingston relatives, took the opportunity of seizing Urquhart Castle, Inverness and Ruthven, then met James Douglas at Castle Sween to renew the pact made with him by his late brother and the Earl of Crawford, the pact that had led to William's murder. A McDonald fleet under Donald Balloch harried the west coast to damage Bishop Turnbull of Glasgow, who was subsidizing the King with church cash. The three-earl pact was then made doubly treasonable by negotiating with Henry VI of England, 'our devout kinsman'.

Meanwhile, James II was working to restore his image. Like a good modern politician he asked for an official inquiry into the murder which he had himself committed. He produced plenty of credible witnesses to prove that he had revoked the safe conduct to William Douglas well before the incident at Stirling. He also had evidence to prove that Douglas had been 'guilty of stubborn obstinacy'. Naturally he was supported in parliament by the Red Douglas Earl of Angus and a majority of well-rewarded supporters, including four brand-new earls and some new lords. So he was cleared. James Douglas persisted with his propaganda campaign, according to Pitscottie sticking up manifestos in the streets of Edinburgh accusing the King of 'breaking the law of hospitalitie and fallis ungodlie thirst of innocent blood'. His twin brother, Archibald, Earl of Moray, based at Darnaway, sponsored a satirical poem called the 'Buke of the Howlat' (Book of the Owl), written by a supporter, Sir Richard Holland, who was later killed in his service. It appeared to poke fun at the King, yet praised Douglas as 'Of a trewe Scottish hart.'

But his revenge was running out of steam. He could see that the King was recovering support and had now collected a considerable army. Moreover, he himself had a difficulty which was insuperable without the King's support. This was his desperate desire to marry his brother's widow, the Fair Maid of Galloway. Without her he was missing out on nearly half the Black Douglas inheritance of which she was the heir:

she had survived her husband, so James could not claim it except by marrying her, and this he could not do without a dispensation from the Pope, any request for which needed the King's backing. So he met the royal envoys at Douglas Castle and formally forgave the King for the death of his brother.

For a while there was an uneasy peace. James II, perhaps thinking it was a good idea to get James Douglas out of the country, appointed him an ambassador to negotiate the long-postponed repatriation of poor Malise Graham, who had been a hostage for James I's ransom for the last twenty-five years. The appointment, however, proved a mixed blessing. English politics were now in an even worse turmoil than Scotland's. Henry VI had become mentally unstable and the Duke of York was making a play for power, a process which was soon to escalate into the Wars of the Roses. In any such civil disruption it was natural for each side to look for support from north of the border, and Edward of York spotted the potential of the four powerful Douglas brothers. Among other acts he had arrested the Duke of Somerset, a royalist Lancastrian, who just happened to be the uncle of King James II of Scotland (Queen Joan was a Beaufort from Somerset). Thus there developed a situation where the Douglas cause became aligned with the white rose of York and James II with the red rose of Lancaster. It was the ideal breeding ground for another major Douglas plot against the throne of Scotland. It was also an opportunity or excuse, if one were needed, for James II to attack the Douglas castles again. He was now once more being advised by the Livingstons, and they doubtless encouraged the latest royal plot to get rid of the Douglases who had contributed to the Livingston bloodbath of 1449. As George Buchanan put it, 'Insolence accompanied this wealth and bands of robbers pillaged everywhere whose leaders it was believed were not unconnected with the projects of Douglas.' James Douglas continued the aggressive policy of his murdered brother in intimidating his local lairds with what Michael Brown calls 'a display of coercive leadership', and it was commented of Threave Castle that 'the gallows knob rarely lacked its tassle'.

Thus in 1455 King James started off with a siege of Inveravon Castle on the Forth: he destroyed it. He had a skirmish with the Douglases near their Newark Castle by Selkirk, then ravaged their estates in Douglasdale, Avondale and Hamilton. He next raided Ettrick and burnt the Douglas mansion there, and turned north again to besiege the massive Abercorn Castle on the south side of the Forth. Its towers were battered by what Auchinleck calls 'a gret gun the quhilk a Frenchman schot richt well'. After a month Abercorn surrendered, with no sign of a relieving force from its earl, and most of the garrison were hanged for not surrendering sooner.

James Douglas could have evaded capture in one of his many hideaways but the King's harassment had the effect that he intended: to force Douglas into the open to defend his pride. So he challenged the King by appearing with a considerable force near Carron, not far from the two destroyed castles of Inveravon and Abercorn. But perhaps in the sometimes sensible Douglas tradition of not accepting pitched battle if the outcome was uncertain, Douglas hesitated. According to Hume of Godscroft, he had the chance to be king and 'he let it slide through his fingers'. His followers were unsettled both by the sight of the royal standard fluttering above the army opposite and the seeming lack of confidence of their own commander. Some of them changed sides, even the Hamiltons who had been strong supporters for many years. Douglas gave up without a fight and headed for England, perhaps in flight, perhaps to seek English reinforcements. James II had won and this time there could be no going back. Douglas *in absentia* was charged with treason.

The Earl's three brothers, however, were still at large and ready for a fight. They too, after all, stood to lose all their estates unless they could force some compromise by a warlike stance. They gathered a small force in the Borders and were met at Arkinholm, near Langholm, by a similar small force of local lairds backed by the Red Douglas. They were trounced. Archibald Douglas, Earl of Moray, was killed outright, and his widow remarried nineteen days later. Hugh Douglas, Earl of Ormond, was wounded and later hanged; John, Lord of Balvenie, escaped to the south, only to be captured and executed some time later. The faithful Douglas of Drumlanrig was also killed, along with many other supporters:

> A Douglas could not have been brought so low
> Had not a Douglas wrought his overthrow.

All four of the Black Douglas brothers, two alive and two dead, as well as their mother, Beatrix, were found guilty of treason by the Scottish parliament, and forfeited all their estates. The main beneficiaries were James II and the Red Douglas, George, 4th Earl of Angus, who acquired many of the old Black Douglas estates to add to his already considerable portfolio based at Tantallon, Abernethy and Dundee. He was also given a substantial salary to act as Warden of the East and Middle Marches. In some ways, therefore, James II had achieved the short-term gain of some much needed cash and the removal of an impudent rival, but he had missed out yet again on the long-term objective of reducing the power of the biggest landholder under the Crown. Though the Black Douglases were no more trouble for the rest of his reign, he left a most unfortunate legacy for his son by promoting the Red Douglas to control most of the power base forfeited by the Black. Sir Walter Scott quotes the saying: 'The Red Douglas had put down the Black.'

One thing James II did prove at this time which was to have a long-term effect on the aspirations of barons like the Douglases was the power of artillery against castles. Before Arkinholm he had already captured and destroyed most of the major Black Douglas castles, and afterwards at considerable expense he transported his bombards to Galloway so that he could capture Threave. Legend has it that the local blacksmith, Brawny Kim, saw the bombards and did not think them big enough to knock down Threave, so he built the famous cannon Mons Meg to do the job. It weighed 6½ tons and was supposedly dragged from a place called Knockcannon. This story, however, lacks some credibility, as such bombards were at that time a novelty being imported from Flanders. What may be true is that special cannon balls made of local granite, and 'as heavy as a Carsphairn cow', were used to hit Threave. Again legend has it that the second shot went straight through the wall and took off the hand of the Fair Maid of Galloway. This macabre incident was slightly corroborated by the finding of both granite balls and a ring inscribed 'MdeD' in a disused well there in 1841. However, another version of the fall of Threave suggests that a combination of money and threat of hanging induced the garrison to surrender.

None of the sieges took long and none of them failed. But the devastation wreaked across southern Scotland in the process of destroying the Black Douglases had a savage side effect: the ordinary peasants paid for it with starvation. As Bower put it, there was 'great pestilence and mortality of men through the whole kingdom of Scotland'.

Ironically James Douglas, the ninth and last of the Black Douglas earls, lived on for thirty-six years after his downfall. A mixture of callous impetuosity and overcautious indecision had meant that his dynasty did not even fall with a bang, more a whimper. His wife, the Fair Maid of Galloway, deserted him and remarried, at last with her third husband producing children, so that it seemed as if the Black Douglases had been fated to become extinct. Yet James outlived his great rival James II, who was killed by one of his own bombards at the siege of Roxburgh Castle, six years after Arkinholm. He also outlasted his last surviving brother, John of Balvenie, who was captured during a border skirmish, fighting on the English side. He was executed in Edinburgh in 1462. For the next twenty-five years James remained mostly in England as a pensioner of the English King. He served the English briefly in the border skirmishes of 1462, and was sent on a mission to revive the old pact with the McDonalds for the partition of Scotland between them and the

Douglases under English suzerainty. This meeting in Ardnamurchan became known as the 'infamous Ardtornish Pact' after the castle of the Lord of the Isles where it was agreed.

Later, Douglas served as a mercenary for Edward IV in France but he did not make any serious effort to recover his estates in Scotland until 1480, by which time he was in his mid-fifties. This was as part of a concerted plan by the Yorkist Edward IV to destabilize James III and replace him with his brother, Alexander, Duke of Albany. The plan persisted after Edward's death when Richard III helped Douglas and Albany to mount an invasion of south-west Scotland, but then withdrew support as he really now wanted peace. So Albany and Douglas attacked Lochmaben themselves. Douglas, on whose head James III had put a substantial cash reward, was no longer the fine horseman who had been champion in the tournaments; he was knocked off his horse and captured. Albany escaped but was killed soon afterwards, jousting in France, and James III was murdered (as we shall see in the next chapter) a few years after that. But James Douglas lived on, outlasting the two Scottish and three English kings with whom he had had to deal. He stayed for the rest of his life as a more or less voluntary prisoner in Lindores Abbey by the Tay, refusing all offers to meddle in politics. As he is reported to have said of himself: 'He that no better be must be a monk.'

When James III was in dire straits he sent to Lindores, looking for support from the old warrior, but got none. One of the few Black Douglases to die in his bed, the 9th Earl did so a lonely and rather pathetic figure in his early sixties. The Fair Maid of Galloway, who had been married to both him and his brother before that, produced children by neither. Like so many of his predecessors, James Douglas had been a champion in the tournaments, and had stood above his fellows not just in wealth and power but also by his personal skill and strength as a warrior. In the earlier days this had led to the huge increase in power and wealth for some of the virtually self-made men in the family, such as the Good Lord James himself, his son Archibald the Grim, William of Liddesdale, William of Nithsdale and others. But now, after ten generations, it seemed as if the energy had run out, the pride had become too great and with it the envy of the rest.

An heir to anything that might be left of the Black Douglas domains was eventually found, but he was Hugh Douglas, Dean of Brechin Cathedral, who had neither the drive nor the circle of friends to help him retrieve any of his inheritance that he might have wanted.

PART II
The Red

He slew my knight to me sae dear
He slew my knight and poin'd his gear
My sweety a' frae life did flee
And left me in extremitie.
Anon., 'Lament of the Border Widow'

CHAPTER THIRTEEN

Bell-the-Cat

And all small fowlys singis on the spray
Welcum the lord of lycht and lamp of day.
                                  Gavin Douglas, *Eneados*

James III (1451–88) inherited the Crown of Scotland aged nine, after the accidental death of his father at Roxburgh. The young man who was to be his chief Douglas adversary, Archibald, the future 5th Earl of Angus (1449–1514), was just two years his senior. This was to be a relationship different from, but just as extraordinary as, that between the last Black Douglases and James II.

Archibald was to be known in history by his later nickname of Bell-the-Cat, which will be explained later in this chapter. His father, George, the 4th Earl of Angus, had been with the King when the cannon exploded outside Roxburgh Castle. He was wounded but still helped to bring the siege to a successful conclusion afterwards. The castle, which had long had an English garrison inside Scottish territory and had been a constant source of irritation to the Scots, was in too vulnerable a position to be worth keeping, so it was then destroyed.

George Douglas had benefited hugely from the share-out of land and jobs after the defeat of the Black Douglases. In particular he had acquired the original Douglas heartland of Douglasdale. In addition to Mains Castle, outside Dundee, his main Angus base, he was also building a new castle by the coast on Broughty Crag, which potentially gave him control over entry to the Tay estuary. This would complement the control he already had over the Forth from Tantallon. As Ranald Nicholson says of his son Archibald: 'Tantallon was a residence calculated to inspire any owner with delusions of unique grandeur.' The addition of Douglasdale and the wardenship of the marches simply added to and confirmed the status of the Red Douglases as rightful successors to the premier role of their Black cousins. As William Fraser puts it of George Douglas: 'He appears indeed without any friendly attachment to his kinsmen the Black Douglases and he did not scruple to make their downfall the stepping stone to his own exaltation and affluence.' Now he became joint tutor of the new boy king, alongside Queen Mary. Also, as lieutenant-general, he became a prominent member of the regency council and entertained Henry VI, the mentally fragile King of England, when he was temporarily ejected from his own kingdom; in fact Henry promised him an English dukedom with all its perquisites if he would help restore him to his throne. As part of this project George Douglas went south to prevent the English Yorkists from capturing Alnwick, which was held for the Lancastrians by a French garrison. Unfortunately he died soon afterwards, and was buried among his forebears at Abernethy.

Of the early career of young Archibald, 'Bell-the-Cat', who succeeded George Douglas as Earl of Angus, we know very little. He attended parliaments, including the one in 1476 when the secret of the two-earl pact put together after his exile by the Black Douglas was leaked to the Scots by King Edward IV. This had been forged at Ardtornish Castle and negotiated in London with Edward thirteen years earlier, so that, if the English helped Douglas to invade Scotland, he and John, Lord of the Isles, would split Scotland between them under English suzerainty. It was similar to the pact made by Douglas's brother which had caused the quarrel with James II and ultimately justified the family's downfall as traitors. In the same way it resulted in the fall of John, Lord of the Isles, as he too was exposed as a traitor. He was deprived of the earldom of Ross and many of his territories, so that the power of the McDonalds, which had been as dangerous at one time for the Crown as that of the Black Douglases, was at last seriously reduced. The west coast began to look less like enemy territory. This fitted in nicely with the fact that the Northern Isles, Orkney and Shetland, had at long last become part of Scotland as a portion of the dowry for James III's marriage to Margaret of Denmark in 1469.

It was not until 1478, when James III was in his late twenties and Archibald of Angus, 'Bell-the-Cat', approaching thirty, that signs of conflict began to emerge, and initially Archibald was not a major player. The conflict centred on the developing personality of the King and his domestic policy, neither of which was liked by the senior barons. James was to some extent a peace-lover, and this was not fashionable among his peers. He also took a great deal further the idea developed by his father of appointing junior lairds or even non-aristocrats to government positions, causing serious offence. Educated by the humanist scholar Archibald Whitelaw, he was genuinely religious and interested in the arts. Literature, architecture and music began to flourish under his patronage, and barons whose main interests were hunting or warfare found this intensely irritating. They also found that it cost them money, for the King's hobbies were expensive. They were infuriated that he gave rewards and prominence to musicians, architects, apothecaries, tailors and fencing masters, rather than his warlike barons.

There is some danger of exaggerating James III's faults in this direction simply because Scottish historians have tended to want to hero-worship his more aggressive son, so any contrast has been overstated. James was far from incompetent even in finance, albeit he perhaps grew bored with some of the detailed administration to which he should have given more care. He was also by no means a pacifist, for he took a very keen interest in the development of artillery, expanded his small navy and in due course showed no hesitation in taking personal command of the royal army. But he was perhaps a bit too much of a dilettante, and certainly he was tactless in handling the barons whose cooperation he would eventually need if there was a war with England.

The result was that some of the barons seem to have begun talking to the King's two brothers, Alexander, Duke of Albany, and John, Earl of Mar, both of whom were somewhat more conventionally warlike than James and presented a potential alternative. The brothers had enemies, however, who procured a handy witch. This lady warned the King that he would be brought down or murdered by a close relative (which was more or less true, as it happens). James III immediately suspected his brothers, perhaps encouraged to this view by the recent events in England. There Edward IV's brother had been accused of treasonable plotting and witchcraft before being mysteriously drowned in a butt of Malmsey wine. Albany and Mar were both arrested, the first later escaping to France via his castle in Dunbar, the other, still a prisoner, dying in suspicious circumstances while being bled by a doctor in the Canongate.

Archibald's role in all this can only be guessed, but he was certainly a supporter of Albany's a few years later and he certainly had a motive for opposing the King. James III had forced him to give up some valuable estates to the royal favourite, David Crichton, just a few years earlier, and had also persecuted relations of his wife, Elizabeth Boyd.

Meanwhile, the plot, if there was one, had come to nothing and Archibald Douglas looked elsewhere for satisfaction. In 1480 he led his private army into Northumberland and laid the area waste for three days, burning Bamburgh. It is not particularly likely that the King had asked him to do this, so his objective may have been to win a reputation, to give his men some fighting practice, or, as Pitscottie suggests, to provoke an English retaliation which would force James III to summon his army and make a public fool of himself. If so, then he may have been partially successful. For there was an English invasion the next year under the Duke of Gloucester which caused 'grete byrnyngis'. James did summon his army but then dismissed it without striking a blow when ordered to desist by a papal letter. The English side did not desist after receiving a similar letter, so he did look rather foolish. Luckily nothing disastrous happened to Scotland as a result, and James had another chance twelve months later. This time the English attacked more seriously with a major siege of Berwick. They had with them Alexander, Duke of Albany, King James's brother, who had returned from France to England and whom the English wanted to put on the throne in his place. They were also accompanied by the elderly James Douglas, the last of the Black Douglases making his final despairing effort to restore the family's fortunes at Lochmaben (see p. 76). Naturally the price to be paid by both Albany and Douglas (and, in the original pact, the McDonalds) for this help was that Scotland would be under English sovereignty.

James III summoned his army again, and this time its leaders, including Archibald of Angus, were in an even worse mood than before. This was partly because the King in his financial difficulties had been churning out large numbers of copper coins which had little value and were leading to food riots in the streets. As the army marched from Boroughmuir, Edinburgh, south past Soutra to Lauder, the barons coordinated their strategy. They knew that if they combined their strength and that of their retainers they would outnumber those loyal to the King. Their essential demands were that the King should withdraw or devalue the new copper coinage and sack all the non-baronial favourites who had been given positions or titles at court. The King refused and the barons had a further meeting in Lauder Church. There, according to Godscroft, Angus made the main speech demanding action against the King. Pitscottie says he was 'principall of the consall'.

In the discussion which followed Lord Gray told the story of the group of mice who had decided to hang a warning bell round a cat's neck, but could find no individual mouse to do the deed. At this point Angus spoke the words which earned him the nickname for the rest of his life: 'I will bell the cat.' He then organized a group to overcome the King's guards, entered his tent and arrested him. So Archibald in one decisive moment had carried out what numerous previous Douglases had dreamed of doing, effectively dethroning a Stewart king.

Soon afterwards Archibald came across Thomas Cochrane, one of the King's favourites. He was the architect, it is believed, of the magnificent great hall at Stirling Castle, had been made an earl, much to the annoyance of the hereditary barons, and was blamed by many for the inflationary coinage. Angus seized his gold chain and told him that a noose would suit him better. One of the Red Douglas henchmen, Robert Douglas of Lochleven, snatched his hunting horn, and then, with others of the royal favourites, Cochrane was arraigned before the helpless King and condemned to death. Several of them, including Cochrane, Thomas Preston and William Roger, the musician, were then hanged. James III was taken back to Edinburgh under arrest. Both the war and the rescue of Berwick from its English besiegers were abandoned for the time being.

With Archibald Douglas's support, Alexander of Albany became unofficial regent for his imprisoned brother, but it was soon evident that he wanted to be more than regent, a step too far for many of the barons. In particular Archibald of Angus had a problem, for if Albany went through with the original London pact of becoming king with English help, by the same token the Black Douglas would be restored to all his former estates and seniority – quite a different outcome from that which Archibald had in mind. It would also mean handing over Scotland to English suzerainty and it is doubtful if Archibald would have supported such an act of treason, unless it brought some very substantial reward for himself, and such was far from obvious. For these reasons Archibald hung back from all-out support for the prospective King Alexander IV of Scotland, and so did an increasing number of his Lauder colleagues.

The English under Gloucester had attacked Edinburgh, and that did not add to Albany's popularity. Gradually James III bought off his younger brother with meaningless words and patiently waited for the tide to turn. It did and in less than a year Albany found that his power base had disappeared. He was forced to flee a second time and died, as we have seen, soon afterwards, in a jousting match in Paris. It is a strange fact that during the period of the early Stewart kings there had been frequent dissatisfaction, frequent violence, but despite several prolonged minorities there was never an occasion when the Crown did not pass on to the rightful heir, whereas in England in the same period there were three palace coups which displaced the heir and brought a change of dynasty.

Bell-the-Cat had kept a low profile, waiting in his massive castle at Tantallon as the mood in Edinburgh changed. He had at least been promoted to the Justiciarship of the South, and his cousin at Dalkeith Castle, James Douglas, 1st Earl of Morton, became Sheriff of Edinburgh. The trouble was that Archibald had shown himself bold and decisive in the negative task of unseating the King, but not particularly constructive in the aftermath. Having engineered the original coup he had perhaps assumed that he himself might have become a kind of permanent regent, but Albany had a prior claim and he had failed. Now that James III was back in control he must have felt extremely uncomfortable remembering his behaviour at Lauder. In 1484 he even went so far as to found a new chapel at St Bride's for the King's soul, an arch piece of hypocrisy which cannot have done much to placate even so pious a man as James III.

Having survived two severe crises James III seemed to feel that he was indestructible. He had learned from the disasters but not enough. He persisted with his policy of favouring junior lairds at the expense of the hereditary barons, aiming understandably for a more centralized state, but treading on toes as he did so. The border barons in particular did not like any restriction on their traditional sport of raiding England for profit. James had organized the successful recapture of Dunbar from the English, but he cracked down on casual border raiding as he aimed to make peace with England. He sealed this by marrying himself to an English royal widow (his previous queen had died in 1486) and his son to an English princess, young Margaret Tudor. But he greatly offended several of the unruly border families, particularly the Homes of Fast Castle by taking away their rights over the valuable priory at Coldingham, and they were to prove dangerous enemies.

Meanwhile, there had been a major change of dynasty in England. Ironically, as Henry Tudor marched towards Bosworth to meet Richard III, he was supported by two senior Scottish officers, a Stewart and a Bruce. Bernard Stewart, Sieur d'Aubigny, led a French contingent, and Alexander Bruce of Earlshall, a favourite of James III, led the Scots. The benefit to James III was that the victorious Henry VII had the same attitude towards war as himself, and there was the real prospect of a proper peace between England and Scotland.

James III, however, still had many baronial enemies, and his offending of the Homes was to trigger the next crisis. There was a Home supporter acting as Governor of Stirling Castle, James Schaw, and as such he was the effective custodian of the King's heir, James, Duke of Rothesay. At the request of the Homes, Schaw let the fourteen-year-old James out of Stirling into the hands of the baronial opposition. To what extent the boy's mind needed poisoning against his father, and to what extent he was already impatient to take over, it is impossible to tell. But his relationship with his father since Queen Margaret's death does not seem to have been totally satisfactory, and he was perhaps jealous of his own younger brother, also called James, who had been made Duke of Ross. Either way, young James allowed himself to be made the figurehead for the baronial opposition to his father. Ironically, as James III saw his support crumble and faced disaster for the third time, he even asked for help from the old Black Douglas, the elderly inmate of Lindores Abbey, but Douglas was too old and disillusioned to help anyone.

This time Archibald 'Bell-the-Cat' does not seem to have played a major role. Early in 1488 he was still at the King's side at Blackness, trying to negotiate a few concessions to avoid war with the prince's supporters. He was still there probably when the King won a minor victory over the

rebels. Either uncertain as to who was going to win or trusting neither of
the two protagonists, he made no immediate move to join the barons
supporting the young Duke of Rothesay. So far as we know he was not at
the battle of Sauchieburn fighting on either side. The opposition won,
James III – still only in his late thirties – was murdered soon afterwards,
young James IV was proclaimed king in place of his father, and Archibald
'Bell-the-Cat' went back to Tantallon:

> I said Tantallon's dizzy steep
> Hung o'er the margin of the deep
> Many a rude tower and rampart there
> Repelled the insult of the air.
>
> Sir Walter Scott, Marmion

CHAPTER FOURTEEN

The Road to Flodden

Remember me when I am dead
And simplify me when I'm dead.
    Keith Douglas, 'Simplify me when I'm dead'

A new James but the same Archibald: now it was James IV who was King of Scotland (1473–1513), one of the most charismatic and potentially successful of the Stewart kings, but it was still Archibald 'Bell-the-Cat' who was what McDougall calls 'the great maverick of the reign'. Yet he was to outlast the son, just as he had already outlasted the father.

The relationship of Archibald of Angus and the new king, twenty-five years his junior, was never to be very relaxed. For a start Archibald had not been one of the early supporters who had brought James to victory at Sauchieburn. While by that same token he did not share the guilt of James III's subsequent murder, a guilt which the son soon felt very keenly, he had not been a friend of the old king's either, and had humiliated him at Lauder. Also it became a natural part of James IV's strategy to continue the process by which his grandfather and father had aimed to reduce the influence of the hereditary barons, so Archibald was a target. After Sauchieburn he had joined with Argyll in the feverish search for the treasure which it was believed James III had amassed, but whether the rumour was true or false, little of it was found either in the vaults of Edinburgh or in the mud of Sauchieburn. Soon afterwards Archibald was deprived of the important office of Warden of the Marches and held briefly the honorific title of Royal Guardian and Court Auditor instead.

For a short period Archibald thrived on the fact that the King's first mistress, Marion Boyd, was a relation of his own wife's. In 1490 we hear of him playing dice with the King at Linlithgow. But a year later, perhaps after a rather suspicious journey he had made to London, supposedly as usual on a pilgrimage, he was told to keep himself at Tantallon, and then he was besieged there by the King with cannon, crossbows and culverins. Clearly Archibald was suspected, perhaps rightly, of plotting to sell out to the English. Soon afterwards, however, he and the King seem to have made it up, and Archibald must have agreed to a request to hand over the vital border castle of Hermitage together with his Liddesdale properties;

so this humiliating demand was perhaps another cause of the quarrel or perhaps a result of it. The castle went to Bothwell, who had been an early supporter of James IV. In its place Archibald was given the lordship of Kilmarnock and Bothwell Castle, with a few other former Black Douglas castles in that area thrown in. This was followed by a Christmas present from the King of a velvet gown with a lambskin lining.

By 1493 Archibald was sufficiently back in favour to be appointed Chancellor, a post he held for five years. As such he was present with the King at Dunstaffnage during the expedition to pacify the west coast and subjugate the McDonalds. This led to the final downfall and imprisonment of John, the last Lord of the Isles. The next year he was with a similar expedition at Tarbert when another McDonald, John of Islay, stormed the castle at Dunaverty and hanged its royal governor within sight of James IV's fleet on its return voyage to the Clyde. Then in 1495 Archibald joined the King on a third expedition against the western clans, this time to Mingary on Ardnamurchan, where they took submissions from more McLeans and McDonalds. Thereafter he seems to have been heavily involved as an ambassador to England, negotiating a seven-year truce and using the prince-in-the-Tower lookalike, Perkin Warbeck, as a bargaining tool. Thus his period as chancellor, which also included parliamentary and judicial appearances, seems to have been quite busy and productive.

From the King's point of view Archibald's chancellorship seems to have ended quite amicably, for Douglas was given Crawford Castle, with various other estates, as his reward and was made Warden of the Middle Marches. Yet the surprising fact is that about this time the now rather middle-aged Earl and the still youthful King were sharing a mistress. The details of this triangle are obscure, but certainly Janet Kennedy had an affair with the King which resulted in a son, and he provided her with Darnaway Castle in Moray for her use. Archibald was either betrothed or married to the same lady in 1498, for he also gave her a castle, Bothwell, but two years later he had either parted from or divorced her, for he married Katherine Stirling, his second or third spouse, in 1500. Whether this was the reason for the two men falling out again we do not know, but certainly Archibald was arrested in 1501 and shut up in Dumbarton Castle. He was then for some reason moved to Rothesay Castle and was there for some time.

The next few years Archibald kept a low profile again, as if he felt the royal distrust. He seems mainly to have been involved in securing the legal transfer of his massive estates to his sons, as if he did not expect to live much longer or feared that he might be forfeited. But a dozen or so years after his latest disgrace he was back in royal employ again, helping to ratify the new alliance with France which was to prove so totally disastrous for Scotland. The signing of this treaty was rewarded with French gold for James IV, money which he needed, as he had been building up his fleet ready for a projected crusade against the Turks. At this point, aged thirty-six, James was beginning to regard himself as the senior king in Europe who might lead the next big crusade – Henry VII had died, as had James's uncle the King of Denmark and the Captain-General of the great fleet of Venice, while Louis XII was too busy with his internal problems to bother. James was ready to be the new Richard the Lionheart to save Christianity from the infidel, not quite so ready to defend Scotland against its nearest neighbour. At the same time the new King of England, Henry VIII, James's brother-in-law but a mere boy of eighteen, was behaving in a far from fraternal manner. As a man deeply imbued with the traditions of chivalry and conscious of his own not inconsiderable talents, James did not take kindly to being treated by his wife's brother as if he was the king under sufferance of a poor English outpost. James preferred the compliments of the French and the Irish. A combination of irritation at Henry VIII's rudeness to him, of quixotic adherence to the French alliance and overconfidence in his own military capacity was pushing him steadily towards an unnecessary war.

Just as the Homes of Fast Castle had precipitated the downfall of James III, so in a way they did the same for his son. In late 1512 they carried out an unauthorized raid into English territory and were badly mauled on their return journey. James felt obliged to retaliate for this defeat, especially as the French were desperate for him to create a diversion against Henry VIII, who was giving them a hard time. He headed towards the border with the largest available Scottish army. It was exactly what Bruce had always said was bad policy and the same that had caused three major earlier disasters for Scotland: Halidon Hill under Sir Archibald Douglas, Neville's Cross under David II and Homildon Hill under Archibald Douglas, the Tyneman, and Murdoch Stewart.

Meanwhile, Archibald 'Bell-the-Cat' had expected to be appointed Admiral of Scotland early in 1513, but just then his rival the Earl of Arran sailed off to France with the fleet, as well as most of Scotland's precious artillery, so he lost his opportunity. He was also at the time involved in rather a messy attack on Kilwinning Abbey in support of a somewhat corrupt Glasgow cleric. Nevertheless, when James called his barons for their views on the situation with England, he was one of several councillors who advised against the invasion. According to Buchanan, he wept when his advice was rejected. Then he was one of a much smaller number who openly disagreed with the King's tactics at Flodden, urging either a very quick attack on the English while they were still moving towards Flodden or a tactical withdrawal to let the English run out of food. Walter Scott gives a description of him at this moment in *Marmion*:

> His giant form like ruin'd tower
> Though fall'n its muscles' brawny vaunt
> Huge, broad and tall and grim and gaunt
> Seem'd o'er the gawdy scene to glower;
> His locks and beard in silver grew
> His eyebrows kept their sable hue.
> Near Douglas when the monarch stood
> His bitter speech he thus pursued.

James accused Archibald of cowardice in the face of the enemy, and dismissed him. According to William Fraser, the Earl burst into tears again. Then he briefed his two eldest sons to lead the Douglas contingent in the battle and headed back to Scotland with just his six personal attendants. He never saw his two sons or James IV again. His eldest son, George, reputedly had a row with the King in the later stages of the battle, when James taunted George to fight on foot and George taunted the King to fight without his royal armour. Both died soon afterwards. William of Glenbervie, the Earl's second son, made a gallant attempt to hold the bridge over the Till so that the survivors of the battle could retreat, but he too was killed, as was Robert Douglas of Lochleven. Of several hundred in the Douglas contingent, only a couple of dozen made it back to Scotland.

Bell-the-Cat lasted barely a year longer, for he died at the monastery of St Ninian at Whithorn, on a border patrol in the area, and that is where he was buried. A particularly large skeleton was uncovered there in 1885 and may well have been his. Godscroft said of him 'He was too much given to women, otherwise there was little or nothing amiss' – perhaps a somewhat superficial judgement on a very complex character.

CHAPTER FIFTEEN

To Marry a Queen

My ears yielding like swinging doors
Admit princes to the corridors.

Keith Douglas, 'Bête Noire'

James V of Scotland (1512–42) was crowned as a baby of eighteen months, and Archibald 'Bell-the-Cat', one of the few high-ranking survivors of the disaster at Flodden, attended the coronation at Stirling. For the brief interval before his death at Whithorn he was provost of Edinburgh and a senior councillor, while one of his younger sons, Gavin, the poet, was Provost of St Giles. Since his eldest son George had been killed, the earldom now went to his grandson Archibald, who was nineteen. He was to have as bizarre a relationship with his royal Stewart opposite number as any in the long catalogue of the two families.

Archibald Douglas, 6th Earl of Angus (1489–1557), was good-looking and appearance-conscious, if perhaps somewhat empty-headed. In the latest fashion he wore his hair and beard short, unlike the late King, who had a longish beard and shoulder-length hair. This might seem a trivial matter but not to the dead King's widow, Margaret Tudor, who at twenty-four found herself on the lookout for a new husband. She had seemed a somewhat downtrodden queen in the glamorous court of James IV, who had several mistresses both before and after his marriage. Now Margaret, who may have had some of the spirit and taste for variety associated with her brother Henry VIII, came out of her shell. According to a rather shocked William Fraser, 'her amorous propensities were strong and were to be indulged at the expense of ambition and decency in precipitate marriages'. She was so besotted by the appearance of Archibald Douglas that she quickly – but, as it turned out, foolishly – picked him as her second husband, though he was five years her junior. He was also a widower, for his young wife had recently died in childbirth. Thus Archibald of Angus instantly became guardian of the new king and joint regent with his wife, Queen Margaret, a position of considerable power. Ironically members of the Douglas family had by this time married into the Royal Stewart dynasty twelve times, but without getting more than an additional earldom out of it. Now a Red Douglas leapt into the regency at the age of nineteen and was to be the ancestor of future kings and queens of Great Britain, not just Scotland.

Archibald was unsuccessful, however, in his efforts to help his uncle, the poet Gavin Douglas (1474–1522), who had tried to make himself archbishop of St Andrews by force and was besieged in the castle there until he was forcibly ejected by his main rival. Eventually, even with the help of Henry VIII, Gavin had to settle for the bishopric of Dunkeld. All this fitted in with the general atmosphere of corruption and nepotism both in Church and baronial circles at this time.

Archibald's position of power did not last very long at this time, for John Stewart, Duke of Albany (1484–1536), a French-born grandson of James III and son of the previous regent, Albany, arrived from France. As the senior adult male member of the Stewart dynasty, he was appointed Governor. He sold James IV's favourite battleship, the *Great Michael,* to raise funds for himself. Archibald and Margaret reluctantly vacated Holyrood for Edinburgh Castle to let him take over. Meanwhile, as so often during royal minorities, the country was descending into chaos, with extortion, robbery and petty warfare between factions. Albany was more French than Scottish, and was well connected on the continent – he was a brother-in-law of Lorenzo de Medici, the ruler of Florence, and had consolidated his position as Count of Auvergne by marrying his own cousin, Anne de la Tour, so that he had now three estates in France. This meant that the regency of Scotland was no great prize in his eyes and he always had another career to return to if it did not work out.

Already the marriage of Archibald Douglas to Queen Margaret was showing signs of friction. When Albany quite naturally demanded custody of the boy king, Margaret fought hard to keep him, but Archibald made little effort to help her. He was even asked by Albany to besiege his own wife in Stirling as a test of his loyalty to him, but he decided to keep out of the way. His brother George Douglas of Pittendreich (1490–1554) had been left to protect Margaret, who was pregnant, and the boy king in Stirling, but he too deserted her. All this, coupled with the fact that Archibald soon consoled himself with a mistress, Janet Stewart of Traquair, hardly helped their relationship. Yet their marriage did produce a daughter, Margaret, who by a remarkable coincidence was to be the mother of Henry Stewart, Lord Darnley. Since Darnley was to marry Mary Queen of Scots, the daughter of Margaret Tudor's son from her first marriage, this resulted in Margaret being the great-grandmother, twice over, of James VI and I. It also means that Archibald Douglas was a prime male antecedent of the Stuart dynasty which was to rule Great Britain for over a hundred years. (From the time of Mary Queen of Scots' period in France the spelling Stuart tended to replace Stewart.)

Meanwhile, Archibald's fortunes continued their temporary decline. He and his brother George were blamed for the murder of a Frenchman appointed by Albany to guard the east march, and George Douglas was imprisoned. Archibald failed to win the appointment of deputy Regent, which to his disgust went to his deadly rival James Hamilton, Earl of Arran. The Hamiltons had been long-term supporters of the Black Douglases, but had deserted them before Arkinholm and done well from their fall. Queen Margaret had found a new lover, another Stewart, Henry Stewart of Avondale, and wanted a divorce. Archibald made grovelling apologies to her, and for political reasons they patched up their relationship for a short while. In 1520, while Albany was out of the way in France, they achieved a small coup. Archibald's youngest brother, William Douglas, Prior of Coldingham, ignored the normal rules of his calling and marched into Edinburgh, with 800 horsemen and bagpipes playing, to support Angus in his street fighting against the Hamiltons, under their leader, the deputy regent, James Hamilton of Arran. They fought a battle, known as Cleansing the Causeway, in Blackfriars Wynd, and Arran's brother, together with many other Hamiltons, was killed. When Albany arrived back from France he forfeited Archibald of all his lands, besieged and captured Tantallon Castle, then tricked Archibald into surrendering. He and his brother were bundled off by ship to one of Albany's dungeons near Boulogne. His uncle Gavin Douglas, the would-be archbishop of St Andrews and currently absentee bishop of Dunkeld, the man who had amazingly translated Virgil's *Aeneid* into Scots and had shuttled between the two sides in the street battle trying to make a truce, was now also disgraced, exiled to London, where he died of the plague two years later, one of the greatest Scottish poets of the Middle Ages.

As so often in Scottish history the winning side self-destructed. Albany's style of rulership, like that of his father years earlier, made him so unpopular that his governorship became untenable, and eventually he went back to his estates in France, where life was more comfortable. Margaret Tudor now wanted to marry Henry Stewart of Avondale and had given her young lover considerable powers in the government, which upset the establishment, so that she lost all credibility. Her enemies put about rumours of her 'ungodlie living'. According to William Fraser, 'she employed her bodyguard more freely than wisely', and her husband accused her of sleeping with the Regent Albany. So her regime and that of her chancellor, Arran, became extremely unpopular. In a vain attempt to rationalize his position Albany stopped the education of the young king at the age of twelve, so that officially he could come of age, albeit still unable to read and write.

Meanwhile, Archibald of Angus had escaped from France by pretending to go on a pilgrimage to Navarre, then skirted round through Germany back to Calais and London. He was joined there by his brother George, who had escaped from France earlier, but they were prevented from returning to Scotland by Henry VIII until he was convinced the time was right. This meant that Archibald had to sign a pledge to support Henry's policies when he at last did return in 1524.

Now came the most important three years in Archibald's life, when as leader of the regency council he was the effective ruler of Scotland, helped by his brother George, who was the abler of the two and had even fewer scruples. King James V was still only thirteen, and during those vital teenage years Archibald was appointed one of four guardians of the boy king, but at the end of his three-month turn he managed to keep the boy away from the other guardians. He has been suspected of deliberately making the young king as corrupt, and therefore pliable, as possible. The boy had been deprived of his father soon after birth and of his mother for many of his boyhood years. Besides, as William Fraser puts it, 'his mother had failings which did not lean to virtue's side'. Now he was not surprisingly showing signs of an unstable background and an uneven education. The red-haired king had a volatile nature and a very suspect temper, and knifed a porter at Stirling Castle who refused to open the castle gate for him. Archibald made sure that he was indulged with plenty of hunting, his favourite sport, money for gambling, exotic clothes and court wenches, to take his mind off the idea of dispensing with a guardian.

Meanwhile, Archibald packed the government with his own family and supporters. Archibald's uncle, Archibald Douglas of Kilspindie (1480–1540), known as a dashing knight, was brought into the royal household to be a hero figure for the young king, who called him Greysteel after a popular ballad of the time. In real life he was more of a robber baron who had an unsavoury reputation in Caithness, where he had acquired a castle near Latheron. He held the all-important Douglas Castle for his brother, became provost of Edinburgh and treasurer of Scotland. Archibald's second brother, the ever-faithful George Douglas of Pittendreich, became Master of the Household or Chamberlain, and was in charge of royal security, sometimes having to guard the boy king day and night at St Andrews to prevent him being taken away by the other three official guardians. During a skirmish between Archibald and one of the other guardians, the Earl of Lennox, at Manuel by Avonbridge in 1526, George seems to have earned the King's lasting hatred by threatening to cut off a physical souvenir if there was any likelihood of the boy falling into Lennox's hands. The threat was unnecessary because Archibald won the battle and Lennox was later killed, but the King remembered it for many years. It was a stupid error by a man who was valued as a conscientious if amoral diplomatist even by judges as demanding as Henry VIII, with whom he exchanged coded messages signed with a heart shape, the badge of the family. James Hamilton of Finnart (d. 1440), a totally unprincipled supporter of the Douglas cause and owner of Craignethan Castle near Lanark, was the party's hatchet man. After Avonbridge it was probably he who murdered the alternative royal favourite, the Earl of Lennox, who had threatened to steal the boy's affections – and his person. William Douglas, Archibald's youngest brother, who through the customary nepotism had become Prior of Coldingham yet still led armed bands of followers, now by devious means became Abbot of Holyrood. The other Douglas women, Marion and Elizabeth, looked after the boy's immediate comforts and health.

In this his peak period of power Archibald did do some useful work in the Borders, attempting to bring order among the border lairds who did not distinguish between authorized invasions of England and downright theft from south of the border. He had done a raid on Liddesdale in 1526 and tried to clean up the east march the year after. Then, just before Avonbridge, he had beaten a group of border reivers under Walter Scott at Melrose when they tried to snatch the King. This to some extent justified the subsidies he was still receiving from Henry VIII.

The whole edifice of Douglas power was, however, quite fragile. It depended entirely on controlling the teenage king in mind and body, and this could not last for ever. Archibald was now Chancellor, and had been busy doing a sweep through the Borders to reduce the banditry of the Armstrongs in that area; then he took the King to St Andrews for Easter, but he himself went off to attend to his own affairs, leaving the boy guarded by James Douglas of Parkhead. According to Lindsay of Pitscottie, the boy asked to go hunting at Falkland and then escaped at night dressed as one of his own servants. He headed to Stirling Castle, whose governor he told to lock out all comers. In Bishop Lesley's words, he announced that he 'was nocht willinge to remane langer under the tutell and governement of the Erle of Angus and his cumpanye'. It is probable that he was egged on to this by his mother, who was at last getting her divorce from Archibald, by Cardinal James Beaton (1470–1539), the Archbishop of St Andrews, and by other barons who were enemies of the Douglases. In fact in 1526 the Douglases had driven the cardinal out of his castle, so that he 'had to keep sheep in Balgrumo'. With Beaton's advice James V called a parliament and arraigned the Douglases for treason. Naturally they were found guilty, and forfeited all their estates some seventy years after the same thing had happened to the Black Douglases – but, unlike the Blacks, the Reds were to achieve a comeback.

Archibald headed first to Tantallon, which the old proverb said was hard 'to ding doon'. But that offered no long-term refuge against heavy artillery, and soon afterwards he took up residence at Ladykirk Church on the Tweed, so that he could cross into England at the first hint of danger, keeping with him his youngest brother the Abbot of Holyrood. Then it was back to Tantallon with some English troops as reinforcements, and in his fury he burnt two Edinburgh villages 'that the king mycht have light to see the rise withall upon Fryday in the morning'. When the King tried to besiege Tantallon, Archibald attacked his artillery convoy, killed most of the gunners and stole some of the guns. All efforts to persuade the two men to make it up seemed to fail. Archibald took to living beside the border, sometimes just to the north, other times just to the south. From there for several years he acted as Henry VIII's man, invading Scotland, burning places such as Coldingham, Cockburnspath and Dunglass in 1532. But neither force nor offers of friendship had any effect in patching up the deep-seated antipathy between Archibald and the King, and George Douglas in particular was loathed by the King. Archibald even went so far as to hand over Tantallon during one of the attempted pacts between them, but whatever the conditions offered by the King he does not seem to have kept to them.

James V's least pleasant act of persecution against the Douglas faction was when he pounced on Archibald's sister Janet, widow of the Lord Glamis and now married to a Campbell. She was tried for treason, murder and witchcraft and found guilty on highly suspect evidence by a tame court, then burnt to death on the Castlehill, Edinburgh. Other Douglas supporters were imprisoned for communicating with George Douglas, who was attempting to act as a go-between from his exile in England. James Douglas, 3rd Earl of Morton (d. 1550), was deprived of all his estates. Numerous other barons were given short spells in prison to try to bring them to heel, yet, as with James I's similar efforts, the effect was often the reverse. James did not enhance his reputation for fairness when he invited the notorious Armstrong reivers to meet him in Liddesdale – and then promptly hanged them.

James V had a strange personality, hardly surprising considering his strange upbringing. On the one hand he enjoyed huge extravagance as he undertook massive rebuilding projects at the royal palaces of Holyrood, Linlithgow, Falkland and Stirling. In a hunting party at Blair Atholl he is reckoned to have personally killed 600 harts and hinds before enjoying a feast of crane and swan in a specially constructed small palace which was burnt to the ground when the meal was over. On the other hand he liked to disguise himself as a poor servant and mix with beggars in the streets, chasing thieves, playing pranks. His love life was also one of extremes. He had an aristocratic mistress, Mary Erskine, who produced a son for him, but he also seduced a serving maid in a vast puddle of beer after the vat had been thrown over him. He was married to Madeleine, the French king's daughter, in Notre Dame, Paris, in 1537, but she died soon afterwards, and he replaced her rapidly with another French princess, Mary of Guise, as he desperately wanted an heir.

The writing was by this time on the wall for the Catholic Church in Scotland, and James demanded reform, but did not set a good example. Four of his young bastard sons were given rich abbacies for which they were totally unqualified. Cardinal David Beaton (1494–1546), who had succeeded his uncle as Archbishop of St Andrews, was allowed to enrich himself with double livings, and kept a permanent mistress. On midsummer's eve 1540 James watched an early version of *Ane Pleasant Satyre of the Thrie Estaitis*, but its message was lost on him. He still milked Church and State to pay for his exotic new apartments and beautifully dressed courtiers. He bullied the week-minded Earl of Morton into signing over his estates to him, a fragrant breach of feudal tradition which was later reversed by the courts. He paid a state visit to the Western Isles with gold plate and an orchestra on board his flagship to impress the local chiefs. The crown and sceptre of Scotland were restyled with symbols of empire so that he would appear equal to Henry VIII and Francis I, who both now called themselves emperors.

In the end it was nothing much to do with the efforts of Archibald Douglas of Angus that James V went into a serious decline. It may have been the after-effects of a hunting fall in 1537 or due to a hereditary disease, porphyria, which was later noted in his daughter and grandson. But he had lost the confidence of his ruling class and had a crisis of confidence in himself. He began to suffer from nightmares, particularly after the execution of Hamilton of Finnart, who had been one of his favourites as both a military architect and a hired assassin. He and his new wife, Mary of Guise, lost both their two baby sons in quick succession. Then he made the mistake of snubbing his uncle Henry VIII, who responded by asserting his imperial superiority over him and sending an army to prove the point. Archibald Douglas joined that army: it was defeated at Haddon Hill, near the border, but Archibald got away.

James V, who had sacked his senior general, summoned a new army to Fala Muir and had to endure the same situation that had been the ruin of his grandfather James III. The baronial officer class simply refused to cooperate, exposing the hollowness of his power. The army dispersed and James was humiliated. He was still only thirty but his regal authority had vanished, and he went into a deep depression. The news that his new general, Oliver Sinclair, had been beaten by the English at Solway Moss in 1542, followed by the news that his wife had produced a daughter, Mary, instead of the much-needed male heir, was all too much for him. He just seemed to will himself to death.

Archibald of Angus was by this time fifty-three and had been in exile effectively for nearly fourteen years, yet on his return to Scotland he survived James by another fifteen. Restored to his estates and a share in the power of yet another regency, he seemed to have no problem changing sides to fight the English instead of his countrymen. Though his basic strategy, unlike that of the widowed queen and his rival Arran, was to make peace with England and avoid messy entanglements with France, he still had to show that the Scots could defend the border.

There was now the beginning of a religious divide, for certainly Archibald's brother George of Pittendreich had become a Protestant and Archibald was probably also moving in that direction, albeit he still wanted the odd abbacy for his bastards. The East Lothian Douglases had been crucially involved in the earliest stages of the Scottish Reformation, for in 1543 John Knox (1513–72) was working as a notary in Haddington and as tutor to the two sons of Hugh Douglas of Longniddrie. George Wishart, a keen reformer who had been in exile in England, arrived back as part of Henry VIII's embassy to persuade the Scots to let young Queen Mary marry his son, Prince Edward. Wishart and Knox both stayed for some time at Longniddrie Castle while Wishart preached the new religion, and perhaps it was at this time that Knox was finally converted, along with a number of the Douglases. Wishart, to whom George Douglas of Pittendreich had in his usual way promised protection but failed to keep his word, was arrested in 1546 on the orders of Cardinal Beaton and burnt at St Andrews. Beaton himself was murdered soon afterwards, and the two Douglas boys were sent with Knox to St Andrews, which was held by Beaton's murderers. Knox was captured soon afterwards by a French force assisting the dowager queen, Mary of Guise, and served two years as a galley slave; the two boys seem to have got away. The seed had been sown, however, and it is significant that Douglas of Whittinghame, a neighbour of the boys, was to be a regular and influential commissioner at the early general assemblies of the new Church of Scotland, while John Douglas, a baillie of Haddington, was a few years later to be one of the first to induct a Protestant minister.

The dowager queen, Mary of Guise, was naturally a strong Catholic and was desperate to maintain the French connection. Her ally James Hamilton of Arran was rewarded with the French dukedom of Chatelherault (later ironically passed on to the Douglases) for his support of her policies. He had harassed members of the pro-English, pro-Protestant party, particularly Archibald's brother George Douglas at Pinkie Tower and his nephew the new Earl of Morton at Dalkeith. This was not wholly unjustified, since George Douglas seems to have been feeding the English with plans of how to invade Scotland. The dealings of the two senior Douglases with Henry VIII had been Byzantine to put it at its mildest. It is hard to tell whether they were playing a double bluff, or, a treble bluff or, as Maxwell in his *History of the House of Douglas* puts it, 'a fair finesse according to the doctrine of Macchiavelli', or, as William Fraser says more bluntly, 'the selfish treachery of the House of Angus'.

Arran had Archibald of Angus arrested, but he needed the old warrior's experience in border warfare, so they patched up their differences. The English under Hertford had been burning Edinburgh and sacking the border abbeys, annoying Archibald particularly by desecrating the Douglas family memorials at Melrose, as well as making specific attacks against the Douglas estates. So in 1544 Archibald was appointed Lieutenant of the South, and swore that he would be revenged against Hertford's men writing 'on their own skin with sharp pens and with bloody ink'. Within a year he had won a victory over the English at Ancrum Moor. He used the old ruse of feigning a retreat, but it worked. As Sir Walter Scott put it in *Eve of St John*:

> He came not from where Ancrum Moor
> Ran red with English blood
> Where the Douglas true and the bold Buccleugh
> Gainst keen Lord Evers stood.

As he said, he knew that he could always avoid capture by hiding 'in the skirts of Cairntable', the secret fort of Parisholm in the hills behind Douglas. Meanwhile, the French were delighted with him for beating the English and sent him cash, a collar of gold and the Order of St Michael.

However, later that year Archibald and Arran had to join forces to face Hertford in a bigger battle at Pinkie, and the old enmity of the two Scottish commanders was their undoing. Arran was convinced that Archibald would change sides and spent too much time watching his back rather than attacking the English. His worries were understandable, because George Douglas was up to his usual double-game, even offering single combat between Huntly (not himself of course) and the English general Hertford – as Huntly said, 'He was a mete man to pick wharels for other men to fight for.' Douglas had written to Henry VIII that if he invaded Scotland with an army 'there is not so little a boy but he will still throw stones against it, the wives will come out with their distaffs and the commons universally will die rather', but he himself was not the kind to fight to the last man.

The battle was a disaster, and the Scots lost 14,000 men. Of the Douglas castles Broughty was taken over by the English, Dalkeith captured and destroyed, Drumlanrig heavily attacked.

Archibald Douglas retired to Tantallon from where he continued to oppose the Regent's policy of alliance with France. The widow Queen Mary of Guise demanded the handing-over of Tantallon. Archibald carried on feeding his hawk with the words 'Confound this greedy gled; she can never have enough.' At Tantallon he died, in 1557, and he was buried in the traditional family plot at Abernethy.

CHAPTER SIXTEEN

To Hurt a Queen

I looked behind their masks and posturings
And saw their souls too rotten to be cured.
Lord Alfred Douglas, Lighten and Darkness

There is at least one unusual aspect to this episode in the long-drawn-out dynastic rivalry between the Stewarts and Douglases: for the first time one of the protagonists is a woman, Mary Queen of Scots (1542–87). Another unusual aspect is that two of the protagonists were executed.

James Douglas, known to history as the Regent Morton (1516–81), was in his mid-twenties when King James V died and was succeeded by his infant daughter, Mary. He was the younger son of George Douglas of Pittendreich, the wily and assiduous brother of the Earl of Angus, so he was in every sense quite a junior member of the family. Since his uncle had no sons, the earldom of Angus was due to go to James's elder brother, but his father, the wily George, had in 1543 arranged a clever marriage for him, to the daughter of the Earl of Morton, who had no male heir. As a result of this James became Earl of Morton in 1552, when his father-in-law died. The earls of Morton were themselves a junior branch of the Douglas family whose main bases were the castles at Dalkeith and Morton itself, which was in Nithsdale, northern Dumfriesshire. They had been the third of the Douglas families to acquire an earldom, which they did in 1457 for services to James II, particularly by marrying his deaf and dumb sister. The Douglases had a knack on the odd occasions when they failed to produce male heirs of making sure that their daughters married other Douglases and kept the title inside the family. Three deaths brought James Douglas unexpectedly to the leadership of the whole dynasty: his father-in-law's gave him an earldom, and his uncle's and his brother's in quick succession meant that the new Earl of Angus was a child with James as his guardian. Thus, as first the Black earls of Douglas, then the Red Douglas earls of Angus, now briefly it was the turn of a Red Douglas Earl of Morton to have centre stage.

Meanwhile, James's father had been taking a devious part in the murky politics of the new regency. As ever he was making use of his wide contacts south of the border, and as a Protestant was closer to the pro-English party in Scotland than to the pro-French, Catholic stance of the King's widow. Mary of Guise. In 1543 he seems actually to have offered to kidnap the infant Queen Mary from Stirling in return for English gold, but this came to nothing. He was arrested and charged with treason. His son James also had to act as a hostage for his father's and uncle's good behaviour. So James had a spell in the dungeon of Blackness and then spent time in disguise, working as a farmer, learning many aspects of estate management which were to be very useful to him later as he tried to revive the run-down Morton earldom. He also suffered during several English invasions over the next few years and was taken away as a prisoner again in 1548 after trying in vain to defend his new home, Dalkeith Castle, against an English siege which followed the bad Scottish defeat at Pinkie. He used his time in the Tower of London to acquire English manners, useful for a potential courtier. Despite the military successes of the English, who wanted Mary as a child bride for their Edward VI, the young queen, still only six, was smuggled away from Dumbarton to Roscoff to be betrothed to the Dauphin of France. She lived at the glittering French court for the next ten years, was married to the ailing Dauphin in 1558 and was Queen of France very briefly a year later. Francis II, who was a year her junior, died after less than a year on the throne and left her a widow at sixteen.

By this time James Douglas – we can start to call him Morton now – had not advanced much in his political career. Naturally his Protestant leanings made him suspect in a court still dominated by Mary of Guise. But when she died in 1560 he came gradually to the fore. He had not wasted his time, for he had worked assiduously consolidating his numerous estates and exploiting his position as guardian of the young Earl of Angus, his nephew. This gave him control of Tantallon and the many other surviving Red Douglas castles. He developed a lust for property and money for which he was later to become notorious. Some additional wealth began to accrue from the development of coal mines round his estates at Dalkeith (by a strange coincidence coal was to be a factor also in the wealth of the Douglases at Douglas itself and at Hamilton, though in both cases it led to the physical downfall of their great houses). Morton had also declared himself a Protestant by being among the first to sign the Covenant in 1557, not so much perhaps because he despised the corruption and wealth of the Catholic Church but because he saw an opportunity to snatch it for himself.

Morton's political career began to take off around 1560, by which time he was in his mid-forties, married with several daughters but no legitimate sons. After the death of Mary of Guise the Protestant lords could at last assert themselves. Morton took part in the illegal parliament of 1560, the Lords of Congregation, which banned the Catholic mass and the authority of the Pope in Scotland. Soon afterwards the now widowed Mary Queen of Scots, returned from France and caused a riot by celebrating mass in private at Holyrood just after landing. So the stage was set for a relationship between the leading Douglas and the head of the Royal Stuarts which was to be as fraught as any in the long battle between the two dynasties.

Morton became one of twenty-four regents working for the newly arrived queen, who was still only eighteen. He served as an ambassador to England, where Elizabeth had been installed two years earlier as a new Protestant queen, with whose policies Morton could identify and who was keen to support the pro-English, pro-Protestant party in Scotland. Elizabeth did not want a renewal of the French–Scottish Auld Alliance, which was always perceived as a potential threat to English security. Morton continued as a special councillor to Mary and tried to calm the heated exchanges which she began to have with John Knox. Knox was a zealot towards the extreme end of the new sect, while Mary was a young but conscientious supporter of the old religion.

In 1562 Morton was promoted to Chancellor of Scotland and joined Mary in her progress round her new kingdom. He played a significant but not militarily very impressive part in the battle of Corrichie, where government forces defeated the Catholic lords under the Earl of Huntly. Morton, leading the cavalry, nearly lost his nerve early on, but his cousin Sir William Douglas of Glenbervie (1532–91), much later to become the Earl of Angus, rallied the foot soldiers with great bravery and turned the tide. Huntly was killed.

After this point Morton's career seems to have stagnated. There were plenty of other clever men around to help manage the Queen and she was enjoying a period of relative popularity. The problem was that she needed a new husband and since the man chosen would almost certainly become king, the choice was very difficult. French and Spanish princes were unacceptable, given the current strength of the Protestant party, and Elizabeth's suggestion of her cast-off, Leicester, was almost derisory. But any Scottish nobleman who aspired to the role would have to overcome the huge jealousy of his peers, who were all extremely sensitive to their status. Morton may have toyed even at this stage with the idea of marrying her himself, though she was more than twenty years his junior. He also still technically had a wife, though Countess Elizabeth had, in William Fraser's words, 'descended into idiocy', doubtless driven into a nervous breakdown by a callous, unfeeling husband who had married her title but then enjoyed himself frequently on the side – there were at least four bastard sons to prove it. Morton must have been conscious that any new royal consort would be a threat not only to his political career, but even worse to his habit of amassing vast wealth and estates, often at the expense of the disused monasteries. He was at this time restyling Dalkeith Castle as a Renaissance palace and rebuilding several of his other castles, including Dalmahoy and Drochil, as well as Torthorwald for one of his bastards. Perhaps, too, he realized he was simply not the type to become a royal favourite in the youthful atmosphere of the new court. In Antonia Fraser's words, 'The small greedy eyes in his florid face covered a cruel mind.' She also referred to him as 'The most profound and perfidious miscreant of a villainous age.'

So whoever Mary chose as a husband would be bad news for Morton, but the eventual choice of her cousin Henry Stuart, Lord Darnley (1547–66), was particularly irksome. The fact that Darnley had both Royal Stewart blood from his father and Tudor blood from his mother, but was also a grandson of the Red Douglas, was even younger than Mary, and was vain and arrogant, clearly got under Morton's skin. The fact that he had largely been brought up in England did not help. Yet within a year of the wedding there was an even more obnoxious person coming between Morton and the Queen. This was David Riccio (1533–66), born in Turin, who came to Scotland in 1561 as a minor attaché with an embassy from Savoy. With the elegant manners of an Italian courtier, a good singing voice and accomplished technique on the lute, he immediately proved useful to the Queen in her continental correspondence. Soon he was effectively the Queen's private secretary and closest adviser, organizing the Darnley marriage and other events. As Mary respected her feelings rather than the staid protocol of the Scottish barons, she was not perhaps wholly professional in her overt promotion of a minor foreign diplomat, and showed considerable disregard for the tender sensitivities of her husband. Such an abuse of the ranking system in court was intolerable to men like Morton, who were obsessed with precedence, and was upsetting to the vanity of Darnley, so they were briefly driven into the same camp.

Judging by the number of stabs he received – more than forty – the plot to murder Riccio involved several dozen people apart from Darnley and Morton, but the Douglases undoubtedly formed the largest single grouping. Two in particular are mentioned: George and Archibald Douglas. George Douglas, known as the Postulate, was the bastard son of the previous Earl of Angus, and had been nominated when very young as the next abbot of Arbroath in 1546, but the Pope had preferred a different, better qualified candidate, one of the Beaton family. Undeterred by this setback, George intimidated his opponent's family by shutting one of them up in Tantallon, and then with his father's help seized the abbey by force. He was referred to by Chambers as 'a man of utter profligacy'. But the murder of Cardinal Beaton that very year cannot be proven as anything other than coincidental, though George did have a motive (as did his half-uncle George Douglas of Pittendreich) and later showed he had the capacity. Twenty years later he was still trying to hold on to Arbroath and became a drinking partner of his distant cousin Darnley, who having been brought up in England had few friends in Scotland. George soon realized how much Darnley hated Riccio and also how much his other cousin, Morton, shared that hatred. He thus offered his services as a conspirator in murder. He inveigled Riccio to Douglas Castle along with Darnley, doubtless for some kind of binge, and then suggested tipping him overboard during a pike-fishing expedition on the lake nearby. This idea was rejected by Darnley, yet back in Edinburgh Darnley kept sending George to Ruthven, another potential conspirator (and George's brother-in-law), three times a day to urge some action. George, according to Ruthven, did not trust Darnley to keep any plot secret, so he wanted the bond (or contract) put in writing: 'The fault is in yourself that cannot keep your own counsel.'

Not long afterwards it was George Douglas who stabbed Riccio first in the Holyrood ante-room, and he made sure that he used Darnley's personal dagger to do it. He was doubtless also involved in the murder of Darnley and spent some time in exile before returning to seize Arbroath Abbey from yet another rival. Mary Queen of Scots was clearly aware of his part in the murder of Riccio, for she referred to him as 'a schameless boutchour'. There had even been a prophecy that Riccio would be killed by a bastard: Moray was seen as the man likely to fulfil it, but George also fitted the description and did indeed fulfil it. Despite an armed attack on Smeaton in 1570 and being arrested for piracy and murder on the River Earn in 1572, he was still promoted to Bishop of Moray by his grateful cousin Morton the following year. Despite also making an extremely poor job of the theology test required by the General Assembly – he was, as Calderwood tells us, 'a whole winter mummilling upon his papers' – and despite being accused of 'scandalous living' and 'fornication with Lady Ardrosse', he held on to the post until his death in 1590. He was clearly one of Morton's least scrupulous aides.

The Archibald Douglas who played a prominent part as Morton's assistant in the murder both of Riccio and of Darnley is harder to identify. He is referred to variously as a parson, first of Douglas then of Glasgow, though he had no Greek and admitted 'I am not used to pray'. He is also referred to as having a house at Whittinghame and being brother of William Douglas of Whittinghame, a member of the gang that killed Riccio and part of the East Lothian Protestant group, a regular and influential attender at the long General Assembly meetings which wrote the rules for the new Church of Scotland. Certainly this Archibald Douglas was the man who kept Morton informed of the Darnley plot and came eventually to trial in 1586, but there were several other Archibald Douglases among Morton's entourage, including Douglas of Kilspindie (1513–85), son of Greysteel, who had just been sacked by Mary as provost of Edinburgh, probably for being an ardent Knox supporter, and survived an attempt to murder him in his home.

Then there was Archibald Douglas of Glenbervie (father of the man who had saved Morton from disaster at Corrichie), who at this time was in charge of Bothwell Castle. And there was Archibald Douglas of Pittendreich, one of Morton's own bastard sons. The Archibald Douglas referred to by Andrew Lang as 'a jackal', the probable murderer of Darnley, was later found to be a forger, for he turned out to be responsible for some fake letters written to Lennox, apparently by Bishop Leslie of Ross, which implicated Lennox in a Catholic plot. He did this to try to protect Morton from Lennox in 1580, but he may well also have been the forger of the so-called casket letters which implicated Mary in the plot against Darnley. Such a hypothesis is suggested by the fact that it was he who 'found' the casket letters when sent by Morton to arrest one of Bothwell's servants after Carberry.

Returning to the night of the Riccio murder, it was Morton himself who organized the capture of Holyrood Palace from its guards with a troop of 150 of his men. Then he was among those who burst into the Queen's apartment shouting the traditional war cry 'A Douglas, a Douglas', and he too stabbed Riccio. Both Lords Ruthven and Lindsay, who were prominent in the murder, had Douglas wives, and Kerr of Fawdonside, who had threatened Mary herself with his pistol, was a Douglas adherent, so it very much had the air of a Douglas enterprise. Another Douglas who took part was Sir James of Drumlanrig (1498–1578), who had acted as a spy for Henry VIII and later fought against Mary at Carberry. His bastard son John was another of the murderers, as was Sir William Douglas of Lochleven, later to be the Queen's chief gaoler. The pious church member William Douglas of Whittinghame was also certainly a member of the team for he was exiled for it in 1566, yet he was a most frequent commissioner at the General Assembly of the Church – in 1561, 1567, 1582 and 1588, often involved in long and tedious debates about sin and procedure. With Riccio's murder the Douglases seemed to justify it to themselves on the grounds of removing a foreign enemy from Scottish soil or a Catholic from Protestant soil. Yet, given Mary's advanced state of pregnancy at the time, it was a particularly unpleasant crime to commit in her presence, and it has to be assumed that the murderers would not have been surprised (or displeased) if the shock had killed the Queen or her baby, or both of them.

Whether it was funk or conscience that led Darnley soon afterwards to disown his co-conspirators is hard to be certain, but it was probably the former. This meant the exposure of Morton, who fled south for safety, and several of the others, but in due course it also meant the exposure of Darnley himself. Naturally the other murderers of Riccio resented one of their number who had signed the bond reneging on his oath, so the second conspiracy sprang from the first. But this time Morton played a slightly less prominent part. The Earl of Bothwell, a friend of the Queen's who was supposed to have been got rid of in the Riccio plot, was the main instigator of the new one. Archibald Douglas was the go-between and organizer, hosting a meeting by the famous yew tree at his brother's house at Whittinghame between Bothwell, Morton and Lethington. Morton later claimed that he had been told by Bothwell that it was what Mary wanted and had been promised this in writing. Certainly he signed the bond and the murder took place at Kirk o' Field, not far from where Archibald Douglas had his lodgings by the Edinburgh city walls. It was Archibald, according to later evidence, who left his mule slippers by the body, though according to Morton he was at this time in the pay of Bothwell, not himself. The gunpowder which blew up the house probably came from a Hepburn or a Douglas arsenal. Darnley and a number of his supporters seem to have escaped the blast and run into the garden, where they were overtaken by Archibald Douglas and his men. As recorded in Labanoff's collection of the Queen's letters, a witness from nearby later stated that she had overheard Darnley's last words, pleading to the Douglases, who were relations on his mother's side: 'Pity me kinsmen for the sake of Jesus Christ who pitied all the world.' He was still only twenty when he died. James Balfour of Pittendreich (1525–83) was also a key player, acting it was said later as agent for Bothwell, but how did he acquire Pittendreich unless as a supporter of Morton's? He had also been part of the team which murdered Archbishop Beaton in 1546 and had been captured by the French from St Andrews the following year along with John Knox. So, when Morton's father, George Douglas of Pittendreich, died in 1554, Morton perhaps rewarded Balfour with this small part of his heritage.

If Morton's real ambition at this time was to be Mary's chief councillor or consort he had now helped to get rid of two men in his way, but he was no closer to his goal, for a third man stepped in to fill their place. This was the dashing Bothwell, now firmly the Queen's favourite, created

Duke of Orkney over Morton's head, who married the new royal widow and threatened to become the new king. So this time it was Morton who reneged on the bond, turned against his co-conspirator and became leader of the faction which rebelled against the Queen. He was leader of the improvised army which faced up to her at Carberry Hill. Bothwell offered single combat with any one of the rebel lords who accused him of the murder but rejected three who offered, the last of whom was Morton himself, supposedly about to don the substantial sword of his ancestor Bell-the-Cat. In the end Bothwell fled without a fight and it was the Douglas underlings, including young William Douglas of Drumlanrig, who arrested the Queen and escorted her back to Holyrood. He had been knighted by Darnley in 1565 and got away with the murder of his neighbour Hugh Douglas of Dalveen until he himself met a violent end in 1572. Mary later referred to him as 'a cowart traitour'. His father, Sir James Douglas of Drumlanrig, who was a close associate of Morton and of John Knox in his final years, and William's bastard brother John were also arrested for complicity in the Riccio murder.

It was to a Douglas prison that Mary was sent soon afterwards, once Morton and his friends had found the casket with the incriminating letters (or forged them) and forced her to abdicate in favour of her baby son James VI (1566–1625). Lochleven Castle on its island (smaller then than now) in the lake had been a Red Douglas stronghold for some years. James Douglas, the laird's uncle, had recently married into the earldom of Buchan and was another strong Morton supporter. The current laird, Sir William Douglas of Lochleven, had taken part in the Riccio murder and was also half brother to the new Regent Moray, since their mother had been a mistress of James V, perhaps welcome respite for a woman living in such a remote, watery castle, particularly for one who was apparently the model for the role of Sensuality in *Ane Satyre of the Thrie Estaitis*. She also produced seven beautiful daughters known as the Seven Fair Porches of Lochleven.

William Douglas had already shown his loyalty to Morton and Moray by taking part in the murder of Riccio. Now he was a conscientious gaoler, and took Mary rowing on the loch or hawking on the other island of St Serf. The same could not be said for his brother George, known as Pretty Geordie, nor for an orphan lad in the castle known as Willy or Little Douglas. Both of these young men seem to have become rapidly infatuated by the Queen's charms. George was shortly suspected of plotting her escape and dismissed from the island. She continued writing to him at the inn in nearby Kinross, using soot and water for ink, with handkerchiefs as paper. She made one nearly successful attempt at escape dressed as a laundress. Willy, still in communication with George and other supporters, exploited the excitement of a May Day pageant to pinch the castle keys, bring Mary out of the gate, relock the castle behind them and drop the keys in the lake. Once across on the other side they were joined by their other supporters and headed for Niddrie.

The showdown between supporters of the Regent Moray, Queen Mary's older half-brother, aided by Morton with his allies on the one hand, and the Queen's party on the other, took place south of Glasgow at Langside. Moray and Morton led the government army; Campbell of Argyll the Queen's men. Mainly because of Argyll's incompetence, it was an unnecessarily bad defeat for Mary, who was watching helplessly from nearby Crookston Castle. She fled south to England, still accompanied by Geordie and Willy Douglas, who remained faithful to her throughout her long imprisonment. Geordie was said by Cecil to have been 'in a fantasy of love with the queen', and according to the biased Burnett had an illicit affair and a bastard child with her at Lochleven, but that is very unlikely. Some said Robert Douglas, the pastor of the Scots troops fighting for Gustavus Adolphus, was her grandson. Willy Douglas was certainly her usher right to the very end in the grim confines of Fotheringay Castle.

During the next five years Morton doggedly pursued his relentless climb towards supreme power in Scotland. But there were four other candidates for the regency whose demise he had to wait for before he achieved his end. First he needed English help to keep out Arran and preserve his own joint rule with Regent Moray. Then Moray was murdered. Lennox (Darnley's father) took over next, and he was murdered within a year. He had helped Morton's climb to even greater wealth by hanging John Hamilton, the Archbishop of St Andrews, ostensibly for aiding the murder of Darnley, but he had stood in the way of Morton's desire to take over church property. The elderly Mar became the next regent with Morton as the real power behind him, and it was at this point, in 1572, that Morton engineered the appointment of John Douglas (1494–1576) as the Protestant Archbishop of St Andrews. He at least up to this point was a Douglas of untarnished reputation, a priest and scholar. Perhaps a bastard son of one of the Douglases of Pinkie or of Pittendreich (i.e. a close relative of Morton), he studied in Paris, was ordained as a Carmelite Friar, and became first Provost of St Mary's College, then Rector of St Andrews University in 1550. He meekly handed over the tithes of the archbishopric to Morton, but he was by this time in his late seventies, unworldly if not senescent, and had worked assiduously to build the foundations of the new Church of Scotland until he perhaps succumbed to vanity in his old age. He dropped dead in his own pulpit three years later. In *The Legend of Patrick Adamson*:

As maister John Douglas weill can tell
How slealie he deceavit himsell
Borrowing ane coffer to keep his claiths
But with his baggage hame he gaes.

Mar died after less than a year as regent and Morton at long last officially took over in 1572, again with English support, mainly artillery. He had already been involved with Lennox in a prolonged siege of Edinburgh and its castle commanded by his old adversary Sir William Kirkcaldy. While Morton and Lennox had been fortifying Leith, Kirkcaldy purloined a wagon train of Morton's best plate, wines and food delicacies *en route* from Leith to Dalkeith for his niece's wedding. Morton retaliated by burning part of Kirkcaldy, then Kirkcaldy retaliated by burning parts of Dalkeith. Morton attacked a Marian squad under cover of truce negotiations, killing fifty for the loss of two.

In this desperate civil war prisoners were tortured and executed out of hand. Gibbets lined the roads. Tradesmen found taking food in to the starving people of Edinburgh were branded with red-hot irons. Kirkcaldy in his final efforts to hold on to the city had cannons lifted to the top of St Giles's steeple and destroyed many buildings. He blew up a new fishmarket, so that bits of fish were scattered over the Edinburgh rooftops. Archibald Douglas, the perpetual double agent, spied on Morton for Kirkcaldy, and when he was rejected as a candidate for the archbishopric of St Andrews he even suggested a plot to murder Morton, to be paid for by Drury, the English governor of Berwick, and carried out by his own murderous servant, Binning. It was about this time that he seems to have smuggled in 5,000 gold crowns from the Spanish Duke of Alva to help Kirkcaldy, but he naturally kept 20 per cent for himself. Morton put up bulwarks on the High Street by the Tolbooth and brought up his English guns. As Governor of Edinburgh Castle, Kirkcaldy continued to hold out against him even after the wells had been poisoned, but his men mutinied and he was forced to surrender. Morton showed no mercy, ordering a public execution. Maitland seems only to have escaped the same fate by dying or committing suicide before they could get to him.

Morton also rather ungallantly allowed the betrayal for £2,000 of the fugitive Earl of Northumberland, who had given him hospitality when he was a refugee in England. Captured in 1569, he had been kept in the cells at Lochleven Castle while the wily Sir William negotiated his ransom money upwards with his wife (who was already paying for his upkeep), only then to offer him to Queen Elizabeth for the same amount. So he was handed back to be hanged by the English, an event portrayed in the

ballad 'Northumberland Betrayed by Douglas'. Nothing stood in the way
of Morton, who was, in William Fraser's words, 'licentious, stern even to
cruelty and avaricious', or, in Walter Scott's, 'of a fierce, treacherous and
cruel disposition'. He did not hesitate to massacre men, women and
children. He burnt down Hamilton Castle, the home of his rivals. The
one man for whom perhaps he had a grudging respect was John Knox,
who died the same week that Morton assumed power. At his graveside
Morton said, 'Here lies one who never feared the face of man.' At least
this meant that Morton did not have to abolish bishops who were helping
him to syphon off the riches of the old Catholic Church.

Morton had a motley band of close assistants, including the two
murderers George and Archibald Douglas, the other Archibald Douglas
of Kilspindie, who was a useful negotiator and who retrieved the artillery
from Berwick, the violent James Douglas of Drumlanrig, and his own four
bastard sons: James Douglas of Spott, Archibald Douglas, of Pittendreich,
George Douglas, who was lame, and William Douglas, about whom
nothing seems to be known. There was also now importantly Morton's
nephew and ward Archibald, 8th Earl of Angus (1555–88), who as a
teenager was now made Lieutenant-General of the South, though he was
not always in total harmony with his uncle. With John Douglas as
Archbishop of St Andrews, George Douglas, Bishop of Moray, and
William Douglas of Whittinghame(whose other brother Robert died
mysteriously at this time) as his regular representative at the General
Assembly, Morton had reasonable control over the Church, particularly
with Knox out of the way.

Morton's rule was naturally not very popular except among his close
adherents, and his key strategy, apart from keeping in with Elizabeth of
England, was to purloin the wealth of the monasteries as her father had
done. His regime was corrupt and inefficient. He retired briefly in 1578 to
potter about the gardens of Lochleven and Dalkeith, his Lion's Den, but
thought it safer to resume power as he saw that the young King James VI
was beginning at fourteen to flex his muscles.

This was not enough to save Morton. James already had two young
favourites: Esme Stuart of Aubigny, now Duke of Lennox, and Captain
James Stewart, who disliked Morton intensely. It was he who started to
poison the boy-king's mind, reminding him that Morton was one of the
men who had murdered his father, Darnley. James was easily led. As
Walter Scott put it, he was bright but 'his childishness and meanness
rendered his good sense useless'. Morton was arrested and taken to
Dumbarton Castle, of which Stewart was the commander, and he refused
the offer of his nephew the Red Douglas Earl of Angus to come to his

rescue. Elizabeth of England demanded his release but James reacted petulantly. The letters supplied by the old spy Archibald Douglas to incriminate Lennox, the King's favourite, were discovered to be his own forgeries when his brother William was threatened with the thumbscrews, so that scheme backfired. Captain Stewart had just been promoted Earl of Arran and there was a prophesy that 'The Bloody Heart would fall by the mouth of Arran.' Morton, current leader of the Bloody Heart dynasty, was condemned to death and executed by the Maiden, a kind of early guillotine which with a sad irony he had himself procured from Halifax to deal with his own enemies. He was sixty-five, older than most contemporaries who had died in their beds. He reputedly left a huge treasure, some according to legend buried at Dalkeith, some, according to Godscroft, transferred to Paris, where it was used up by the many Douglas exiles of the next few generations.

Archibald Douglas, the spy and forger, was also charged with 'The cruell horibl abhominabill and tresonabill murthour of umqhile Henrie King of Scottis'. But his brother William was one of the judges and Archibald was too useful to the King to be allowed to go to prison. He was helpful in the exchanges between James VI and Queen Elizabeth as they prepared the ground for Mary's execution and also in buying stallions for James in England, but then he was dispensed with and spent some time in prison, dying in extreme poverty round about 1600.

Morton's nephew the luckless Archibald, 8th Earl of Angus, did not survive him for long. After the Regent's fall, James VI had a fixation that Angus was plotting his death, perhaps rightly, and drove him into exile. Angus's wife had an affair with the Earl of Montrose and betrayed his secrets, as did Douglas of Whittinghame, who as usual revealed all after a very short spell in the torture chamber. Angus had his way to London prepared by the retired spy Archibald Douglas, Whittinghame's brother, and made friends with the poet–knight Sir Philip Sidney, who read his *Arcadia* to the young Scot. A year later Angus was allowed to return to Scotland and at least had Morton's head taken down from the Tolbooth spike, but King James still did not trust him. Neither did Mary in Fotheringay, who wrote 'his line never have been friends to the Stuarts'. In 1585 the Earl had a brief taste of power after the fall of Arran, but the King was now an adult and Angus's policy against bishops did not please him. He was fobbed off with the earldom of Morton, joined now to that of Angus, and died childless in 1588 at Smeaton, near Dalkeith, aged only thirty-five. The death seemed mysterious, referred to initially as 'an infinite flux', and was in fact probably caused by consumption, but there was a fashion at this time, much encouraged by James VI, to suspect witches. As Maxwell tells us: 'His bodie pynned and melted down with sweats', and in the meantime the witches were 'trying his picture in waxe before a fire'. So one of the North Berwick coven, Barbara Napier, was accused of the murder by his nurse, Agnes Simpson; Barbara escaped burning only by 'pleading her belly' – she was pregnant – so the court picked on Agnes Simpson, the accuser, and executed her instead. She was sent to Edinburgh Castle 'and thair bund to ane staik and wirreit [garotted] till she was deid and thairafter her body to be brunt in assis'.

Meanwhile, the old scoundrel James Douglas of Drumlanrig had also died in 1578, but not before rebuilding Drumlanrig Castle and his Drumlanrig Tower in Hawick, as well as his other tower houses at Ross, Mouswald, Kirkhope and Locharben, thus paving the way for the Queensberry empire of the next century. He had acquired Mouswald by intimidating its two heiresses into marrying his nephews and handing the property over to him, but one of the heiresses, Marion Carruthers, was so distraught that in 1564 she jumped off the ramparts of Comlongon, 'wifullie breking of her awin creg [neck] and banis quhairof sche diet' – hence the ghost at Comlongon. James's brother Robert Douglas, the Provost of Lincluden, was not much better, carefully transferring all the valuable estates of the Church to his own name.

Queen Mary did not outlive her old adversary Morton by long either. Archibald Douglas, the double agent, had recommended to Elizabeth that she be murdered by smothering. Elizabeth was more scrupulous but recognized that Mary was a permanent danger to her throne until she was taken out of circulation once and for all. She was executed, aged forty-five, at Fotheringay in 1587, with Willy Douglas still at her side. The spy Archibald Douglas was present when James heard the news of his mother's death and noted that he showed not the faintest sign of grief, though for dynastic propaganda purposes he did later build her a fine tomb in Westminster Abbey.

Morton at least was posthumously avenged, for in 1588 James Douglas of Parkhead murdered Arran, the instigator of Morton's fall, as Calderwood put it 'for mocking God and his carcase was left in the open kirk'.

One man from that generation outlasted them all – William Douglas, the gaoler of Lochleven and betrayer of Percy, who survived the two earls Morton and Angus and thus, since they had no sons, became Earl of Morton himself. One of his sons disappeared in the Mediterranean and was never seen again, apparently having been captured and enslaved by some Algerian pirates.

CHAPTER SEVENTEEN

The Wisest Fool and the Fanatic

The specimens, the lilies of ambition
Still spring in their climate, still unpicked.
Keith Douglas, 'On a Return from Egypt'

It is ironic that the disagreements between our two families in this and the previous chapter sprang from the same source, religion, yet were totally different. Mary and Morton had fallen out mainly because, for doubtless quite cynical reasons, he supported the Reformation, while she had been brought up a devout Catholic in France. In the next generation it was the Douglas who was by a strange chance a fanatical Catholic, and King James VI a convinced, almost obsessive Protestant, referred to as 'the wisest fool in Christendom'. After the early and childless death of the 8th Earl of Angus the main line of the Red Douglases had become extinct, so the title went to the Douglases of Glenbervie, who had acquired this Aberdeenshire castle about fifty years earlier. The first of the Glenbervie Douglases to be Earl of Angus was William (1532–91), the hero of Corrichie, but his succession was strenuously resisted by James VI, who perhaps saw this as an opportunity to snatch a few extra estates for himself, especially as his own great-grandfather had been a Red Douglas earl. William won his case eventually but he survived for only three years and was in deep financial straits because of the huge legal expenses of fighting the King. The two men seem to have made it up – Angus carried the sword of state at the royal wedding of King James to Anne of Denmark – though not entirely, for William was imprisoned later for a fortnight for not allowing one of the King's favourites to arrest one of the Douglas retainers.

William's son, the prospective 10th Earl, was William Douglas of Kemnay and Glenbervie (1554–1611), who had studied at St Andrews and assisted his cousin the Regent Morton for two years. Then he was sent to France, perhaps to take some of Morton's fabled treasure to a foreign bank in case of emergencies – officially it was to learn aristocratic manners at the ostentatious court of Henry III. This turned out to be a disaster for the family: instead of concentrating on swordsmanship and tilting, as Douglases were expected to do, William attended lectures on

113

theology at the Sorbonne round about 1579, and he was dramatically converted to Catholicism by his teachers there. When he came back to Scotland his father was horrified by this dangerous act of subversion, as was the dying 8th Earl of Angus: both then wanted to disinherit him. They even married the young man to a staunchly Protestant wife in the hope that she would reconvert him, but he seems to have turned the tables on them and converted her instead. The newly-weds were pelted with stones by the fanatical students of Aberdeen and were hunted round the country as fugitives. However, the 8th Earl and his successor, William's father, died in fairly quick succession before anything could be done about it, so, despite being excommunicated and under arrest in Stirling Castle, and despite further opposition from King James, William succeeded as the 10th Earl in 1591. Like his father he was heavily mortaged and he had to sell Glenbervie itself to his brother. His career as earl was to be as extraordinary as any of his predecessors.

As with Catholic members of the English aristocracy at this time, William's position in adhering to an illegal religion was both dangerous and delicate. Even in Scotland the threat of a Spanish invasion was not taken lightly, and the Armada episode had occurred only three years earlier. A distant cousin, William Douglas of Mains (Milngavie), was executed in 1585 for an alleged plot to murder the King. James VI suspected William of plotting against him and put him under house arrest at Drumlanrig. Then he seems to have relented and decided to give William a chance to prove himself, or perhaps enough rope to hang himself. William was appointed a justice and lieutenant for all Scotland north of the Tay to quash the feuding which had followed the murder of the Bonnie Earl of Moray by Huntly. William did the job well enough, but the effect was ruined by the discovery of one of those 'popish plots' which were to make James VI paranoid. This one was known as the 'Spanish Blanks' because it emerged from the discovery of eight blank sheets of paper signed by three Catholic earls: William of Angus himself, Huntly and Errol. An agent was caught embarking on a Spanish ship off Cumbrae in the Clyde and confessed under torture, whether it was the truth or not, to a plot to bring a large Spanish army to destroy Protestantism in Scotland. William was immediately put back under house arrest, then seized by a crowd and frogmarched to Edinburgh Castle.

William, who was by this time nearly forty, must have been physically agile, for he managed to escape from the castle, abseiling down a rope which his long-suffering wife contrived to smuggle in to him, hidden in 'a large stoup'. The unfortunate keeper of the castle was later hanged for allowing this escape to happen. But William's problems were not over either. He was formally excommunicated by the Synod of St Andrews and forfeited all his estates in 1594. Ostentatiously waylaying James VI by the road at Fala Muir and bending his knee to the impressionable King had some effect, but not enough. William went into hiding in Aberdeenshire but does not seem to have been at the battle of Glenlivet when Huntly beat off a government attack led by the Campbells. He also tried a lightning attack on Edinburgh but it did not come off. What proved more effective was a showy and barely convincing conversion back to Protestantism in 1598. This won him back all his estates and appointment as Lieutenant of the Borders, a post which he held with some distinction, suppressing the robber barons of the area such as the Johnstones and his own cousins the Douglases of Drumlanrig. It is perhaps surprising that a king as understandably paranoid about 'popish plots' as James VI should be so apparently gullible with a man like William Douglas, but then perhaps William was potentially an effective and reliable officer with just the one fault in James's eyes, his religion. James VI was after all a man of pretty sound judgement, though he did succumb occasionally to a pretty male face. He was in many respects the most effective King of Scotland produced by the Stewart dynasty and managed to avoid war in the Borders throughout his adult career, far longer than any predecessor. Also, despite his often overt bisexuality, he managed to sustain a happy marriage which produced seven children. His reputation may be more that of a rather effete and bumbling scholar, yet his main passions were hunting and horse breeding.

Inevitably William, Earl of Angus, was soon caught attending mass again, so all his successes in the Borders were of no avail; Catholicism was equated at that time with treachery. He was excommunicated for about the fifth time and sent into exile, this time for good. The last two years of his life he spent on the outskirts of Paris, attending the Abbey of Saint-Germain-des-Prés every day. That is where he was buried and a black marble monument marks the spot. James VI had by that time long transferred his residence to London, where he had inaugurated a new era in the history of the Stewarts, adding the throne of England to the one of Scotland which they had already occupied for more than 230 years. For the Douglases too this would present new challenges.

CHAPTER EIGHTEEN

Wars Civil and Otherwise

To find a friend one must close one eye. To keep him – two.
Norman Douglas, *An Almanac*

Ironically the Douglases were more supportive to the Stewart/Stuart dynasty when it was in dire trouble in England than they had ever been during its ups and downs in Scotland. Charles I (1600–49) was the last British king to be born in Scotland, at Dunfermline, when his father was still the King of Scotland only, not also of England and Ireland. It was his fate to adhere to the kind of obsession with authority and precedence which was so characteristic of the Scottish baronial class throughout the two previous centuries. James VI, despite his hatred and fear of Catholicism, had withstood all opposition in his enthusiasm for keeping bishops in a Scottish Church that did not want them. His son went even further, adhering fanatically to a kind of deromanized Catholicism which was even less acceptable to the country of his birth than in the newer Stuart kingdom of England. Ironically, if it had not been for Scotland, Charles I might never have had to fight a civil war and might never have lost his throne.

So far as the role of the Douglases during the reign of Charles I is concerned, it was much less dramatic than in previous generations, but does help to illustrate the changes which were occurring in Scotland at this time. There are several reasons why the Douglas–Stuart relationship was less fraught at this time. For a start, Charles I was based in London and none of the senior Douglases had moved south in 1603, as some other Scottish courtiers had done, so there was more distance between them than before. Secondly, the three main branches of the Douglas family had all rather petered out; the Black Douglases were extinct, as was the original line of the Red Douglases, and the brief supremacy of the Morton branch was over. So there was now a period of regrouping which in the end was to bring forward two different lines, the Douglases of Drumlanrig, who had been around for a long time but in a minor role, and a branch of the Red Douglases, which married its way into the dukedom of Hamilton. The third reason was that in this particular generation none of the family heads was a man of very exciting character,

The ruins of Lesmahagow Priory, with the more modern church behind. Its need for protection led to the founding of the Douglas family. (Author)

All that remains of Douglas Castle, a single tower. (Author)

" Now praised be God, the day is won !
They fly o'er flood and fell—

A nineteenth-century engraving of Sir James Douglas's last battle at Teba in Andalucia. (Mary Evans Picture Library)

St Bride's, Douglas, burial place of the
Black Douglases. (Author)

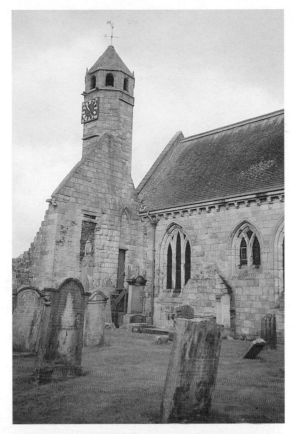

Two of the embalmed hearts at
St Bride's Church, Douglas. (Author)

Bothwell Collegiate Church, founded by Archibald the Grim. (Author)

Lincluden Collegiate Church, near Dumfries. (Author)

The heart and crown carved together on the tomb of the royal princess Margaret Douglas at Lincluden, symbolizing the ambitions of the family. (Author)

Dalkeith, St Nicholas Collegiate Church, founded by the Douglases of Morton. (Author)

Bothwell Castle by the Clyde. (Author)

Strathaven Castle, Lanarkshire. (Author)

The grassy mound where Abercorn Castle stood by the Firth of Forth. (Author)

Threave Castle on its island in the River Dee. (Author)

Tantallon Castle, looking towards the Bass Rock. (Author)

Morton Castle in Dumfriesshire, with its lake below. (Author)

Lochleven Castle on its island, looking towards Kinross. (Author)

Aberdour Castle on the north shore of the Forth. (Author)

Dalkeith Palace, original family seat of the Morton Douglases, restyled for its later owners. (Author)

Chatelherault hunting lodge, all that remains of Hamilton Palace built for the Douglas dukes of Hamilton. (Author)

Drumlanrig Castle, built by Douglas, 1st Duke of Queensberry. (Author)

James Douglas, the Regent Morton.
(Scottish National Portrait Gallery)

Statue at Douglas of the Earl of Angus
who founded the Cameronians.
(Author)

James Douglas, 2nd Duke of Queensberry. (Scottish National Portrait Gallery)

William Douglas, 3rd Duke of Hamilton. (Scottish National Portrait Gallery)

Top left: David Douglas the plant collector. (Author's collection)

Top right: Lord Alfred Douglas with Oscar Wilde. (Mary Evans Picture Library)

Sir Alec Douglas-Home. (Mary Evans Picture Library)

while the more exciting lesser Douglases mostly had their adventures outside Scotland.

William Douglas, 11th Earl of Angus (1589–1660), was the third of the Glenbervie family to lead what was left of the Red Douglas empire, and in many respects his career marked a watershed. He was not a Catholic like his father, but pretty close to it, for he studied at both Paris and Rome, where he ran into the future Marquess of Montrose. He came back obsessed with the usual notions of precedence, concerned only that the Earl of Angus should have his rights as crown bearer at the coronation, to be the first earl to vote in the Scottish parliament and theoretically at least to lead the van in battle. Doubtless it was partly his staunch Episcopalianism which led to his being made Marquess of Douglas by Charles I in 1633, the same year that Robert Douglas (1574–1639) of Mains was made Viscount Belhaven. It was the new Marquess's misfortune that, when religious dissatisfaction boiled over in Scotland in 1638 and the Covenanters demanded the end of bishops, the village of Douglas just happened to be one of the hotbeds of Covenanting fervour. Douglas Castle was taken over by the Covenanters while the Marquess was away in England, and when he returned he had the indignity of being reprimanded for poor attendance at the now strictly Presbyterian kirk.

It is not perhaps surprising, therefore, that William was almost the first Douglas to risk his life to help save the Royal Stuarts. As John Buchan put it in *Montrose*: 'the prestige of the bloody heart had not wholly died.' It was William who commissioned Hume of Godscroft to write his remarkable portrait of the family and he who went specially to Orleans in 1622 to meet up with Antonio Scoto, Count of Agazano, who claimed with some credibility to be a descendant of the Good Lord James. This Italian branch of the Douglas family had silver stars on its coat of arms and a bloody heart, and had settled as supporters of the Emperor Henry IV at Agazano, near Piacenza, where the church contained some of their tombs. A William Douglas on his way back to France from Rome had fallen ill at Piacenza, fallen in love with the daughter of Antonio Spettino: they 'begett manie children', so he settled there and made himself useful to the Duke of Milan, so starting a dynasty of Italian Douglases.

When the English Civil War began in earnest the Marquess became Montrose's main recruiting officer for the south of Scotland. Though he does not seem to have taken part in any of the battles which Montrose won so spectacularly, he was there at the final disaster of Philiphaugh. Reputedly after a brief display of gallantry which was not emulated by his bonnet lairds, he and the Douglas cavalry left Montrose's Irish mercenaries to their fate once they saw that defeat was inevitable.

Many of the Irish and Scottish McDonalds, men, women and children, were massacred by the Parliamentarians in the nearby Douglas castle of Newark. In Sir Walter Scott's time skulls were still being found in a field nearby known as the Slain Men's Lea. Most of the Douglas contingent got away but many were captured later, including the Marquess himself. He spent a year or so in Edinburgh Castle before he was released.

The Marquess's cousin William Douglas, 6th Earl of Morton (1582–1648), was one of the ablest Douglases of his time. He had commanded a Scottish regiment of 2,000 men which went to the relief of La Rochelle in 1627, and was made Lord Treasurer of Scotland by Charles I on his return. Later in 1641 he was also given Orkney and Shetland by the King. He was supposedly favourable to the Royalist cause but was too old to join Montrose, though his brother Sir James Douglas, later himself Earl of Morton, was a diehard Montrose supporter, as was another brother John who came to him in an Orkney sloop in 1649 and died in the last despairing battle at Carbisdale a year later.

Yet another cousin who joined Montrose was James Douglas of Drumlanrig, whose father had been made the 1st Earl of Queensberry by Charles, also in 1633. Unfortunately he was captured by the Covenanters before the battle of Kilsyth, and was later roughly treated by Cromwell.

As with so many civil wars, this one divided families. Archibald Douglas (1609–55), eldest son of the Marquess, opposed his own father and supported the Covenanting side as an elder in the General Assembly, though not on the battlefield. He chose to go abroad but came back to welcome Charles II for his coronation at Scone in 1651, and as usual bore the crown. For his pains he had his great castle at Tantallon pounded to destruction by Oliver Cromwell. He died before his father and so never inherited the title. Another very remote cousin who was a Covenanter rather than a Royalist was Sir James Douglas of Cavers, who had nine nephews killed fighting against Montrose at Auldearn.

The second youngest brother of Marquess William was James Douglas (1617–45), who took no part in the Civil War as he was a professional soldier serving in the French army. He had gone as a page-boy to the court of Louis XIII in 1630. Seven years later he took over as colonel of the Regiment of Scots from John Hepburn, who had fought with them under Gustavus Adophus at Saven. This regiment thus became Le Regiment de Douglas or Douglas Ecossais with 1,200 men, later increased to 2,000. They fought under Turenne for Louis XIV, who supposedly thought of giving James Douglas his field marshal's baton, but the Scot was killed still in his twenties while leading a flying column of troops near Arras. He was given a black marble monument beside other members of his family in the Abbey of Saint-Germain-des-Prés. Remarkably, his prestige was such that command of the regiment went to two of his brothers in turn. The first was his elder brother Archibald, who did not, it appears, actually fight with them, but brought over a significant group of troublesome Aberdeenshire men who had fought for Montrose and now had nowhere else to go.

The third brother to command the regiment was George Douglas (1636–92), later Earl of Dumbarton in 1675, so that it was then called the Dumbarton Regiment after him, and is still remembered in the popular piping tune 'Dumbarton's Drums':

> Dumbarton's drums they are so bonny,
> When they remind me of my Johnny.

In due course the regiment became known as the Royal Scots Guards, which still marched to the tune of 'Dumbarton's Drums' three centuries later. Meanwhile, as a Catholic, George Douglas found it more acceptable than many of his relations to remain in the service of James II. He led the forces which suppressed the Earl of Argyll's rebellion in 1685, organizing his arrest at Renfrew, albeit with the offer of a drink and a few pleasantries to which Argyll responded with stoic good humour.

A fourth brother, William (1634–94), was made Earl of Selkirk as a twelve-year-old by Charles I in 1646 and later married the Duchess of Hamilton, thus acquiring for the family its first British dukedom. Despite his early promotion, his relationship with the Royal Stuarts was to prove far from totally loyal.

Meanwhile, in 1649, three years after the remarkable campaign by Montrose in which the Douglases had played by their standards a fairly inglorious part, the King whom they had half-heartedly supported was executed at Whitehall. Given the similar fate of his grandmother, the record of Stuart sovereigns in England was not looking particularly healthy.

This perhaps partially accounts for the renewed exodus of Douglases at this time to the continent, where they could once more find profitable employ as mercenaries. Robert Douglas (1611–62) came from the ill-famed Whittinghame branch of the family, his father being Patrick Douglas, son of one of the henchmen of Morton. Robert served his military apprenticeship with the charismatic King Gustavus Adolphus of Sweden and developed into one of the dashing cavalry leaders of the Thirty Years War. He won his field marshal's baton after a brilliant attack during the battle of Jankau or Jankowitz near Prague in 1640, when he all but destroyed the Bavarian army of the Emperor. He captured the town of Wollmar in 1657 and defeated the Lithuanians in 1659. Constantly in debt and short of money, he regularly had to beg for advances on his salary, pleading on one occasion the fact that three of his brothers had died in the war. He was presented with a barony as Count of Skenning and Lord of Skalby together with the castle of Linköping, leaving a new line of Swedish Douglases who still live there. Another Douglas, Sir George, also served in the Swedish army and rose to be Governor of Kreuznack, though he was later sacked by Gustavus Adolphus for his oppressive treatment of the inhabitants.

More attractive was another Robert Douglas (1594–1674), who served as padre with the Scottish soldiers in the Swedish army and was much respected by Gustavus Adolphus. Referred to in a contemporary report as 'One of the noblest characters of the period', as minister in Edinburgh after his return to Scotland he preached at the coronation of Charles II in 1651. He was offered the archbishopric of St Andrews but turned it down on principle, as he thought bishops inappropriate. His refusal was also wise since James Sharp, the man who did take the job, was murdered, while Douglas ended his days quietly as the minister of Pencaitland.

Meanwhile the Douglas family had produced the first in a line of adventurous sea captains. The mysterious Archibald Douglas seems to have begun his career as a privateer and captured three Spanish ships in the English Channel in 1625, one of them holding six chests of gold coin. He was arrested briefly, but was released by Charles I to become Captain of the Scottish Royal Navy ship *Lyon*. James McHarg has identified a Bloody Heart emblem on the stern of a warship, probably the *Lyon*, depicted in a painting now in Aberdeen Maritime Museum.

PART III

The Queensberrys

That reptile wears a ducal crown.
> Robert Burns, 'On the Destruction of
> the Woods near Drumlanrig'

How shall I sing Drumlanrig's Grace
Discarded remnant of a race.
> Robert Burns, 'Stanzas on the
> Duke of Queensberry'

CHAPTER NINETEEN

Red, Black and Orange

Many a man who thinks to found a home discovers that he has
merely opened a tavern for his friends.
Norman Douglas, *The South Wind*

The late Stuart period saw a greater proliferation of high-sounding titles
among the Douglases than had been evident in all their amazing years of
valiant service and rebellion. Within a short space of time they acquired
three dukedoms. William Douglas, as we have already seen, was made an
earl by Charles I, married into the dukedom of Hamilton and took over
the title in 1660. William Douglas of Drumlanrig was made Duke of
Queensberry in 1683 by Charles II for services as High Treasurer of
Scotland, and Archibald Douglas of Douglas was made Duke of Douglas
in 1703 by Queen Anne. Yet despite all this aggrandizement there was
little sign of gratitude among the Douglases as their old rivals the Royal
Stuarts renewed their long process of self-destruction.

The main Douglas line at Douglas itself, still using the titles of Angus
and Douglas, was somewhat undistinguished at this time. James
Douglas (1646–1700), the 2nd Marquess of Douglas, has been
described as 'morose, peevish and incapable of managing his own
affairs'. He fell out with his wife, allowed his estates to be ruined by a
corrupt factor, was close to bankruptcy and was forced to sell the
ruinous family seat at Tantallon. The distress of his wife gave rise to the
popular ballad 'Lord Jamie Douglas', which struck a familiar chord as
she complained:

> Thou thocht that I was just like thyself
> And took everyone that I did see
> But I can swear by the heavens above
> That I never knew a man but thee.

But she was not without allies:

> O what need I care for Jamie Douglas
> More than he needs care for me

For the Lord of Murray's my father dear
And the Duke of York's daughter my mother be.

Like his ancestors, James Douglas, Marquess of Douglas, was obsessed with precedence, but he made no real effort to play any major role in politics, content to be rid of James II, last of the male Stuarts to reign, and welcome the arrival of William of Orange (though even he was a grandson of Charles I). As his reward he received some of the estates of Bonnie Dundee, who had just died in his last-ditch effort to help James II retain his throne. The Marquess's eldest son, James (1671–92), bore the title Earl of Angus and founded a local regiment, called after himself, which joined (without him) in the defence of Dunkeld against the remnants of Bonnie Dundee's army after Killiecrankie. He did, however, want to see action with his own regiment and, despite his father's pleading, he went to join it, fighting for William of Orange against the French in the Netherlands. He was killed two months later at Steinkirk, aged twenty-one. The regiment he founded later became famous as the Cameronians, and in recent years they still paraded in front of his statue at Douglas on the anniversary of the founding. In the same battle a distant cousin, Sir Robert Douglas, was also killed in the act of recapturing the colours of the old Douglas Ecossais (later Dumbarton) Regiment now renamed Douglas again. They had had a chequered history when sent back to England in 1665, as they had made a poor showing of defending the Thames against the Dutch fleet and even took to looting the nearby English. They had boasted of having been on duty in Jerusalem and acquired the nickname of Pontius Pilate's Bodyguards, but in due course redeemed themselves and ultimately became the Royal Scots Guards. Thus two famous Scottish regiments had Douglas origins.

It was James's younger brother Archibald Douglas (1694–1761) who inherited the title and was promoted to the dukedom at the age of seven. He also inherited considerable debts from his eccentric father and was to prove even more eccentric himself. At the age of nineteen he won some praise for raising 300 troops from his estate to fight for the Hanoverians against James Stuart, the Old Pretender. He himself made it to the battle of Sheriffmuir and, according to witnesses, 'behaved very well', but ten years later he killed a young friend, Captain Kerr, in a mysterious shooting episode. Either he lost his temper because of a rude remark about his sister, of whom he was exceptionally fond, or about his factor, to whom he was unnecessarily overloyal. Either way it was apparently murder rather than a duel. He went abroad for a while and only his ducal status saved him from public trial, but he never quite seemed to regain his youthful confidence. We shall return to the extraordinary events of his later life in the next two chapters.

Meanwhile, his uncle Archibald Douglas (1653–1712), younger brother of the morose 2nd Marquess, had been promoted to Earl of Forfar by the Stuart King Charles II in 1670, and was given Bothwell Castle. Despite this, in 1688 he was one of those who played a prominent part in welcoming William of Orange to the throne of Great Britain. He had a son, Archibald Douglas (1680–1715), who briefly became the 2nd Earl and was an envoy to Russia, but had his leg shot away as a brigadier fighting for the Hanoverian side at Sheriffmuir in 1715, so the title and family died out.

Archibald's own uncle William, as we have seen, married Anne, Duchess of Hamilton, in 1656, and inherited his father-in-law's dukedom four years later. He took a prominent part in Scottish politics during the Restoration years, though he fell out with Lauderdale, the Scottish Secretary of State. He was restored to the Privy Council by James II, but this did not deter him from deserting the Stuarts in 1688, and he was president of the Council of Scots nobles who welcomed William of Orange.

The Duke's brother the Catholic soldier Lord George Douglas, by this time made Earl of Dumbarton by Charles II, was one of the few Douglases to stay loyal to the Stuart cause. He was general in charge of putting down the Scottish end of the Argyll and Monmouth rebellion in 1685 and did not desert James II when he succumbed to the Orange party in 1688, instead following him into voluntary exile at Saint-Germain. When he died four years later he was buried in the family vault at Saint-Germain-des-Prés. George had a son who succeeded him, but then, as with the earldom of Forfar, the family and the title of Dumbarton also died out.

Now we turn to the third branch of the Douglases who made the most rapid advance at this time, the Douglases of Drumlanrig. They had been one of the junior branches founded by a bastard of the 2nd Earl back in 1388. They had built a small castle known as the House of Hassock at Drumlanrig and acted as little better than robber barons or hired henchmen for patrons such as Morton. Then they had become respectable, being made viscounts in 1628 and earls in 1633 by Charles I, then marquesses in 1681 and finally dukes in 1683 by Charles II. The 1st Duke, William Douglas (1637–1695), had been playing his cards right. Queensberry, the small mountain from which they took their title, stood to the east of Drumlanrig and Morton, to the south of Douglas. They became the dominant family in Scottish politics in the 1670s. The Duke's sons James Douglas, Earl of Drumlanrig (1662–1711), later known as the

Union Duke, and his brother Lord William, were both captains in the army of Jack Claverhouse, soon to be Viscount Dundee, as he attacked the Covenanters in 1685. Claverhouse had used his influence at court to help their father on his way to his dukedom, though he reckoned the favour was not properly returned, for the two young captains rapidly became colonels, while his own brother remained a cornet. As Lord Treasurer of Scotland, Queensberry was now – alongside his distant cousin the Duke of Hamilton – in a position of considerable power. He was turning the old castle at Drumlanrig into a much grander stately home, fit for a duke, but it cost a vast amount of money, and having spent one night there he disliked it so much he went back to his old castle at Sanquhar. When someone queried the cost, as Brown tells us, he replied, 'The deil pyke out his een that looks therein.' He also bought Queensberry House as his residence in Edinburgh.

Having thus lined their pockets serving Charles II and James II, the Queensberrys abandoned James II for the Orange cause in 1688. The 1st Duke was described as 'an atheist in religion, a villain in friendship, a knave in business and a traitor in his conduct to the king'. When he died, a Scottish sailor on shore at Palermo claimed to have seen a coach and four headed for Mount Etna and shouted 'Open to the Duke of Drumlanrig.' Yet to be fair, if that is necessary, Queensberry had made it clear to James II that he would not accept any move to Catholicize Scotland, and, unlike his son, he did not actually go over to William of Orange until James had abandoned the throne. Few of the Douglases felt able to support the cause of James II as he dug himself into an ever deeper hole, just like his father and his great-grandmother before him. Religious style rather than substance was at the base of the irreconcilable disagreement of the Royal Stuarts with the majority of their countrymen. Yet it was an issue that cost them their thrones and sometimes their lives.

James Douglas of Drumlanrig, the 1st Duke's brother, trained as a lawyer, served with Claverhouse at Bothwell Bridge and was made a brigadier for exterminating Covenanters. The name of Colonel Douglas is found on numerous martyrs' tombstones in south-west Scotland as the man who hanged them without trial. He also made himself generally unpopular as a compulsive martinet, going apoplectic if his men grew their beards too long or his officers drank too much, but in 1688 he changed sides, like so many others, and led two brigades for William of Orange at the battle of the Boyne. By 1689 he was a general in Schomberg's infantry which led the attack on Athlone. Schomberg said of him, 'Whatever he does he is never content and finds fault with everything.' He died of fever at the siege of Namur in 1691. His younger brother Robert had been killed at the siege of Maastricht in 1676.

One of many Douglas soldiers who returned home at this time was William Douglas of Fingland, one of the Morton side of the family, who gave up soldiering in 1694. He fell in love with a girl called Annie Laurie, who was locked up by her father until she came to her senses. In the song which William wrote he said he would 'lay me doon and die', but in the event he found another girl to marry and like so many of this generation was not quite as good as his word. At least, however, he did leave a set of immortal lyrics. Yet another Douglas soldier was Sir William Douglas, who was commanding the Scots Dragoons or Greys in 1689.

One Douglas who did undoubtedly stick to his principles at this time was Captain Archibald Douglas (d. 1667), serving on the *Royal Oak* when the Dutch fleet came up the Thames. Refusing advice to retreat he said, 'It shall never be told that a Douglas quitted his part without orders', and he remained on board as his ship sank in flames. Equally gallant was Captain Andrew Douglas, who began his career as a privateer, captaining the *Phoenix* out of Glasgow. He became a hero during the siege of Londonderry by Stuart supporters in 1689. He took his ship upriver right under the Royalist batteries, burst through the boom and delivered valuable supplies to the starving populace. He was twice court-martialled during a colourful career.

CHAPTER TWENTY

The Three Dukes

Like as the rose in June with her sweet smell
The marigold or daisy does excel.

Gavin Douglas, *Eneados*

Queen Anne (1665–1714) was of course the last of the Royal Stuarts to sit on a throne, and her death ended 344 years of dynastic survival, a remarkable feat in itself, even if some of the occupants of the throne had not been particularly distinguished. She was to a large extent a constitutional monarch based in London, so the behaviour one way or the other of a few errant noblemen in Scotland might not seem to matter. But the three Douglas dukes did still have massive wealth and manpower at their disposal, and if they had all had a concerted policy for the Jacobite cause or for an independent Scotland they might have made a very serious difference to the course of history.

The three Douglas dukes were James Douglas, 2nd Duke of Queensberry, the Union Duke, Archibald Douglas, 1st and only Duke of Douglas; and James Douglas, 4th Duke of Hamilton and Chatelherault (1658–1712), eldest son of William Douglas (see p. 123).

The first was the most astute politician of the three. Born in Sanquhar, he had been the first prominent Scot to reject James II, who had stalled his promotion in the army. He had supper with the King at Andover, slipped out of the house when the King went to bed and headed off to welcome William of Orange at Sherborne. In 1690 he was still involved in rounding up highlanders for the new king, and five years later inherited the dukedom. Despite his huge wealth, his father, William Douglas, had almost bankrupted himself building a huge new mansion at Drumlanrig, but he had in the family tradition married another Douglas, Isabel of Angus, so James inherited the Red Angus portfolio to add to the basically Black Douglas estates of Drumlanrig.

James had seen military service with Claverhouse, suppressing the Covenanters in 1684, but his dislike of this duty helped turn him against the Stuarts, and in 1688 he was one of those fighting against his old colleague, now Viscount Dundee. He became the leading Whig in Scotland at the turn of the century, dominating Scottish politics, but was dismissed by Queen Anne in 1703. Three years later he was back in power, and it was he who manœuvred the Act of Union through the suicidal Scottish parliament of 1707, he who officially touched the Act of Union with the sceptre, despite being stoned by rioters in the streets of Edinburgh. Though frequently threatened with assassination, he continued to be driven in his coach from Holyrood to the parliament, and so he went down in history as the Union Duke. As his reward he was also given an English dukedom, Dover, to add to the Scottish one. Whether the Union of parliaments was a benefit or a disaster will always be the subject of argument, but certainly the way it was achieved was undemocratic.

Hamilton was the nearest to a rebel of the three dukes. Unlike his father, the first of the Douglas dukes of Hamilton, who had welcomed the Orange changeover in 1688, he was an almost open Jacobite and had served on an embassy to France in 1683. He fought for a while in the French army of Louis XIV as an aide-de-camp and then for James II in England during the Monmouth rising. As Macaulay put it, 'Hamilton's abilities and knowledge though by no means such as would have sufficed to raise an obscure man to eminence appeared highly respectable in one who was the premier peer in Scotland.' After the accession of William III he had two spells in the Tower of London for his part in Jacobite plots, the first time in 1688 on the recommendation of his own father, who was far from Jacobite, and again in 1696. William said of him: 'I wish to heaven that Scotland were a thousand miles off and that the Duke of Hamilton was king of it. Then I should be rid of them both.'

For the vital five years from 1702 the Duke led the opposition in the Scottish parliament. Thus remarkably a James Douglas led both sides: Hamilton the opposition, and Queensberry the government party. Both of them were major investors in Scotland's disastrous colony in Darien, and Hamilton in particular spent a lot of energy on it. Robert Douglas, a prominent London merchant, was a key supporter of William Patterson, the financier born in Tinwald who promoted the Darien Scheme and also founded the Bank of England. Hamilton subsequently led the resistance to the Act of Union of 1707, but in a most erratic and unpredictable fashion. He let down his supporters in one of the crucial debates, and later he was totally indecisive on the question of armed rebellion. His motives are suspect as he too accepted an English dukedom, that of Brandon and Suffolk, to add to his Scottish one, and was perhaps even angling for the throne himself. In fact he was probably the last and least likely of the Douglases to have any ambition for the Crown. Ironically, since so many Douglases had married Royal Stewarts, in his case it was thanks to one of his Hamilton ancestors who had done the same that he now had sufficient Stuart blood to be theoretically next in line to the Crown after the Old Pretender – if you ignore the reality of Queen Anne.

Hamilton spent a lot of his time on his new English estates and made very little effort to harness the opposition which undoubtedly existed in Scotland to the destruction of its parliament. He was arrested again in 1708, still indulging in facile plots for the restoration of the Old Pretender to the Stuart throne. When he was provoked into fighting a duel in 1712 he killed his opponent, as the partisan Tory ballad recorded:

> Duke Hamilton thrust with all his might
> Unto Lord Mohun thro' his body right
> And sent him to eternal night

but was fatally wounded himself, probably stabbed from behind by Mohun's unstable second.

Archibald Douglas of Douglas, the third of our dukes, was only thirteen when the Act of Union was passed so he cannot be blamed for it, but he was undoubtedly pro-Hanoverian, as shown by his presence at Sheriffmuir on King George's side, and was to turn into an eccentric, a murderer, as we have already seen, and an ill-tempered old man. The exploits of his bitter senility fall in the next chapter.

Two other Douglas noblemen were actively involved in pushing through the Act of Union. James Douglas (d. 1715), 10th Earl of Morton, had been an active Orange supporter in 1688 and was a commissioner for the Union in 1707. He had his overlordship of Orkney and Shetland restored to him as a reward. Also in support was his later successor, George Douglas (1662–1738), the future 12th Earl, who in 1685 had killed a friend's footman because of an insult to his dog. This did not stop him becoming a colonel in the army and a member of the last Scottish parliament of 1707 who supported its abolition.

Meanwhile Queensberry's eldest son, James of Drumlanrig, turned out to be a homicidal maniac, not perhaps surprising, given his pedigree. He was supposed to be kept locked up in a basement room at Queensberry House in the Canongate, Edinburgh. But he escaped one day during the celebrations for the Act of Union and knifed a cook boy before roasting him on a spit in the family kitchen, and then enjoying a few mouthfuls before his minders returned. He was apparently extremely tall, as evident from the huge coffin in his elaborate monument at Durisdeer Church (though he actually seems to have been buried in York).

CHAPTER TWENTY-ONE

Politics and Madness

> For here the lover and killer are mingled
> Who had one body and one heart.
>
> Keith Douglas, 'Vergissmeinicht'

The history of our two families would not lead us to expect large numbers of the Douglases to turn out in favour of Bonnie Prince Charlie. They were lowlanders after all, they tended to be Protestant, and they had always envied the success of the Stuarts. As it turned out the most well-known Jacobite among the Douglases was a lady, Jane Douglas (1698–1753), sometime favourite sister of the first (and last) Duke of Douglas.

The Duke, as we have already seen, developed into an eccentric, perhaps plagued by conscience after his murder of the young Captain Kerr. He fought a duel over some obscure quarrel with the Duke of Buccleuch, perhaps with regard to his sister's honour, perhaps after he had beaten up one of his retainers. He then became convinced that there were plots afoot to kidnap him with drugs and transport him to St Kilda, which all suggests that he was becoming unhinged. He did not marry until he was over sixty, and then only because a remarkable young woman, Miss Peggie Douglas from the Mains branch of the family near Milngavie, set out deliberately to snare him. Shortly afterwards, in 1758, the old castle of Douglas was destroyed by a fire, some said caused deliberately by the new Duchess, who wanted her husband to mix more in Edinburgh society and in whose jewel room the fire started. Not surprisingly the castle was believed to be haunted by a black dog. The Duke commissioned a new castle from the Adam brothers, modelling the design on Inveraray Castle, but since the Campbells were regarded as junior dukes, the new Douglas Castle had to be 10 feet bigger in every direction. The castle was never completed, as funds ran out. The Duke died a mere four years later, in 1761, but the lively Peggie became a hostess in Edinburgh, entertaining Dr Johnson in St James's Court, where he described her in a letter as 'talking broad Scots with a paralytick voice scarcely understood by her own countrymen'. James Boswell enjoyed her company regularly and on one occasion when he asked for a warm bed for the night she wrote back that 'the warmest bed in the house was her own to which I (Boswell) should be welcome'.

The Duke's sister Jane also had a bit of an eccentric streak. Despite being an acknowledged beauty she was jilted by a promising suitor, perhaps because of the machinations of Kitty, the match-fixing Duchess of Queensberry. Gossip had it that Jane was so hurt by her rejection that she then ran off to France disguised in male clothing and determined to hide herself in a nunnery, but her relations chased after her and she was brought home. Romance bloomed again some years later, when she was close to forty, with Sir John Steuart, a widower, a near penniless professional soldier and a Jacobite. He had fought for the Old Pretender at Sheriffmuir and then done a stint as a colonel in the Swedish army. However, she heard some bad gossip about him and this time it was her turn to do the jilting.

About nine years later, when Jane was living in Drumsheugh, Edinburgh, came the news that Bonnie Prince Charlie had been defeated at Culloden. He had stayed at Douglas Castle on his way north, much to the annoyance of the Duke, who was Hanoverian to the core. But Jane took a different standpoint. At huge personal risk to herself she gave shelter to one of the Prince's aides, the Chevalier Johnstone, who had escaped the battle in disguise, like his master. That she did this for two whole months in the heart of Edinburgh speaks highly of her courage and determination.

Meanwhile, the evil gossip she had once heard about Sir John Steuart was proved to be false and she contacted him to apologize. Thus after a ten-year gap they met again, eloped to France and married in secret, Jane by this time forty-eight. The reasons for the secrecy were understandable: she expected her crusty old brother to object to the marriage and to cut off her cash allowance and her inheritance. This was, of course, exactly what he did as soon as he heard what had happened. He was even more angered, or genuinely incredulous, to hear that she had produced boy twins at the age of forty-nine. He had as yet no wife or children so hers, if genuine, would inherit the vast estate. Refusing to believe that his middle-aged sister could have produced twins, he cut off her source of finance so that her husband ended up in a debtors' prison. To her chagrin she could scrape together only half a crown to send to the poor man with whom she was clearly very much in love. The Duke also repudiated his supposed nephews, changing his will to make the Duke of Hamilton his heir. When Jane tried to visit him at Douglas he would not let her in the gate, and soon afterwards one of the twins died.

Not until Jane herself died in poverty in 1753 did the Duke of Douglas at last begin to relent, goaded to it partly by his new wife, who surprisingly took the part of her sister-in-law against her husband. Two years before his own death in 1761 he at last restored his previous will so that Archibald Steuart Douglas (1748–1827), the surviving twin, was made his official heir. It was too late, however, to avoid upsetting the Hamilton branch of the family, who had been looking forward to receiving such vast additional estates. They sued, and for eighteen years (1762–79) the legal wrangling went on before the Lords at last settled finally in favour of Archibald. The Douglas Cause resulted in massive costs and considerable anguish. Archibald, one of whose advocates was James Boswell, inherited all the estates, but not of course the dukedom, which became extinct with his uncle's death. He represented Forfar in the Commons and was made a peer in 1790, but though he and his wives had eight sons none of them managed to produce male heirs: his daughter's daughter married a Home, so that the two dynasties merged into the Douglas-Homes, who in due course took over the main Douglas inheritance; several generations later they produced a Prime Minister of Great Britain, Sir Alec Douglas-Home (see p. 144).

Slightly younger than the Duke of Douglas was Charles Douglas (1698–1778), 3rd Duke of Queensberry, known as the Good Duke, who if nothing else followed family tradition by falling out with his king, George II. He is mainly remembered for the vivacity of his wife, the famous Kitty, the most popular hostess of her day, and for their patronage of the poet Gay, whose efforts they subsidised as he wrote the *Beggar's Opera* to poke fun at their least favourite politician, Sir Robert Walpole. They entertained Pope, Congreve and most of the best-known writers of the day in their Buckinghamshire mansion. Kitty, about whom Walpole wrote 'Thank God the Thames is between me and the Duchess of Queensberry', was eccentric in her adherence to the fashions of her youth and to vegetarian feasts; she died of eating too many cherries. She was given to massive tantrums, for example when guests followed the normal Scottish upper-class manners of that time and ate food off their knives. Their great house at Drumlanrig, like Douglas, was slept in by Bonnie Prince Charlie on his way northwards in 1745. The highlanders stabbed a painting there of William of Orange and damaged the place so badly that it was abandoned. Anyway, it seemed to be cursed, for Thomas the Rhymer had predicted:

> When the Marr Burn runs where never man saw
> The House of Hassock is near to fall.

The 3rd Duke had indeed moved the Marr Burn to make a fountain and soon afterwards, in 1754, the disasters began. One son, referred to as a promising young officer, though he was as unstable as his mother and was regularly seen weeping with his wife in the grounds of Drumlanrig, shot himself, and the other died of an illness, aged only thirty. The Duke himself died after a fall from his carriage nearly a quarter of a century later. He had dabbled in canal building, industry and banking, the last of which caused huge financial difficulties in his later life. In fact the family's main bank, Douglas Heron and Company Bank, collapsed in 1773.

The next and last Douglas Duke of Queensberry, William Douglas (1724–1810), known as Old Q, was a fairly distant cousin of the previous incumbent, whose two sons had both died. Since he himself died a bachelor and there were no male heirs left, the dukedom and Drumlanrig went in 1810 to the Scotts of Buccleuch. Thus within a space of fifty years the Douglases lost two of the dukedoms it had taken them so long to acquire. It is strange that at this stage in a dynasty's life cycle they often produced a superfluity of bachelors.

Old Q led a long but uninspiring life, his main achievements having been to improve the breeding of racehorses – he lived for many years at Newmarket – and pioneer better rules for the turf. He was an addicted but successful gambler who made a lot of money by it, once for example betting that he could do 19 m.p.h. in a two-horse cart – he had a carriage specially built with whalebone and silk for lightness. But to pay for his extravagance he cut down trees, so that Robert Burns said of him, 'That reptile wears a ducal crown.' William Wordsworth was appalled at the way he had so many trees cut down at Drumlanrig and Neidpath to pay for the marriage of his mistress's daughter, whom wishful thinking suggested to him that he might have fathered. Wordsworth wrote in 'Sonnet composed at —— Castle':

> Degenerate Douglas, oh the unworthy lord . . .
> To level with the dust a noble horde
> A brotherhood of venerable trees
> Leaving an ancient dome and towers like these
> Beggared and outraged.

The old man kept himself alive with vast numbers of pills, and played the classic role of an ageing Regency buck. During the first period of madness of George III he 'ratted' on the old king and threw in his luck with the Prince of Wales, earning himself some disgrace when the King recovered again. He entertained the Prince frequently with large quantities of champagne at his house near Piccadilly. As a contemporary wag wrote:

> Insatiate yet with folly's sport
> That polished sin-worn fragment of the court
> The shade of Queensb'ry should with Clermont meet
> Ogling and hobbling down St James's Street.

The one dukedom the Douglases retained into the twenty-first century was the one they acquired by marriage and there too, like the Douglas-Homes, they became double-barrelled, calling themselves Douglas-Hamilton after 1895. In 1724 James Douglas, the 5th Duke (1702–43), had started building Chatelherault, the most exotic hunting lodge and dog kennel, designed by Adam, in the park above his main palace at Hamilton. The most remarkable scion of this branch of the family was Thomas Douglas, 5th Earl of Selkirk (1771–1820), who founded several settlements for emigrating highlanders in Canada, the best known on the Red River by Lake Winnipeg (see below).

Of the very small number of Douglases who did risk their lives for Bonnie Prince Charlie, one was George Douglas (d. 1745), 5th Lord Mordington, who was taken prisoner and died in prison. Another possibility was James Douglas (1702–68), 13th Earl of Morton, who seems to have been some kind of Jacobite, as he was arrested in France in 1746 and spent some time in the Bastille. Apart from selling the Orkney and Shetland Islands, his main claim to fame was his work as a physicist and astronomer. A member of the well-known longitude group, he was a significant proponent of Captain Cook's voyage to Tahiti to plot the transit of Venus in 1769. Certainly Alexander Douglas of Banchory was killed at Culloden fighting for the Prince, Sylvester Douglas of Whiterig was captured at Carlisle, and three Glenbervie Douglases had been captured at Preston.

Two other exotic Douglas soldiers of this period both began their military careers on the continent. A William Douglas served in the French army until 1703, when he transferred to the Swedish and won acclaim as the first to storm the gates of Reusch Lenberg in 1705. He did well at Frauenstadt but was captured by the Russians at Poltava. He was transported to Siberia, where he met an attractive Dutch girl who became his wife. He died in his bed with the rank of general and having been made a count at Stjinarp in Östergötland.

Otto Douglas was also made a count. He too had served the Swedish army and been captured by the Russians at Poltava, but had the wit to change sides and was made governor of Finland by Peter the Great. However, his rule there was so harsh that he became hugely unpopular. In 1719 he killed a Russian girl in a drunken quarrel and was condemned to hard labour, but the Tsar had a soft spot for him and obtained his release. He promoted him soon afterwards to lieutenant-general, making him a knight of the Alexander Nevsky Order and a count. But he finally went too far and was sacked in 1757 for condemning a Livonian nobleman to corporal punishment. Another colourful Douglas of this period was Jane Douglas (1700–60), a noted London brothel-keeper.

CHAPTER TWENTY-TWO

Postscript: Fir Trees and DC-10s

> I am a pillar of this house
> Of which it seems the whole is glass.
>
> Keith Douglas, 'The House'

If anyone typified the better qualities of the Douglas family in the nineteenth century it was Thomas Douglas, Earl of Selkirk (1771–1820). Born on St Mary's Isle, Kirkcudbright, the youngest of seven brothers, he was the only one who survived to take his father's title. At Edinburgh University he became a friend of Sir Walter Scott, and, though he had no prior connection with the Highlands, he 'interested himself in the fate of the natives' at the time when the clearances were beginning to cause real distress. He learned Gaelic and toured the Highlands. His first successful project, in 1803, was to organize around 800 emigrants to go to a new colony on St John's, now Prince Edward Island, Canada. Considerable difficulties had to be overcome, but in the end the settlement worked very well. His next plans were interrupted by the Napoleonic Wars, but he did manage to start another new colony at Baldoon (called after one of the Douglas baronies near Wigtown) in Kent County on Lake Erie, and tried to build a proper road from it to York (now Toronto).

Selkirk's schemes were held up by the war or other obstacles, but in 1810, helped by the fact that his wife had already inherited a large shareholding, he began to buy up a substantial number of shares in the Hudson Bay Company, which was going through a rough patch at the time. Thus for a nominal sum he was able to get a grant of 45 million acres of land on the Red River in 1812 and send out the first 100 colonists to Fort Douglas and Daer. He had the imagination to appreciate the food-producing potential of these vast prairies, but realized that it would take a massive human effort to create the new arable land.

The settlement was plagued with very severe difficulties – not just the harsh climate but the violent rivalry of the North West Fur Company, which did not want settlers on its hunting grounds – but by 1815 the first harvest had been reaped. Twice the colony was destroyed. Then Selkirk came out to Canada himself again, and with the help of some Swiss and German mercenaries attacked the North West Fur traders on their own ground at Fort William, taking prisoner some of those who had destroyed his own settlement. As James Hunter remarks, he was 'conducting himself very much as his Douglas ancestors might have done'. He made peace with the Indians and founded a new colony called Kildonan, after the area in Scotland from which the emigrants had come. Unfortunately the effort of these years ruined Selkirk's health, and he died two years later in the south of France. Selkirk town and county and the whole of Manitoba are his monument. Walter Scott, who was a lifelong friend, said of him: 'I never knew a man of more generous and disinterested disposition.' Soon after his death the two rival fur companies finally amalgamated. He was of course a paternalist – the Indians actually called him father – not a democrat, and frequently became too absorbed in petty detail, yet his achievement was still massive. As his admirer William Wilberforce put it, everything he had done was 'with the aim to the improvement and benefit of your fellow creatures'.

There were a number of other early Douglas colonists in Canada. Colin Douglas sailed in 1773 on the *Hector* to Pictou, from Loch Broom, losing two of his children during the voyage. James Douglas from Sweetheart in Dumfries settled in Georgetown, Prince Edward Island, in 1775. John Douglas from Kirkbean sailed on the *Lovely Nellie* to Prince Edward Island in 1775, as did a William Douglas.

Several other Douglases feature in the early history of Canada. Sir Charles Douglas (d. 1789) of Lochleven, later a rear admiral, was involved in several actions during the capture of Quebec, most notably when he took his ship in through the ice with vital supplies in 1775. Douglastown in Gaspe County, near the CNR terminal, was named after him. As captain of the *Formidable* under Admiral Rodney it was he who broke through the line to help win the victory of Dominica in 1782. His son Sir Howard Douglas (1776–1865) was an artillery officer initially, who spent a couple of years hunting and fishing among the Cherokee Indians in 1797. He once skated all the way from Montreal to Quebec to attend a ball, then saved a sinking timber ship by his prompt action. He spent some time off the African coast helping to suppress the slave trade, then fought with Wellington during the Peninsular War. He pioneered new designs of military bridge and has even been credited with passing on to Telford his idea of a suspension bridge. Then he turned his attention to raising standards of naval gunnery at Whale Island, where he helped found the famous gunnery school. In 1823 he was back in Canada as governor of New Brunswick, where he founded the University of Fredericton. His versatile career ended in 1832 with a spell as Lord High Commissioner of the Ionian Islands, where he introduced a number of improvements.

Sir James Douglas (1803–77), referred to as 'a man of imperial mind', was born in Demerara, the son of a Glasgow sugar merchant. He joined the North West Company in 1820 as a fur trader, and by 1830 was with the Hudson Bay Company based at Fort Vancouver. He led an expedition to the Stikine, trading with the Russians in Alaska, building Fort Conolly, named after his half-Cree wife. In 1843 he was in a party which landed on Vancouver Island and founded Victoria. As chief factor for the company he was the self-appointed governor of Vancouver, then of British Columbia, controlling thousands of lawless diggers by sheer force of personality. In the end his position as governor of British Columbia was made official.

Doctor George Douglas was the medical supervisor of Gross Isle, the quarantine island on the St Lawrence, known as Cholera Bay in the 1840s, as further waves of immigrants were brought in for health checks during the Irish potato famine. Thomas Douglas was a clergyman who became premier of Saskatchewan in 1904, and was a pioneer of welfare.

Also involved in the capture of Quebec in 1759 was Admiral Sir John Douglas (1703–87) from Friarshaw, near Cavers, Roxburgh. He was later with Rodney in the West Indies, helped the capture of Martinique in 1761 and captured Havana with minimal losses in 1762. He had earlier won acclaim in the fast sailing frigate *Alcide* which overtook and captured the rich prize of the *Felicité*. By coincidence another Cavers Douglas was a captain in the navy, commanding the *Greyhound* in 1745, and he made his name by capturing two French privateers. Similarly, Sir Andrew Snape Douglas was the most successful frigate captain of 1793, and when in command of the *Phaeton* captured the French ship *General Dumouriez* of 22 guns and a cargo of 680 cases of silver, following this up by capturing the Spanish galleon *Iago* on the same day; he died of a head wound three years later. Back in Canada, Captain W. Douglas (b. 1788) was at Nootka on the Cook River with a cargo of sea otter and visited the Sandwich Islands. Admiral Sir Archibald Douglas was commander-in-chief at Portsmouth in 1905 and a keen supporter of the building of Dreadnoughts. Lieutenant D. Douglas escaped with only six others from the flooded submarine *Stratagem* after it had been bombed by the Japanese in the Malacca Straits. He was tortured to reveal the position of other submarines and suffered extreme privations, which caused the death of four of the other survivors.

David Douglas (1798–1834), the botanist, also spent time in Canada, though he is perhaps more associated with California. This remarkable man came from Scone, near Perth, where his father was a stonemason and he trained as a gardener. He then trained further at the Glasgow Botanical Gardens before being sent out to the United States to look for samples in 1823. He went plant hunting in Vancouver in 1825, and discovered the fir that was named after him. He brought back to Britain several species of pine including the noble silver fir, the lodgepole pine, the grand silver pine and perhaps less happily the fast-growing Sitka spruce. He noted the Californian vulture and the ribes before crossing the northern Rockies to Hudson Bay, where he met Franklin. He was then based in California for five years (1829–34) before setting off to walk back to Europe via Alaska and Russia. This expedition was halted because of Indian wars, and on his way back south again he and his dog Billy were nearly drowned when their canoe capsized in the Fraser River. He then headed for the Sandwich Islands, where a monument was erected to him at New Scone, and Honolulu, where he was the first man to climb several of the local peaks. There he died in mysterious circumstances, being gored to death by a wild bull after falling into a trap set by a former Botany Bay convict, with whose wife he is thought perhaps to have been having an affair. In all he introduced some 50 tree and 100 herbaceous species to Britain, including lupins, sunflower and mahonia. His collection of dried specimens is spread between Kew and other major museums.

His humble origins and great achievements stand out against men such as Alexander Douglas, 10th Duke of Hamilton (1767–1811), who was obsessed by his pedigree and married Susan Beckford, daughter of the eccentric but rich novelist, 'one of the handsomest women of her time'. Among his other possessions at Hamilton Palace he had Leonardo da Vinci's *Laughing Boy*. He worked briefly as British ambassador to Russia in 1806, and stayed on in Poland afterwards for a year or two. When he died he was buried like a pharaoh in an Egyptian sarcophagus laid in a huge stone mausoleum built beside his palace. William, the 12th Duke, who died in 1895, had married a relative of Napoleon's first wife, the famous Josephine, and had his illusory dukedom of Chatelherault confirmed by Napoleon III in 1864. Well known in sporting and racing circles, he had no children and was succeeded by Alfred Douglas. It was his son, Douglas Douglas-Hamilton, the 14th Duke (1903–73), whose influence Rudolf Hess so greatly overestimated when he made his extraordinary flight in 1941, aiming his Messerschmitt at Hamilton, and parachuting not far off his mark at Eaglesham in the hope of ending the Second World War. The Duke was a pilot who had taken charge of the first flight over Mount Everest in 1933 and as a flying ace had been introduced to Hitler in 1936 in Berlin, so they had that in common, but the peace had to wait. Of his near contemporaries John C. Sholto Douglas, 21st Earl of Morton (b. 1927), was managing director of the family country club at Dalmahoy, his son Lord Aberdour born in 1952, and David Douglas, 12th Marquess of Queensberry, was professor of ceramics at the London Royal College of Art, his son the Viscount Drumlanrig born in 1967.

The Douglas Marquesses of Queensberry entered the twentieth century with a highly controversial third son in the shape of the athlete and poet Lord Alfred Douglas (1870–1945), who wrote some elegant sonnets and whose attractions had brought about the tragic downfall of Oscar Wilde. It was Alfred's father, the irrascible 8th Marquess, John Sholto Douglas (1844–1900), who had given his patronage and name to the new Queensberry Rules for boxing in 1867 and then pushed Wilde into suing him for criminal libel in 1895. After Wilde's release from Reading Gaol Lord Alfred still met him in Paris and Naples, keeping up the friendship until Wilde's death, but then two years later he defied the rumours by eloping with a wealthy young bride. Lord Alfred played a hysterical role in the politics of the First World War with a shrewish attack on Prime Minister Asquith, followed by an even more bitter one on Winston Churchill, whom he accused of falsifying the reports on the battle of Jutland. Churchill therefore had no choice but to sue him for libel, and with some difficulty and considerable mental anguish managed to win. Douglas was sentenced to six months in prison.

Drumlanrig and the Dukedom of Queensberry had passed to the Scotts of Buccleugh in 1810, after the death of Old Q meant that the title went to a female heir, Jane Douglas, who had married a Scott. In subsequent centuries they more normally used the title Dukes of Buccleugh, to avoid confusion with the other Queensberrys, but even they persisted with the Douglas pedigree, giving themselves the triple-barrelled surname of Douglas-Montagu-Scott.

The best of the other Douglas poets since the remarkable Bishop Gavin Douglas was probably Keith Douglas (1920–43), known for his evocative descriptions of the war in North Africa in the 1940s, when he served as a tank commander. Sadly he was killed in action. The best of the novelists was Norman Douglas (1868–1952), whose *South Wind* of 1917 was a paean to hedonism set among the pleasure-seekers of Capri.

On the military side the Douglases produced three generals during the Napoleonic Wars: Neil Douglas (1779–1853) was at Corunna and Walcheren, was a colonel at Nivelle and despite being badly wounded led his regiment at Waterloo, reaching the rank of general in 1838; Sir Kenneth Douglas (1752–1833) fought in the West Indies in 1791 and Egypt in 1804; Sir James Dawes Douglas (1785–1862) was at Salamanca and Corunna, was made a colonel in the Portuguese army in 1809, lost a leg at Toulouse and was made a general in 1825.

General Charles Whittingham Douglas (1850–1914) was Chief of the Imperial General Staff from April 1914, taking over from John French, and was responsible for the mobilization of the British army when the

First World War began in August. Born in South Africa, he had served in the Afghan wars of 1879, including the Kabul to Kandahar march and the battle of Kandahar, then in both the Boer Wars, rising to major-general by 1901. He was a keen reformer and an excellent organizer and is said to have died of overwork in October 1914, as much a casualty as any who died in the field. Major-General William Douglas led the Manchester Brigade against the Turkish trenches at Gallipoli and commanded the 8th Corps at Helles in 1915. Lieutenant-Colonel Angus Douglas-Hamilton won a posthumous Victoria Cross commanding the Cameron Highlanders on Hill 70, leading the last of four heroic charges. There were two other Douglas recipients of the VC: Henry Douglas, a doctor from Jamaica, won it in the Boer War, and a Canadian doctor, Campbell Douglas, won it for saving life at sea off Little Andaman Island in 1867.

As well as Afghanistan, Canada and South Africa, Douglas soldiers had also seen service in the West Indies, a very unhealthy posting at that time. Two elder brothers of Thomas Douglas of Selkirk died there. Walter Douglas of Baads was governor of the Leewards in 1712 and Robert Douglas was treasurer of Honduras. A number of Douglas minor criminals were among the early convicts transported to Australia, including John Douglas, for rioting in Inverness, and Joseph Douglas, a thief from Dumfries.

Of the American Douglases perhaps the best known was Stephen Douglas (1813–61) of Vermont, who was the great proponent of America's westward expansion as its 'manifest destiny'. He supported the annexation of Texas, opposed slavery and lost as presidential candidate to Abraham Lincoln in 1860. In the same period H. Ford Douglas (1831–65), a Virginian abolitionist with a white father and a slave mother, became one of only thirty black officers in the Union Army, and probably the only black captain serving in the front line. Another Afro-American Douglas who was an influential abolitionist was Frederick Douglass (1817–95) from Maryland, who worked as a slave in a Baltimore shipyard until he escaped in 1838 and became a leader of the Massachussets Anti-Slavery Society and founded an abolitionist newspaper in New York. He came to Glasgow in 1860 to speak against slavery. David and John Douglas were with Oglethorpe among the founding colonist in Georgia, while there were also significant groups of Douglasses in North Carolina and Mississippi.

William Orville Douglas (1898–1980) was a keen supporter of Roosevelt's New Deal, a justice of the supreme court where he began to uphold civil rights, and a pioneer in the conservation of wilderness areas, supporting John Muir as the champion of national park areas. Other supporters of Roosevelt were Helen Douglas (1900–80), the actress who became a senator and ran against Richard Nixon – who said that she was soft on Communism – and Lewis W. Douglas (1894–1974), the Arizona opponent of the Ku Klux Klan. James Douglas (1837–1918) founded an iron smelting empire at Douglas, Arizona, before dying in New York. Of the academics perhaps the most able was Andrew Douglas (1867–1962), the Arizona astronomer who discovered the relationship between sunspots and the growth rings on trees, thus inventing the science of dendrochronology, which had a major impact for archaeology and studies of long-term climate change. Lloyd Cassel Douglas (1877–1951) was a religious teacher from Indiana who projected a new optimism for the human race and wrote two best-selling religious novels, *The Robe* and *The Big Fisherman*. Another Douglas religious teacher was Neil Douglas (1750–1823) of Glasgow, a poet and powerful preacher who was sent to prison for referring to George III as Nebuchadnezzar and parliament as a den of infernal corruption. He was a small man with a big voice who in the heat of his sermon would snatch off the huge brown wig from his head. Equally fanatical was the left-wing economist Major C.H. Douglas (1879–1952), who advocated universal bank loans for the poor, hated Jews but was much admired by the poets MacDiarmid and Pound.

One of two pioneering pilots was Donald Wills Douglas (1892–1981), the New York plane designer who founded his own company in the back room of a Californian barbershop in 1920. He had visited the Wright brothers when he was only sixteen and was now determined to develop a fast monoplane. He started with a torpedo-carrying seaplane, but his first transcontinental effort was a failure. He persisted and his Douglas World Cruisers flew round the world in 1924. The all-metal Douglas DC-2 with fourteen passengers was second in the 1934 Britain to Australia Air Race. He designed the DC-3 Dakota in 1936: described as one of the most important advances in aircraft design, it became the standard Allied troop transport of the Second World War and enabled paratroopers to be dropped behind enemy lines for the liberation of Europe in June 1944. He also made the successful B-19 bomber at that time and some successful post-war propeller airliners such as the DC-7, but he was late in adapting to jet airliners with the DC-8, -9 and -10 and he was outsold by Boeing, so that his company had to merge with McDonnell in 1967.

The other pilot was William Sholto Douglas (1893–1969), an ace fighter pilot in the First World War and Marshal of the RAF in 1946. He had a two-year period in charge of Fighter Command just after the battle of Britain and has been perhaps unfairly accused of increasing RAF losses by his tactic of 'dragging a coat' along the coast of France to try to provoke counter-attacks by the *Luftwaffe*. These mass sweeps failed and were nicknamed 'rhubarbs'. He then led Middle East Command up to 1944, before moving to Coastal Command, where he oversaw the successful anti-submarine campaign that was a decisive factor in the later stages of the war of the Atlantic.

In Italy Count Marco Antonio Scoto d'Agazano came from Count Scoti Douglas in the castle of Vigoleno, near Parma. The family had silver stars and a bloody heart on their shield in the reign of Henry IV, whom they had supported in the murky world of Italian politics. These Italian Douglases survived until modern times, as did the descendants of Robert Douglas, Baron Skalby, the Swedish field marshal who owned Linköping. In Germany there was Count Hugo Sholto Douglas (1837–1912), descended from a family which came to Germany in 1760; he became a major industrialist. In France there was a Douglas family that had lived there since the days of the Hundred Years War, when so many of the family had fought there, including an Antoine Du Glas. François Douglas de Richnagnard moved to Montreal in 1755 as a captain of the Languedoc infantry and had a son there in 1758 who later became a Paris Deputy, while a Louis Archambaud Douglas was born in the Château Quincieu in 1814 and became a railway pioneer.

The historical contribution of the Douglases had begun to ebb in Scotland, but throughout the world the family continues to produce some remarkable characters. The same could to some extent be said of the Stewarts or Stuarts and the Bruces. In 1762 John Stuart, Marquess of Bute (1713–92), became Prime Minister of Great Britain, albeit for only a short, fairly unsuccessful period, as he was intensely unpopular. Then in 1812 Robert Stewart, Viscount Castlereagh (1769–1822), became Foreign Secretary and though more successful he too was unpopular and cut his own throat ten years later. The Stewarts produced another Foreign Secretary, Michael Stewart (1906–90), and the Douglases their Prime Minister, Sir Alec Douglas-Home (1903–95), who was Foreign Secretary twice, under both Harold Macmillan and Edward Heath. Heir to the Douglas estates, he celebrated his twenty-first birthday at Douglas Castle in 1924, when it was already beginning to subside because of the neighbouring pits.

The Bruces produced one Prime Minister of Australia, Stanley Melbourne Bruce (1883–1967); Thomas Bruce, Lord Elgin (1766–1841), most famous for removing the Parthenon marbles; James Bruce (1730–94), who discovered the source of the Blue Nile and was referred to by David Livingstone as 'a greater traveller than any of us', and Sir David Bruce (1855–1931), who discovered the tsetse fly parasite, which causes sleeping sickness, and identified the bacterium causing the fever known thereafter as Brucella.

Two notable criminals came from the Douglas family. Joe Douglas was a well-known New York thief and kidnapper working for the notorious Marion Frederick Mandelbaum until he was finally caught in 1874. The bullet-ridden body supposed to be that of Wattie Douglas was found in a canal near Amsterdam in 1991 and he was presumed dead, but two years later Interpol intercepted a yacht called the *Britannia Gazelle* and found him on board with cannabis worth $60 million.

Of the Douglas film stars, Melvyn, Kirk and his son Michael, none of them was a real Douglas, but they were of East European origin and took the name because it had the right sound, a tribute perhaps to the adventurous qualities of the family over the last 750 years. For four of those centuries the family had played a dangerous game of power politics in Scotland and later England. Then it had spread its energies over a wider area in Europe, Canada, the United States and Australasia. In peace and war its achievements had been extraordinary.

A Tour of the Sites

But we should weep to see today
How on his skin the swart flies move.
Keith Douglas, 'Vergissmeinicht'

My brother Douglas may upbraid
And strive with threatening words to move me
My lover's blood is on thy spear
How canst thou ever bid me love thee?
Anon., 'The Braes of Yarrow'

For the sake of travelling convenience, rather than historical or any other thematic order, we start in Glasgow and after a quick trip westwards head anticlockwise round Scotland, finishing in Orkney. (L = Scheduled Monument number.)

Note on heraldry: of the various motifs frequently seen on monuments in our trip, three silver stars signify Moray; a red triangle, Liddesdale; a silver lion, Angus or Galloway; a red lion, Abernethy; a buckle, Bunkle; a cross, Annandale; a criss-cross, Lauderdale, and a red heart, Douglas. In our context the fleur-de-lis means Touraine.

GLASGOW AND CLYDE COAST AREAS

Sadly little remains of the quite considerable number of castles built or owned and refurbished by the Douglases round Glasgow. A combination of medieval violence, subterranean sapping by the coal industry and general neglect or vandalism has robbed us of important parts of this heritage. Yet a glance at their positions shows how the Douglases established control of the Clyde from estuary to source, and there must be hope that more conservation effort goes into preserving what is left, for these remains form an important part of Scotland's history and should not be allowed to deteriorate further.

Rutherglen has the site of **Farme Castle**, which was demolished in the 1960s for the sake of short-term industrial development and was a Douglas property in the fifteenth century up to 1482.

Little remains of **Drumsargad Castle** on a mound beside the Clyde near Calder Glen, off Hallside Road. This was a Black Douglas property from around 1370, when Archibald the Grim of Douglas married Joanna of Moray, until the family's fall in 1455.

Carmunnock was a Douglas estate shortly after Bannockburn and the family took over a Comyn castle at what is now called **Castlemilk**, of which a few basement stones from the fifteenth century remain beside Machrie Drive housing scheme. As with other Black Douglas properties, this was lost to them after the disaster of 1455: it passed first to their rivals the Hamiltons, then to the Stewarts of Castlemilk in Dumfriesshire, who gave it its new name. To the south also are **Carmunnock Motte**, perhaps also a Douglas site, and **Busby Peel**, a privately owned sixteenth-century L-plan tower house, dating from after the fall of the Black Douglases but built on the site of one of their castles in this area.

Glasgow itself is the site of the battle of **Langside**, in which James Douglas, the Regent Morton, was a principal player in the defeat of Mary Queen of Scots, and her supporters.

To the north-west of Glasgow was **Mains Castle**, beside modern Milngavie, a Red Douglas outpost from 1373, one of whose owners, Malcolm Douglas, was executed for a plot against James VI, yet whose son Robert was made Viscount Belhaven. It remained in Douglas hands for more than five centuries, producing Peggie, the one and only Duchess of Douglas. A few stones of the old castle survive but the mansion built to replace it was demolished to make way for a school, Douglas Academy.

Moving to the west we head for the remnants of the Stewart presence in Renfrewshire. Their great seat at **Kingsinch**, originally an island fortress in the Clyde, was destroyed during the Cromwellian Civil War, and any remains are buried beneath tons of industrial rubble and housing near Renfrew Ferry. Fine remains of their foundation dedicated to St Mirren and St Milburga at **Paisley** are still visible, built into the west side of the more modern Paisley Abbey. A quarter of a mile to the south is **Blackhall Manor**, restored for private use in the 1980s, built by the Stewarts in the sixteenth century on the site of one of their original castles from the twelfth century. Half a mile to the north is the monument showing where Marjorie Bruce, wife of Walter the Steward, gave birth to the future King Robert II at **Knock Hill**, also the battle site of the defeat of Somerled by the Stewarts, the monks of Glasgow Cathedral and others in 1164.

Heading west on the north side of the Clyde we come to **Dumbarton Castle** (Historic Scotland L90107), which in our narrative figures in the imprisonment of William Wallace by his betrayer Stewart of Menteith, who was its governor, also in the early history of David II and his queen,

Joan, who sought safety here, as did Mary Queen of Scots. Two prominent Douglases were arrested and held here: Archibald 'Bell-the-Cat' and James Douglas, the Regent Morton. A fourteenth-century gateway survives from this extremely important royal castle, but most of the buildings still standing date from after the Cromwellian destruction.

Beneath the castle on the other side of the River Leven stood Robert Bruce's favourite country mansion of **Cardross**, where the legend of the Bloody Heart actually began as the King passed his dying request to James Douglas. Sadly for such an important site nothing has been preserved but a few stones of the stable. This area at the mouth of the Leven was also the scene of the escape route of Bruce and Douglas and their party after the disastrous defeat at Dalry, near Tyndrum, by John of Lorne and their dash for safety down Loch Lomond, where Douglas had procured a waterlogged boat.

Further west on the south side of the Firth of Clyde, half a mile south of Kempoch Point, is the site of **Gourock Castle**, a smaller outpost of the Black Douglas empire, but characteristic of their strategy of dominating the mouth of the major navigable rivers in Scotland.

Across the Clyde from here, ten miles away, is the magnificent Stewart castle of **Rothesay** (Historic Scotland L90252) which was captured by the Vikings in 1236 and 1263, then by the English in 1298, and retaken by Bruce in 1334. Built on a raised mound surrounded by a water-filled moat, it has a massive twelfth-century keep surrounded by four round towers. An additional keep was built to create more comfortable quarters for James V as conditions generally became less spartan. It was popular with the early Stewart kings as a summer residence, and it was here according to one chronicler that Robert III died of grief after hearing of the capture of his young son, later James I, by English privateers. It was Robert II who had first made his son and heir the Duke of Rothesay, albeit with tragic consequences, and this tradition has been preserved by his successors, the modern British royal house of Windsor.

Ten miles to the south is **Brodick Castle** (National Trust for Scotland) on the Isle of Arran, a fifteenth-century keep on top of thirteenth-century foundations. Originally built by the Menteith branch of the Stewarts, it was captured by the English around 1289 and was recaptured reputedly by the Good Lord James Douglas for Bruce in 1307, as the first stage of their remarkable fightback for the throne of Scotland. It had a chequered history until in 1510 it came into the ownership of the Hamilton family who extensively rebuilt it in the 1540s. It had Douglas owners from 1660, when William Douglas became 3rd Duke of Hamilton by marrying the Duchess, until 1895, when the 12th Duke's heiress married the Duke of Montrose. The substantial art and silver collection owes much to the marriage of Alexander Douglas, 10th Duke, to the extremely rich Euphemia Beckford, whose grandfather made a fortune from slave-run sugar plantations in the West Indies and whose father was a compulsive collector.

Returning to the mainland at Ardrossan gives the opportunity to head up to that other popular Royal Stewart castle at **Dundonald** (Historic Scotland L90112), with a thirteenth-century keep which seems to have been the gatehouse of the original castle. This was the home of Robert the Steward before he became Robert II in 1370. He refurbished it in the 1350s after his first and for a long time non-legalized marriage to Elizabeth of Rowallan, and he lived there frequently afterwards with his massive brood of children, probably dying here in 1390.

Also in Ayrshire, 3½ miles south-west from Mauchline, is **Trabboch Castle** (L5281), now very much ruined, a strong fourteenth-century castle which was surrounded by a ditch. Given originally to the Boyds by Bruce, it passed to the Douglases about 1450 and its remains have been incorporated in a farm at Trabboch Mains.

To the south-west are the ruins of thirteenth-century **Turnberry Castle**, which surmounted an even earlier castle. Standing on a promontory jutting out into the sea, it had a curtain wall and a keep, but little survives. As the main seat of the earls of Carrick, it was inherited by Robert the Bruce's mother, and was the scene of her extraordinarily forceful wooing of his father in 1270. Thus it was probably the place where the future king was born and it was certainly the scene of his first landing on the mainland in 1307 after the previous year's wandering and exile. It was part of his policy to destroy castles which could be used by the enemy, so he set an example by dismantling his own at Turnberry in 1310, and never rebuilt it.

On the way back north towards Glasgow is **Loudoun Hill**, where Bruce and Douglas scored one of their early victories against the English in 1307.

Mauchline was the site of some legalized murder of covenanters by Douglas officers and an epitaph there recorded:

Bloody Dumbarton (George Douglas) Douglas and Dundee
Moved by the Devil and the Laird of Lee
Dragg'd these five men to death with gun and sword.

North-east of Glasgow was **Cumbernauld Castle**, seat of the Flemings, who were close supporters of the Black Douglases and held it from them. Here the widow of Archibald Douglas the Guardian sheltered from the English in 1333 after his defeat at Halidon Hill. A couple of vaulted chambers and a few outbuildings survive, built into the more modern

Cumbernauld House. One of its owners was murdered by James Douglas in 1406 after being involved in the secret departure of young James I to the Bass Rock, and another, Sir Malcolm Fleming, was executed alongside the two Black Douglas brothers after the Black Dinner of 1440.

CLYDESDALE

Returning to Glasgow, we can now head south-east to the main Douglas heartland of Lanarkshire. At Bothwell are the majestic ruins of one of the finest of the Douglas castles, **Bothwell Castle** (Historic Scotland L90038), standing on a promontory jutting out into the River Clyde, which formed part of its defences. It has a strong curtain wall up to 60 feet high and had the additional defence of a moat. It had three large round towers, one of them ruined, surrounding a large courtyard with a massive round keep at one end, built in the thirteenth century on to the solid rock which had been cut away to make the moat. The castle was in English hands in 1298, recaptured briefly in 1300, retaken by the English in 1301 and surrendered to Bruce in 1314. In 1336 it was captured and refurbished as his base by Edward III but captured again by the Scots and dismantled a year later. It came into Black Douglas hands in 1362 when Archibald the Grim married its Moray heiress and substantially rebuilt it, so that along with Threave in the south it became his favourite seat. His son Archibald, the 4th Earl and famous loser of battles, added a palatial hall to make it even more impressive for entertaining his retainers and potential rivals. In 1455 the Black Douglases lost Bothwell along with all their other castles after their defeat at Arkinholm. By coincidence the Red Douglases acquired it in 1492 in exchange for Hermitage Castle as James IV tried to loosen their grip on the Borders. Then Archibald, 'Bell-the-Cat', rather rashly gave it to his fiancée or third wife, Elizabeth Kennedy (it is not clear if they ever actually married), as an espousal gift, though she was King James IV's mistress at the time. The Douglas earls of Forfar held it in the seventeenth century but abandoned it in favour of a Palladian mansion which they had built nearby, but which was demolished in 1926. As one of the barristers in the Douglas Cause, Boswell met his client here. The ground in due course passed to the Douglas-Homes, who handed it over to the state in 1935.

On the opposite bank of the river are the scant remains of **Blantyre Priory** (L2251). Also in Bothwell is **St Bride's Collegiate Church**, founded in 1398 by Archibald the Grim, St Bride being the patron saint of the Douglas family. Here two years later his daughter Marjorie married the ill-fated David, Duke of Rothesay, and would have been Queen of

Scotland had he not died in suspicious circumstances soon afterwards at Falkland, while in the custody of her brother Archibald the Tyneman, by then the 4th Earl of Douglas. He was Duke David's brother-in-law twice over as he had married the Duke's sister, the Princess Margaret Stewart. The old collegiate church is no longer in use but is attached to a more modern parish church. It is the earliest known example of a church with its roof consisting of overlapping stone slabs supported by a pointed barrel vault, similar to Lincluden (see p. 161), which was also founded by Archibald the Grim. The stone slabs are carefully curved to keep water away from the joints, so the standard of masonry is very high. There are some fine areas of carving, including the elliptical arch over the doorway and the sedilia, and the work here and at Lincluden has been attributed to the French master mason John Morrow. There are some ancient Douglas tombstones and slightly more recent ones for the Douglas earls of Forfar, the last one of whom was fatally injured in 1715 fighting for the redcoats at Sheriffmuir.

South of Bothwell is the site of **Hamilton Palace**, or The Orchard, which was burnt down on the orders of the vengeful James Douglas, Regent Morton, in 1579. It was rebuilt by the Hamiltons in 1591 as a Renaissance-style mansion. Charles McKean describes it as 'a U-plan palace . . . note the flanking rectangular towers, the viewing platforms, the ornamental cappings to the chimneys and their alternating rhythm with the dormer windows'. It first came into Douglas ownership in 1660 when William Douglas married his way into the dukedom of Hamilton. It was revamped in the early eighteenth century by the 5th Duke and again about 100 years later as a vast palace for the increasingly megalomaniac Douglas dukes of Hamilton, but it started to fall apart in the 1920s as the nearby coal mines, which had helped to pay for it, began to sap its strength from below. The Douglas lifestyle had been enhanced by the rich seams of coal beneath their properties but in the end they paid the price, and the palace had to be demolished in 1927 when the dukes bought a new seat at Lennoxlove in East Lothian. **Hamilton Mausoleum**, a huge domed structure built to house the sarcophagus of Alexander Douglas, 10th Duke, known as Il Magnifico, stands 200 yards from the site of the palace and has been restored. It dominates the skyline of the M74.

Chatelherault Lodge was completed by William Adam between 1732 and 1744 for James Douglas, 5th Duke, who still claimed the title Duke of Chatelherault given to his Hamilton ancestors in the reign of Mary Queen of Scots. It was seriously damaged by mine works and rot, but has been painstakingly restored. This exotic hunting lodge sits above the Avon gorge and looks down on the site of the palace. It incorporates the most elaborately designed picnic accommodation and dog kennels for the eighteenth-century hunting party. The 5th Duke of Hamilton also employed William Adam in 1732 to build the fine octagonal **parish church of Hamilton**.

Across the Avon are the ruins of **Cadzow Castle**, once a royal seat, with a line of oak trees reputedly planted for King David I and its own herd of wild white cattle descended from those of the ancient Caledonian Forest. It was after Bannockburn the home of the original Hamiltons, who were staunch supporters of the Black Douglases until they fell out in 1454 as they became disillusioned by the vacillations of the last earl. It was destroyed in 1570 out of spite by James Douglas of Morton, who had an ongoing feud with the Hamiltons, but came into Douglas hands finally in 1660. Sadly it was converted into a Gothic folly in 1820 by the 10th Duke.

One of the stranger episodes of more recent Douglas history was when Rudolf Hess, successor designate to Adolf Hitler after Goering, flew a Messerschmitt fighter from Germany to Scotland in 1941 and landed at Eaglesham, with the intention of meeting the Duke of Hamilton to organize a peace treaty. He greatly overestimated the influence of dukes in that period and spent the rest of his long life as a prisoner in Spandau.

Turning south again, 2 miles south-west of Carluke is **Hallbar Tower** (L21148), associated with the Braidwood estate of the Black Douglases, who held it from the fourteenth century. The sixteenth-century tower house has been restored for holiday lets in private ownership.

To the south-west is **Strathaven or Avondale Castle** (L2619), a fifteenth-century keep, now ruined, standing on solid rock above the River Avon, which joins the Clyde at Hamilton. It is associated with the Black Douglases from the period of James the Gross, and was besieged and sacked by James II in 1455 as part of his policy of destroying the power of the Douglases. It then passed to the Stewarts of Avondale, who rebuilt it, then to the villainous James Hamilton of Finnart, military architect and hired assassin, who further extended it as well as rebuilding nearby Craignethan, before he was beheaded on the orders of James V.

Craignethan Castle (Historic Scotland L90083) itself is further down the valley, standing high above a deep ravine overlooking the River Nethan as it flows down to the Clyde. With its large tower and curtain wall on three sides, it was a Black Douglas base until the family's forfeiture in 1455. In its subsequent form it was an example of the outstanding engineering skill of James Hamilton of Finnart, who owned it and rebuilt it in the 1530s, for the first time in Scotland using carponiers, stone-vaulted musketry emplacements which enabled defenders to harass incoming gunners from the side. He was also responsible for the building of sophisticated fortifications at Blackness, Edinburgh and Linlithgow to meet the challenge of the new artillery then arriving from the continent.

Craignethan became a Douglas property again in the more modern period when it was bought by the Duke of Douglas and then passed to the Douglas-Homes with the rest of the Douglas patrimony. **Belstane Castle**, of which virtually nothing remains, was a sixteenth-century tower house 1½ miles north of Carluke owned briefly by the Douglases.

Moving south now into the original Douglas heartland we come to **Lesmahagow Priory**, whose need for protection on behalf of the monks of Kelso was the original reason for inviting the Freskin family from Flanders to settle on land nearby at the Poniel Burn. The priory was established by the River Nethan for the Benedictine order of Kelso under the patronage of David I in 1144, and the Freskins were brought in to protect it six years later, changing their name to Douglas in about 1200 when they built their first castle on the river of that name. At about this time Brice or Brixius Douglas was Prior of Lesmahagow before moving north in 1202 to become Bishop of Moray. The monks of Lesmahagow became well known as pioneers of fruit-growing in the fertile and sheltered Clyde valley, an industry which still struggles to survive. The modest ruins of the priory are visitable beside the elegant parish church built in 1803 to replace the one founded by David I.

Douglas Castle, of which bits of a tower and cellars survive, was the starting place for the entire Douglas story, as it was the river here which gave the Flemish Freskins their new name when they were given this land in 1150. Their policies stretched from Tinto Hill in the east to Cairntable in the west. The castle originally stood on a mound two-thirds surrounded by the winding river, but this was later diverted into ornamental lakes which now dominate the site. When Sir Walter Scott visited it while researching his last novel, *Castle Dangerous*, which was set here, he reputedly wept at the dilapidation even then of such a historic site. There was 'a single tower embosomed in ash trees' which were reckoned to be 600 years old. One of them, the Doom Tree with its hanging hook, still stood in 1861. Pennant, visiting in the 1770s, noted the untidy state of the agricultural land in the area and commented 'near the castle are several ancient ash trees whose branches groaned under the weight of executions'. The Doom Tree has gone but is still represented by some wooden artefacts in the Douglas Heritage Museum (see below), and several other very old ash trees survive.

The castle was attacked three times by its most famous owner, the Good Lord James, from 1307 to 1313, and twice deliberately destroyed by him so that it would be of less use to the enemy. The English, however, persisted with it, presumably because even then it was close to the main westerly route from England into Scotland. After Bannockburn Lord James seems to have made no immediate effort to restore it, being of a roving spirit and preferring his hideaways in the border forests, so for a while it became one of the minor castles of the Black Douglas empire. It was forfeited along with the rest in 1455 but soon afterwards came into the hands of the Red Douglases, and was somewhat modernized in the seventeenth century to house the marquesses of Douglas. It was here that the one and only Duke of Douglas murdered or accidentally killed his friend Captain Kerr. Then it was burnt down in 1758, shortly after the Duke's belated marriage; his young wife lost all her jewels in the blaze but has been blamed for starting it as she not surprisingly found the place boring and gloomy. The eccentric old duke was still unwilling to move with her to the bright lights of Edinburgh and promptly hired the Adam brothers to build a replacement. It was based very much on the design of Inveraray Castle, new home of the Campbell Dukes of Argyll, but had to be 10 feet larger in every direction for reasons of ducal prestige. It was thus, like Inveraray, a castellated mansion with round towers, but it was never finished, and in the 1930s, like Hamilton Palace, it began to subside as the rich seams of coal were moved from beneath its foundations. By 1938 it was demolished, a few years after the twenty-first birthday party held there for its heir at the time, and its best-known modern owner, Sir Alec Douglas-Home, then Lord Dunglass, the future Prime Minister. Pennant describes his visit there in 1772: 'Continue my journey through dreary glens or melancholy hills . . . procure a guide over five miles of pathless moors and descend into Douglasdale, watered by the river of its name; a valley distinguished by the residence of the family of Douglas a race of turbulent heroes celebrated throughout Europe for their deeds in arms; the glory yet the scourge of their country; the terror of their princes; the pride of the Northern annals of chivalry.' He describes the house as 'an imperfect pile begun by the late duke: in the front are three round towers. Beneath the base of one lies the noble founder, and tears of the country painted above. He was interred here by his own directions, through the vain fear of mingling his ashes with those of the injured dead [Captain Kerr, presumably].' The site is reputedly haunted by a black dog. It is sad that not more has been done to conserve what remains of the castle. It is reachable by a path from the village or an estate track leading from the A70 near New Mains. Just to the west is a monument marking the site of the first gathering in 1689 of the Cameronian Regiment whose first commander, James Douglas, the heir of Douglas, was killed in his first battle. One carved stone, an obelisk dial, was moved to King's Park, Glasgow.

The Douglases seem to have protected their headquarters with two additional small castles or outposts as early warning stations or additional retreats. **Thorril** (L5425) or Torthorl or Thirwall Castle, about 2 miles to the south-east, near Parkhall Burn and Parkhead on the east side of the modern motorway, was perhaps originally put up by the English in 1308 when the governor of the main castle was called Thirwall, the second of the commanders killed by the Good Lord James. It later belonged to the Douglases of Parkhead, one of whom, George Douglas, featured as a violent henchman for Angus during his virtual imprisonment of young James V and another murdered Arran, the nemesis of Morton. Some ruins of a sixteenth-century two-storey bastle house or fortified farm were discovered during the excavations for the M74 in 1990. There is also a raised site of a structure known as the **Park of Douglas** where tradition said the Good Lord James was buried.

Parisholm is an even more obscure site, but seems to have been the ultimate hideaway of the Douglases, up near the source of the Douglas Water on Cairntable, which rises to over 1,900 feet, with two scheduled cairns (L4632). Archibald, Earl of Angus, boasted he could always escape capture by hiding in 'the skirts of Cairntable' where he would never be found. This small fort, the site of which is now on the edge of Muirkirk Country Park further to the west on the A70, had its own chapel at Andershaw between it and Douglas and the hill nearby is called Chapel Hill.

The original **St Bride's Church** (Historic Scotland L90265), Douglas, of which a few finely carved Norman stones survive, including one of a man with a fierce moustache, dated from the late twelfth century, when Brice Douglas was prior of Lesmahagow under the wing of Kelso Abbey. From an early stage, perhaps because of the dedication of this church, St Bride was regarded as the patron of the Douglases. In 1307 it was presumably in this church that the Good Lord James locked up and killed the English garrison of his castle on Palm Sunday. It was rebuilt again at the end of the fourteenth century, probably by Archibald the Grim, and by then had come under the control of Glasgow Cathedral. Only the elegant little choir of this building survives, though the large arch of the nave is still visible, plus its south aisle with a turret put up in the reign of Mary Queen of Scots. A monument on the north side of the choir is reputedly that of the Good Lord James, killed in Spain, though the canopy is fifteenth century, with its shield bearing the image of the Bloody Heart. His heart in a leaden casket was brought back here. Barbour mentions that Archibald the Grim:

> Of alabaster both far and fyne
> Ordered ane tomb full richly
> As it behufit to sae worthy . . .

To its east is the monument to Archibald, 5th Earl of Douglas, Count of Longueville, who fought in France and died of fever in 1439. His effigy

155

bears the ducal coronet of Touraine inherited from his father, the Tyneman. In the south wall is the monument of James the Gross, 7th Earl, who died in 1443, and his wife, Beatrix Sinclair – an unusual double effigy tomb which required the whole wall to be widened to accommodate it. Two small heart shapes set in the floor contain two of the famous Douglas hearts below an effigy of the Countess of Home. An early, damaged female effigy on the south-west wall may have been that of Marjory of Abernethy, wife of Hugh Douglas. The vanished Dickson Aisle commemorated Thomas Dickson, the retainer who died helping the Good Sir James.

The best-known priest to have charge of this church was George Douglas, the later postulate of Arbroath, murderer of Riccio and then first Protestant Bishop of Moray. He is alleged to have brought Lord Darnley and the Queen's secretary, Riccio, for a weekend of jollity at Douglas in 1564, and suggested to Darnley that they should tip Riccio into the loch while out in a boat fishing for pike. Darnley rejected the idea, but George Douglas was the first to stab Riccio when a few months later a plot was agreed to trap the Italian favourite in Holyrood.

In the village of Douglas north of the church stands the statue of James Douglas of Angus, the heir of the 2nd Marquess, who raised the Cameronian Regiment in 1689 but died in his first battle, aged twenty-one. Also nearby is the **Douglas Heritage Museum**, established in the former dower house of Douglas Castle. It contains a number of stained-glass windows transferred from the castle which commemorate various Douglas earls, as well as numerous other artefacts from the demolished castle. Next to the Sun Inn is the **Red Hall**, once lived in by a Fleming family who may have arrived at Douglas early as henchmen to the barons, whose ethnic origin they shared. The **monument to James Gavin** commemorates a tailor who had his ears cut off and was transported to Barbados in the purge of Covenanters which was led by Colonel James Douglas.

At the mouth of the Douglas Water, where it joins the Clyde, is **Crookboat**, site of a fourteenth-century church dedicated by the famous William Douglas of Liddesdale on a site of an earlier one founded by Hugh Douglas the Dull, son of William le Hardi. Once a small ferry took travellers across the river here.

Three little-known Douglas castles are in the area of Carnwath. **Westhall Tower**, 8 miles to the east, was a sixteenth-century L-plan tower owned by the Red Douglases; modest remains survive. **Dunsyre Castle**, 6 miles to the east, was Douglas from 1368 presumably until 1455, and again was part of the Bothwell package offered to the Red Douglas in exchange for Hermitage in 1492, but nothing remains above the surface. Other components of this package were Weston, 2 miles away, and

Dolphinton, east of Dunsyre, also now completely disappeared. Nor is there any sign of **Todholes Castle**, 4 miles east of Carnwath, another sixteenth-century Douglas tower house.

To the south was **Edmonston**, a fifteenth-century keep 4 miles north of Biggar, which had a longer Douglas ownership, from 1322 until 1650; it is substantially ruined but in private ownership, with a new house alongside. The original castle at **Kilbucho Place**, replaced by a seventeenth-century L-plan tower, 4 miles south-east of Biggar, was acquired through his marriage to a Graham by William Douglas of Liddesdale, Flower of Chivalry, at the same time as Hermitage in 1350, and remained Douglas probably until 1631, when it was rebuilt by the Stewarts. It is still habitable.

To the south are two castle sites which were Douglas for a relatively short period. **Crawford Castle** was an important one, built on an artificial mound once surrounded by water just north of the Clyde and east of the M74. Some walls survive to a reasonable height. The Lindsays of Crawford were partners with the Black Douglases in the pact which led to the disaster of 1455. Crawford then belonged to the Red Douglases from 1488 up to their forfeiture in 1528. James V is recorded as having spent the night here and made the daughter of the house pregnant.

Nothing survives of **Crawfordjohn Castle**, 3½ miles west of Abington, which was a Black Douglas stronghold from 1366 to the forfeiture of 1455. It was later occupied by the ubiquitous Hamilton of Finnart, who seems to have quarried the stones from it to make nearby Boghouse. To the south-west 3 miles away are the remote remains of **Snar Castle**, a sixteenth-century tower house used by a branch of the Douglas family who made their money out of mining lead and gold in the nearby **Leadhills**, where parts of the old lead mine by the B797 have been restored with a small museum. The conditions for miners were appalling.

NITHSDALE

> To thee lov'd Nith, thy gladsome plains,
> Where late wi' careless thought I rang'd,
> Though prest wi' care and sunk in woe,
> To thee I bring a heart unchanged.
>
> Robert Burns, 'To thee lov'd Nith'

Heading west from Crawfordjohn on the B740 we come to **Sanquhar Castle** near the upper reaches of the River Nith, which boast a string of Douglas castles from here southwards. The ruins of Sanquhar, standing by the Southern Upland Way, date from the thirteenth century and include a four-storey tower at the corner of a courtyard, the remains of a keep and a semicircular tower. This castle's early occupants were the Ross and Crichton families (one of whom was murdered by a Douglas), but it was bought by William Douglas of Drumlanrig, later 1st Earl of Queensberry, in 1639. His grandson the 1st Duke was born and died here, although he had by then built the huge new mansion of Drumlanrig, 7 miles to the south. Though he himself took an instant dislike to it after a single night there, his family moved out of Sanquhar after his death and it fell into ruins. Douglas of Fingland, the writer of 'Annie Laurie', was born here, and the properties of Fingland are nearby.

Coshogle Castle, of which there are no visible remains except the odd stone built into the nearby farm, was another seat of the Douglases of Drumlanrig, built in 1576 just north of Enterkinfoot. In 1621 it was the scene of a macabre fight between Douglas of Coshogle, who lost an ear ('his left lug', says the chronicler), and an adherent who lost his life, defending the castle against other Douglases. Nearby is an ancient chapel of **Kirkbride**, doubtless an extension from St Bride's in Douglas and patronised by the Douglases.

Cutting across from Enterkinfoot towards Durisdeer, we hit the A702 coming south from Elvanfoot running parallel to the old Roman road, later a toll road, connecting Nithsdale to Clydesdale by the Dalveen Pass. Guarding the pass at one time was **Dalveen Castle**, of which nothing visible remains, though it was rebuilt in 1622, as the farm at Nether Dalveen has a panel bearing that date built into its wall. This was a Douglas stronghold, and we know one of its owners, Hugh Douglas, was murdered by the Douglases of Drumlanrig in 1565. They made up for this by giving Hugh's son control of Mouswald Castle. Further up the road is another Fingland, of 'Annie Laurie' fame. Here the Southern Upland Way crosses both the ancient and modern roads on its route south from Wanlockhead. The walker can cut across here to the Daer Water, now partly dammed into a reservoir, further up which is **Kirkhope Tower**, of which minimal remains of a bastle or tower house survive beneath Watchman's Brae. This remote outpost was built by the Drumlanrig Douglases and later was the focus of the barony of Daer awarded by Charles I to the Douglas earls of Selkirk. Their most famous scion was Thomas Douglas, founder of several important settlements in Canada, including Selkirk, Daer and Winnipeg itself in Manitoba. To reach the road turning to the reservoir you need to do another 2½ miles further up the A702. Robert Burns met Lord Daer and, as he described in 'Lines on Meeting with Lord Daer', liked him:

Nae honest, worthy man need care
To meet wi' noble, youthful Daer
For he but meets a brother.

Returning to **Durisdeer**, a place of great strategic importance, as shown by the remains of a Roman fort, medieval motte and early Christian site, we find the now almost vanished castle, which was was held by the English in 1307, guarding their supply lines. It was recovered by Bruce but destroyed along with Morton Castle by David II as part of his ransom package for his release from English captivity. Rebuilt by the Menzies, it had several royal visits, but does not seem to have ever been occupied by the Douglases. In the small village James Douglas, 2nd Duke of Queensberry, built the church in the late seventeenth century, and adjoining it is the mausoleum containing a marble monument by Van Nost for the Union Duke and his Duchess who died in 1711 and 1709 respectively. One extra-long coffin is supposedly that of their mentally retarded eldest son, James Douglas of Drumlanrig, who cooked and ate one of the family's cook boys in their home on the Canongate.

Two miles further south is the site on a steep ravine by the Carron River of **Enoch Castle**, which was captured by William Wallace in 1296 and was also a Menzies stronghold, though bought by the Queensberry Douglases in 1703 and held by them until handed over to the Buccleuchs in 1810.

Drumlanrig Castle itself is about 2½ miles to the south-west on the west side of the River Nith. The original fourteenth-century castle was begun by the enterprising William Douglas of Drumlanrig, bastard son of James the hero of Otterburn, and a notable fighter himself. It was badly damaged by the English in 1547 after Pinkie and again in 1575 by the Regent Morton, their neighbour, as he did not like the way this branch of the family had switched sides to support the exiled Mary Queen of Scots, who had stayed here in 1563. It was rebuilt by 1617 when James VI stayed here and it was used as a base for Cromwellian troops during the Civil War. Meanwhile, the Drumlanrig Douglases won promotion, becoming Earls and then Dukes of Queensberry, taking their title from the hill which rises over 2,000 feet some 8 miles to the east. William Douglas, 3rd Earl and later 1st Duke, employed the architects James Smith and William Wallace to build a magnificent mansion round the castle in 1675. Charles McKean describes it as 'a resplendently harled renaissance palace . . . entrance facade in polished red ashlar . . . ogee-capped stair towers and ducal coronet above the baroque centre-piece'. It took fourteen years and most of his fortune to build, yet, as mentioned, he only spent one night in it and disliked it so much he went back to his old castle at

Sanquhar. The Union Duke, his successor, liked it better, though his life was made somewhat miserable by the fact that his wife took to the drink, his eldest son was a lunatic and two other sons died in the wars. During the life of the 3rd Duke the castle was occupied and seriously damaged by Bonnie Prince Charlie and his army of highlanders. This bad luck was later compounded by the suicide of his elder son on his honeymoon, a disaster attributed to the fact that the Duke had diverted the Marr Burn to make an ornamental fountain, an act which Thomas the Rhymer had prophesied would bring doom. It was this duke's wife, the famous Kitty Hyde, who had constructed the Duchess's Walk along the banks of the Nith, which at one dramatic point is known as the **Devil's Cauldron**.

Old Q, the reprobate 4th Duke and a distant cousin of his predecessor, is mainly remembered in this area for his savage cutting-down of beautiful woodlands. Robert Burns had little time for him and wrote:

> How shall I sing Drumlanrig's grace
> Discarded remnant of a race
>   Once great in martial story?
> His forbears' virtues all contrasted
> His very name of Douglas blasted –
>   His that inverted glory.

In 1810, since Old Q had no wife, legitimate children or surviving male relatives, the castle and the dukedom passed by marriage to the Scotts of Buccleuch, who refurbished the castle in 1827. It is now open to the public and houses a valuable collection of paintings.

Within the grounds of Drumlanrig are the scanty remains of **Tibbers Castle** (L711), which was a century older at least than Drumlanrig, having been captured by Edward I in 1298, recaptured by Wallace, retaken by the English again soon afterwards and by the Scots again in 1313. Like Drumlanrig it was burnt by the English invaders in 1547 and the Douglases took over its remains. It had a rampart and ditch with square walled courtyard, towers at each corner and a hall along one side.

A couple of miles south on the A76 and on its east side is **Morton Castle** (Historic Scotland L90221), just south of Morton Loch and a mile from the nearest road. Built on a strong site commanding the old road north from Dumfries, this castle went through a number of hands before coming to Sir William Douglas of Liddesdale in 1342 from the Good Lord James's priestly brother Hugh the Dull. Thus it came to the Dalkeith or Lothian branch of the Douglas family, and James Douglas of Dalkeith was probably the man who had it rebuilt in the 1440s. Reputedly owing to a legal technicality it was a different Morton, near Calder, which was the official source for the family's new title as Earls of Morton, though this one was an important seat and was held by the family until 1715. It has a ruined fifteenth-century keep, triangular courtyard and two-storey hall house, one tower still standing to four storeys. As an unnamed local poet put it:

> Timeless no more hath vandal hand marred thee
> There's beauty yet in thy tranquility.

Morton Church has the gravestones of a number of Douglases.

To the west and south of Thornhill are two more castles in this cluster. **Killiewarren**, 5 miles to the west, is a seventeenth-century tower house built in 1617 and now converted into a whitewashed farmhouse. To the south **Barjarg Tower** is a sixteenth-century L-plan tower house, now incorporated in a nineteenth-century mansion. It seems to have been one of Regent Morton's properties and was lost to the family with his disgrace in 1581. Further to the east on the slopes of Queensberry itself is the remote Drumlanrig outpost of **Locharben**. Little but the name remains of the monastic hospital founded at **Holywood** by Sir Robert Bruce, the king's bastard son, who was killed at Halidon Hill in 1333, but the Douglases maintained it later.

Ten miles further down the Nith valley on the outskirts of Dumfries is **Lincluden Collegiate Church** (L90200), founded on the ruins of a Benedictine nunnery by Archibald the Grim, 3rd Earl of Douglas, who rightly or wrongly accused the nuns of 'insolence' to justify disbanding them, but seems to have benefited himself somewhat from the changeover. Situated where the Cluden Water flows into the Nith, it had a keep and a hall above cellars and stood on raised ground so that it doubled up as an additional residence and meeting place for the Earls of Douglas when they were conducting business as Wardens of the Western March. Robert Burns had a farm here for some years and is believed to have composed 'Tam o' Shanter' while walking up and down the banks of the Cluden. His 'Ca' the Yowes' was certainly written here:

> Yonder Cluden's silent towers,
> Where at moonshine's midnight hours,
> O'er the dewy bending flowers,
> Fairies dance sae cheery.

In 1469 William Douglas, on behalf of his ward, the 5th Earl of Angus, had a parliament here of border lairds to settle on new rules for border warfare. It was ruled by provosts, many of whom went on to become bishops, though the last one, Robert Douglas, held on after the Reformation to turn the church into a private estate for himself. Traces of Norman masonry from the first church have survived. The choir is beautifully carved in the local red stone and reasonably well preserved, with musical angels carved on the corbels of the vaulting shafts. The groined vaulting has been compared with that of King's College Chapel, Cambridge, though it also has similarities with St Mirren's Aisle in Paisley Abbey and with Archibald's other foundation at Bothwell. A richly ornamented monument in the north wall commemorates Margaret, daughter of King Robert III, and widow of Archibald Douglas, 4th Black Douglas Earl, who was killed fighting the English in France. It combines the heart symbolism of the Douglases and the chequered napkin of the Royal Stewarts. The sacristy door bears the arms of Archibald the Grim and his wife, the heraldic decorations on the shaft caps carrying the bloody heart and other Douglas motifs. The last word goes to Burns in 'A Vision':

> As I stood by yon roofless tower
> Where wa'flower scents the dewy air
> Where the howlet lines her ivy bower
> And tells the midnight moon her care.

About 6 miles to the south-east are the scant ruins of one wall of **Mouswald Tower**, a sixteenth-century tower house which was acquired by the Douglases of Drumlanrig by trickery and intimidation. Its two orphaned heiresses were wards of Drumlanrig and both were forced to marry Drumlanrig bridegrooms. One of them, Marion Carruthers, jumped off the battlements of nearby **Comlongon Castle** (L688) to avoid such a marriage and is said to have haunted the place ever since. James Douglas of Mouswald later killed another of the luckless Carruthers 'with schotis and hagbutis' (shot and arquebus). Mouswald churchyard has a number of memorials to these families.

Caerlaverock Castle (Historic Scotland L90046), 6 miles to the south-west, is one of the most beautiful and dramatic castles surviving in Scotland. It was never a Douglas property but the family were regularly involved in several sieges which the Scots had to undertake to recover it from the English. Duke Murdoch Stewart of Albany was imprisoned here in the tower named after him before his execution by James I in 1425. It had a crucial position guarding the Nith estuary. Its main owners were the Maxwells, originally supporters, then rivals, of the Douglases in this area; they later moved to Terregles, which had also earlier been a Black Douglas estate.

Sweetheart Abbey (Historic Scotland L90293) stands directly opposite Caerlaverock on the other side of the Nith estuary and is one of the finest examples of Scottish Gothic architecture. Founded by Devorguilla, the mother of King John Balliol, it was managed by the Cistercian order and dedicated to her husband, who died in 1269. She was eventually buried with him in front of the high altar when she died twenty years later, aged seventy-six. This wealthy lady also founded Balliol College, Oxford, and built the old bridge over the Nith at Dumfries, some lower parts of which survive. Archibald Douglas, the 4th Earl, was a prominent patron and protector of this and other border abbeys.

High above the abbey on the summit of Criffel at nearly 1,900 feet is a large cairn known as the **Douglas Cairn**. It was probably a Bronze Age cairn reused as the site of a bale fire or signalling station to warn the Douglases of any English attack across the Solway. Near here on the A701 beyond Kirkbean (birthplace of Admiral John Paul Jones) was the once prominent royal burgh of **Preston** with its market cross and an early base of the Black Douglases. Preston Castle was held by James the Gross, 7th Earl of Douglas. **Wreath's Tower**, a couple of miles south of here before Southerness, is a very much ruined sixteenth century tower house which belonged to James Douglas, the Regent Morton, until his execution and forfeiture in 1581.

GALLOWAY

Buittle Castle (L1115), just north of Dalbeattie by the Water of Urr, is an important site of great antiquity. The castle built here by John Balliol senior, father of the king and husband of Devorguilla, is sadly ruined and overgrown, though one arch at least survives. Here the future King of Scotland was born in 1250. He took over as Lord of Galloway and of large tracts in northern England in 1269, and for a very short time nearly thirty years later became king because Edward I thought he would do as he was told. The castle was captured by the English in 1297 and retaken by the Scots in 1313. They rendered it completely defenceless in case it was recaptured by the English. Since the Balliols had banished themselves to France, it was given by Robert the Bruce in 1325 to Lord James Douglas, but after his death and the disaster of Halidon Hill, Edward Balliol came back to reclaim it (and the kingdom of Scotland) for himself, with English help. He held on to it until ejected by William Douglas of Liddesdale, the Flower of Chivalry, in 1348. A century later it passed to the Douglases of Dalkeith, who held it probably until Morton's fall in 1581.

Buittle was a substantial courtyard castle with ditch and drawbridge. Excavation has shown that there had been timber towers and a palisade burnt down, perhaps in 1313, when the Scots wanted to render it useless. Nearby is **Buittle Place**, a sixteenth-century L-plan tower house made with stone quarried from the older castle. It has been refurbished and is in private ownership. The **Church of St Colmanel** at Buittle (L1108) was restored by Archibald the Grim and was granted to Sweetheart Abbey. It is now an ivy-covered ruin.

To the south of Dalbeattie is the small offshore island of **Hestan** with a small ruined castle burnt by Edward Bruce and which Edward Balliol used as a safe refuge in the 1340s. It was later given to Dundrennan Abbey.

The small town of **Castle Douglas**, previously Carlingwark, was given its name in relatively recent times by William Douglas of Gelston, a former pedlar who made a fortune out of tobacco in the late eighteenth century and bought the village in 1789 to build mills here.

Threave Castle (Historic Scotland L90301) is 1½ miles west of Castle Douglas and set on a 16-acre island in the River Dee. There was an earlier castle here destroyed by Edward Bruce in 1308 but the present one was built by Archibald the Grim in the 1370s as the headquarters for his lordship of Galloway, a position he acquired in 1369 after clearing the area of English supporters. According to legend, it was built overnight with an army of stone-handlers stretched in a lengthy queue, and certainly the huge tower with walls 8 feet thick is constructed with vast numbers of small slatey stones. In its time it was revolutionary in design, with a very strong five- or six-storey keep surrounded by an outer four-towered curtain wall and moat – as well, of course, as by the river, which in spate is quite deep. The entrance to the keep was at the first- and second-floor levels, with a two-tier bridge leading to it from the impressive gatehouse. Beneath this floor were the kitchens and beneath them again the castle's well and a pit prison reached by a trapdoor. The gatehouse also had its famous gibbet stone, which was rarely 'without its tassle'.

Archibald the Grim died here in 1400 and forty years later his two great-grandsons set out from here on their way to be murdered at the Black Dinner in Edinburgh Castle. It was used frequently by the two brothers, the 8th and 9th Earls of Douglas, as an important base from which to overawe their neighbouring lairds. It was their execution of Herries of Terregles and the unfortunate McLellan of Bombie, who was beheaded here in 1451, which in some respects precipitated the final crisis for the Black Douglases.

After the defeat of the Douglases at Arkinholm in 1455 and the exile of the last earl, Threave was besieged by James II, who based himself for the period at **Tongland Abbey** (only an arch of which survives) on the Dee.

A variety of legends surround the artillery used for his attack, including the tale that the great cannon Mons Meg might have been transported here from Edinburgh or, improbably, that the huge gun was made by a local blacksmith who noticed that the king needed something big to knock down such huge walls. The story of granite cannon balls made from local stone is more credible, as some were found in an early excavation. There is also the story of the Fair Maid of Galloway, wife of both the last two Douglas earls, losing her hand as the second ball came through the wall, backed up by the supposed finding of a ring with her initials in the castle well by one of Sir Walter Scott's researchers. Another version of the siege story suggests the defenders were persuaded to give up by an offer of cash from James II. After this the castle became a royal fortress, though it was captured by the English after their victory at Solway Moss in 1542. Its final use was as a prison for French soldiers during the Napoleonic Wars. Visitors are now ferried across to it in a small boat.

To the north on Loch Ken is an island known as **Brent** or **Burnt Island**, which had an older castle used by Archibald the Grim while he was building Threave. **Kirkcudbright Castle** (L2459) stood to the west of the town on the east bank of the River Dee at Castledykes, but nothing is visible except the defensive ditch. This was an early fortress of the Lords of Galloway which passed to the Balliols when they married into the lordship in 1260 and was captured and held by the English from 1300 to 1309. Then, like other Balliol properties, it passed to the Black Douglases, who held it until their fall in 1455. After that it was royal property, and the fugitive King Henry VI of England sheltered here during the Wars of the Roses in 1461.

Bombie Castle was a large moated castle about 1½ miles east of Kirkcudbright. Nothing much remains and the castle is famous in our context only because of the provocative execution of its master Sir Patrick McLellan of Bombie by the Douglases at Threave in 1451, just because he had tried to resist their authority. Hence the help given by the McLellans to the King when he besieged Threave in 1455. In the sixteenth century the family acquired a new site from the former Franciscan monastery in the town and built **McLellan's Castle**, a more modern tower house.

St Mary's Isle, south of the town, was the early home of Thomas Douglas, later Earl of Selkirk and pioneer of Manitoba, Canada. It was raided in his father's absence by an American naval party under John Paul Jones, who had been born nearby and perhaps believed that if he captured Thomas's father it would help the independence negotiations. He was not at home and when the admiral heard his sailors had removed the family jewels he had them returned. This was the time when he made his daring raid on Whitehaven. It was in this house that Robert Burns first spoke the famous Selkirk Grace in honour of his host.

Dundrennan Abbey (L90014), some 4 miles east of the town, was another foundation of David I and Fergus, Lord of Galloway, completed originally about 1180. Later it was given protection by the Black Douglases, doubtless at a price, and there is a monument to Sir Patrick Douglas who was cellarer here in 1480. Mary Queen of Scots spent her last night in Scotland here before embarking from nearby St Mary's port to cross over to exile in England.

Forty or so miles to the west off the A75 we come to the site of **Wigtown Castle**. This was a large, round thirteenth-century castle at the mouth of the River Bladnoch of which little survives but its moat, which was originally kept filled by the incoming tide. It was probably built for King Alexander III in the 1280s, captured by the English in the 1290s, retaken by Wallace in 1297, taken back by the English in 1298 and retaken by Bruce again around 1310, when it was dismantled to prevent its use by the enemy. It was later rebuilt by Archibald the Grim when he was forging his lordship of Galloway, driving out the English and intimidating former supporters of the Balliols in the 1370s. It remained with the Black Douglases until their fall in 1455, and the eldest sons of the earls used the title Earl of Wigtown until they took over the main earldom of Douglas from their fathers.

To the north of here lie two battle sites where in 1307 Bruce and the Good Lord James shared victories over the English: the first, **Glen Trool** (Forest Enterprise), where they defeated the Earl of Pembroke, and Clifford, the man who had been given the barony of Douglas over James's head by Edward I, is marked by a stone in the Forest Park; the Southern Upland Way passes nearby. Also here is one of the **Martyrs' Tombs**, commemorating the killing in 1685 of six Covenanters at prayer by a party under Colonel James Douglas, the brother of the Duke of Queensberry who executed numerous Covenanters without proper trial. The stone was reputedly repaired by the mason who inspired Sir Walter Scott's novel *Old Mortality*.

The other battle was **Raploch Moss**, now marked by Bruce's Stone at Clatteringshaws (National Trust for Scotland). It took place after Bruce had been trailed using one of his own captured dogs by John of Lorne, the victor over him at Dalry the year before. The legend went that Bruce had his morale restored and his hunger assuaged by an old woman whom he later rewarded and after whom the spot was renamed Craigenlachie, Crag of the Old Woman. It is close to the A712 and the Southern Upland Way. This is also the landscape made famous by John Buchan in his *Thirty-Nine Steps*.

A couple of miles south of Wigtown are a few remains of **Baldoon Castle**, which had an association with Thomas Douglas, Earl of Selkirk, who named one of his Canadian settlements after it. It is also famous as the home of the tragic Jane Dalrymple, who inspired the story of the *Bride of Lammermoor* by Sir Walter Scott, later turned into an opera by Donizetti.

Seven miles to the south of Wigtown off the B7004, **Cruggleton Castle** (L3811) stood on a cliff to the south of Garlieston on Wigtown Bay. Preceded by an Iron Age fort, it was a thirteenth-century courtyard castle built by the Lords of Galloway, with fifteenth- and sixteenth-century additions. Like Wigtown, it was captured by the English, then retaken by Wallace, and as it was then owned by Bruce's great rivals the Comyns, it was destroyed by Edward Bruce in about 1310. Like Wigtown, it was taken over by Archibald the Grim in about 1370 and he built a new keep, but it was destroyed by James II along with several other Black Douglas castles in 1455. It then went through a chequered history with various other families until being abandoned for good in the seventeenth century. A ballad by Andrew Glass recalls some forgotten romance here:

> Cruggleton beneath thy archway
> Leaning o'er the restless sea
> Have I sat beside a maiden
> Fairer, dearer far to me
> Than the azure of the ocean
> Than ambition fame or glory
> Or ancestral pedigree.

Cruggleton Church (L2006) on the B7063 is a delightful twelfth-century church, the key of which is kept in a nearby farm. It has a fine Norman chancel arch.

At Whithorn a further 3 miles to the south, the famous **Priory of St Ninian** (L3851) is relevant in our story as the burial place of Archibald, 'Bell-the-Cat', most famous of the Red Douglases, who died here pursuing his duty as a March Earl. In 1885 a particularly large skeleton was unearthed here and has been attributed to the mighty Angus.

The original **Lochnaw Castle** was on an island in the loch 5 miles from Stranraer and was an Agnew stronghold destroyed by Archibald the Grim as he brought the whole of Galloway under Black Douglas control in the 1360s.

We now have to backtrack to Dumfries, passing the site of **Greyfriars** in the town, where Robert the Bruce murdered the Red Comyn in 1306. Four miles beyond the town on the A709 is **Torthorwald Castle** (L713), which has an ancient history, though it did not pass to the Douglases until the 1570s, when the Regent Morton procured it for one of his bastard sons, who was later made Lord Torthorwald by James VI. It has a ruined fourteenth-century keep with its entrance at first-floor level and stands on a motte surrounded by a ditch. The bastard was succeeded by a daughter who kept it in the family by marrying one of the Douglases of Parkhead.

ANNANDALE

A further 4 miles up this road is **Lochmaben Castle** (Historic Scotland L90205), one of the largest castles of the Bruce family before they became kings, and a possible birthplace for Robert the Bruce (the other claimant of this honour is Turnberry Castle in Ayrshire). Annandale was the original patrimony of the Bruce family when they first migrated to Scotland from Yorkshire, but sadly little of this heritage remains. Of the original thirteenth-century Lochmaben Castle which stood between Kirk Loch and Castle Loch, only the motte is now visible. The English captured it in 1298 and Edward I decided to build a replacement castle in a more secure position south of the Castle Loch. It was about this time that Robert the Bruce, still then on the English side, captured William le Hardi Douglas's wife and brought her here. Later the new castle was besieged three times by Bruce: in 1299, 1301 and finally in 1306, when he captured it but lost it again to the English until 1314. Almost twenty years later, after Bruce's death, the Scots were weakened by the defeat of the Guardian Archibald Douglas at Halidon Hill, so Lochmaben fell yet again to the English and Edward Balliol. This time it remained in English hands for fifty years. In 1384 Archibald the Grim at last recaptured it and it came under Douglas control, with Maxwells as hereditary keepers until the disgrace of the last Black Douglas earl in 1455.

Ironically, it was here that the last earl, James Douglas, made his disastrous attempted comeback in 1483 with the help of an English army and the Stewart Duke of Albany. It failed and he was captured to end his life as a prisoner at Lindores. Douglas of Drumlanrig was one of the few casualties on the Scottish government side. Mary Queen of Scots and Darnley stayed here in 1565, but the castle was abandoned forty years later. The ruined keep is from the fifteenth century and had a strong, much older curtain wall surrounded by a moat.

Annan itself was the first place where the Bruces established their presence in Scotland in 1142 with a motte and bailey castle (L702), probably of timber, as was the custom of migrating Norman knights. The castle was rebuilt in stone and captured several times by the English.

It was also the scene of the night attack by Sir Archibald Douglas, the Guardian, in 1333, when he came close to capturing Edward Balliol by surprise and sent him scurrying south in his nightclothes. However, it was a short-lived success, as Douglas was soundly beaten and killed by the English at Halidon Hill soon afterwards. The castle was abandoned in the 1570s and has now completely disappeared.

One of the more eccentric ladies of the Douglas family was Lady Margaret, who married a man called Jardine in the 1650s. She always went around in rags and stood by the River Annan, offering to carry anyone across for a penny.

Kelhead, a few miles further on, produced the branch of the Douglases who succeeded to half the Queensberry inheritance on the death of childless Old Q. They became Marquesses of Queensberry and produced among others Lord Alfred Douglas, the poet friend who caused the downfall of Oscar Wilde.

We now head east again to Gretna, near which is **Lochmabenstane**, site of the victory by the River Sark achieved by Hugh Douglas, Earl of Ormond, along with the Red Douglas Earl of Angus over the English under Percy in 1449. It is not far from the site of the humiliating defeat of the Scottish army sent by James V to meet the English at **Solway Moss**. It was the news of this defeat which seems to have thrust the King over the edge into terminal depression.

To the south is **Carlisle**, where Bruce and Lord James Douglas conducted an unsuccessful but morale-boosting siege in 1314.

Turning north onto the M74, we can now take in three castles in the Moffat area which all had Douglas connections. It was just north of here, at **Ericstane** by the Devil's Beef Tub near the source of the Annan, that the Good Lord James first met Robert the Bruce and offered his services.

Blacklaw Tower, 2 miles north of Moffat and on the east side of the motorway, was a sixteenth-century tower house held at one time by the Douglases of Fingland (of 'Annie Laurie' fame). Only the basement survives.

Auchen Castle, 2 miles to the south on the west side of the motorway, was a thirteenth-century castle of enclosure built by Thomas Randolph and later held by the Douglases of Morton. There is a newer Auchen Castle nearby which is used as a hotel.

Cornal Tower, south-east of Moffat by the Moffat Water and in woods just off the Southern Upland Way, was a sixteenth-century tower house of which there are scant remains. It belonged to the luckless Carruthers girls of Mouswald, who, as we have seen, were driven into loveless marriages by their unscrupulous guardian, Douglas of Drumlanrig. In due course this tower too became part of the Drumlanrig empire.

YARROW

We now head north-east up the A708 into Yarrow, past Polmoodie and Polboothy, parts of the ancient Douglas barony, and the Grey Mare's Tail, a majestic waterfall in the care of the National Trust, then St Mary's Loch. Beside the loch under **Capper Law** is the ruined chapel and graveyard of St Mary, where are buried according to tradition the victims sung of in the 'Douglas Tragedy', a ballad (not to be confused with the play by Home, which was performed in Edinburgh in 1756). The ballad refers to the sad love story of Lady Margaret Douglas:

> Lord William was buried in Saint Mary's Kirk
> Lady Margret in Mary's quire
> Out of the lady's grave grew a bonny red rose
> And out of the knight's a briar.

Just over a mile to the east, past the loch, we come to **Craig Douglas**, site of one of the favourite castles of the Good Lord James and a hiding place in the ancient hunting forest of Ettrick during the years of border warfare. Nothing now remains, as this was one of the castles attacked and destroyed by James II in 1450 while the penultimate Black Douglas earl, William, was visiting the Pope in Rome, just two years before he was murdered by the King at Stirling.

Two miles north up a farm road from Craig Douglas, or slightly longer up the Southern Upland Way from Dryhope, are the ruins of **Blackhouse Tower**, supposed site of the Douglas Tragedy; the present ruin is of a sixteenth-century tower house which had a round stair tower. Coincidentally it stands beside a burn called the Douglas, which flows from the Blackhouse heights. Here, according to the ballad, Lord William wooed Margaret, daughter of the Lord Douglas, and here he killed her seven brothers and father before dying himself and leaving his bride to die of grief:

> Lord William was dead lang ere midnight
> Lady Margret lang ere day
> And all true lovers that gang thegither
> May have mair luck than they.

The fight took place according to tradition on Bught Rig a mile to the north through the woods, where seven stones at Rispdyke still mark the spot. Remarkably also the well-known eighteenth-century poet James Hogg, author of *Confessions of a Justified Sinner*, worked here as a shepherd for ten years.

At **Williamhope**, then called Galsewood, on Minchmuir by an ancient drove road in the Ettrick Forest, William Douglas, known as the Flower of Chivalry, was ambushed and killed by his godson William, Lord of Douglas, and William's Cross was put up to mark the spot, near where the Southern Upland Way heads from Traquair to Hare Law. This old drove road was used by Edward I when he invaded Scotland and is featured in Sir Walter Scott's 'Two Drovers'. It was a regular haunt of bandits, and the **Cheese Well** was an offering point for wary travellers to leave titbits to appease bad fairies and robbers.

A further 10 miles down the Yarrow and we come to Bowhill, now a Buccleuch estate, in which are the remnants of several Douglas castles. Along this stretch are **Tinnis** and **Erncleugh**, two other popular meeting places for Douglas troops heading south on expeditions over the border. The best preserved of the castles is **Newark** (L1729), a ruined five-storey keep from the fifteenth century standing on a high bank above the Yarrow. It was built about 1423 by Archibald, 4th Earl of Douglas, and held by the Black Douglases until their fall in 1455, when it became a royal hunting lodge, used by Margaret of Denmark, wife of James III, hence the royal arms carved on the west wall. The courtyard of the castle was the scene of the massacre of Highland and Irish troops, plus their female camp-followers, who had been captured by the Parliamentary, Presbyterian forces at the nearby battle of **Philiphaugh** in 1646. Their ghosts are said to haunt the area. A Douglas cavalry contingent under the Marquess of Douglas took part in this battle, fighting for Montrose and the Royalist side alongside the Highlanders, but when they saw the first signs of impending defeat they beat a retreat and suffered few casualties. Wordsworth visited Newark and in 'Yarrow Revisited' wrote

> Flow on for ever, Yarrow stream!
> Fulfil thy pensive duty

and Walter Scott set his *Lay of the Last Minstrel* here:

> He passed where Newark's stately tower
> Looks out from Yarrow's birchen bower.

Newark replaced an **Auldwark** slightly to the east, and this may have been the Douglas stronghold referred to in chronicles as Eddybredshiels or Etybredscheles, but the precise site is hard to find. Pont's map of 1608 has it half a mile east of Newark, but another tradition placed it on the Newark burn.

In Selkirk itself are the ruins of the **Kirk o' the Forest**, where William Wallace is supposed to have been declared Guardian of Scotland.

ESKDALE

Now as part of our ongoing zigzag to take in the spread of sites in this area we head south again on an inevitable diversion past Hawick (to which we shall return) down the A7 towards the Debatable Lands and Langholm. **Langholm Tower**, yet another ruined sixteenth-century tower house, had belonged to the infamous Armstrong border reivers and was acquired by the Douglases of Drumlanrig about 1550. It was abandoned in 1725. Nearby is **Arkinholm**, now part of Langholm, site of the famous battle fought and lost by the three Black Douglas brothers in 1455, three years after the murder of their eldest brother by James II. Archibald, Earl of Moray, was killed; Hugh, Earl of Ormond, was captured and executed; while John, Lord of Balvenie, escaped only to be captured and executed a year later. James, the last Black Douglas earl, was not present, as he had already escaped to England, and it was nearly thirty years before he attempted to return.

Stabilgordon in Eskdale was one of the estates given by Bruce to the Good Lord James in the 1320s, as was **Westerkirk** or Watskirker, also on the Esk.

LIDDESDALE

Cutting over by a side road from Langholm to Newcastleton, we can now head north again on the B6357 and B6399 up Liddesdale to **Hermitage Castle** (Historic Scotland L90161), one of the most dramatic and furthest south of the castles associated with the Douglases in the Borders. Earlier it had belonged to the De Soulis, yet another Norman family which had pretensions to the Crown of Scotland in the Balliol period. As opponents of Bruce they had been expelled and the castle given to his bastard son, Sir Robert Bruce, who was killed at Halidon Hill in 1333, after which it was captured by the English. Liddesdale then became the springboard for the rise to fame of William Douglas of Lothian, later known as the Knight of Liddesdale and the Flower of Chivalry. Using the tactics of the Good Lord James of quick raids and ambushes against the English, followed by rapid retreat into the depths of the forest, he made life unbearable for the occupying army until he at last got the opportunity to seize the huge castle of Hermitage itself. There is some doubt as to how he legalized his ownership; possibly his marriage to a Graham heiress helped his case. The Steward seems to have staked a claim, but William Douglas had done the work of clearing the area of English and in due course in 1352 David II recognized this by giving him the official title. Meanwhile, William had pursued an erratic career carving out his own new patrimony and doing good service for David II, particularly with his spectacular capture of Edinburgh Castle. He was not content, however, and became jealous, it seems, of his neighbour Sir Alexander Ramsay, who had captured Roxburgh Castle just as spectacularly and been appointed its justice. William kidnapped Ramsay while at church in Hawick and reputedly starved him to death in the dungeons of Hermitage. Ironically, he was captured himself soon afterwards, along with King David, at the disastrous battle of Neville's Cross and was locked up in his own dungeons until he promised to support the English cause. He was released but by this time his reputation was tarnished, and he was murdered a few years later by his godson while hunting in the Ettrick Forest at Minchmuir.

The original castle was put up by the Dacres and De Soulis and was a key fortress of the middle march. The thirteenth-century courtyard and huge fourteenth-century keep had towers added at the corners, probably by the 1st or 2nd Black Earls before Otterburn, and the overall impression is of brooding grimness. After the 2nd Earl's death at Otterburn it was held for the Red Douglases by Douglas of Cavers, and by the end of the fifteenth century had been handed over at the King's request to the Bothwell family in exchange for Bothwell and a group of Lanarkshire castles, a move intended to reduce Red Douglas dominance in the Borders. By this time the castle was not without its comforts. As Charles McKean puts it, there was 'an English-seeming manor house immured within the castle'. Two hundred yards away are the remains of a medieval **Church of the Virgin Mary** associated with the castle, presumably on the site of the original hermitage which gave the castle its name and had been started by a hermit from Kelso called William. Near here James V hanged a large number of Armstrong border raiders.

TEVIOTDALE

We now head back up to Hawick and **Drumlanrig's Tower**. This property was acquired by the first William Douglas of Drumlanrig, the daring and able bastard of the hero of Otterburn. It was an L-shape sixteenth-century tower house which originally had a moat. It survived the burning of the rest of Hawick by the English in 1570 and has since done service as a prison, an inn, a hotel and a visitor centre. Also in Hawick was the church where William Douglas of Liddesdale kidnapped the luckless Sir Alexander Ramsay before shutting him up in Hermitage Castle.

The remains of **Cavers House** stand about 2 miles east of Hawick. This site belonged to the Balliols in the thirteenth century but came into the hands of the Black Douglases about 1350 or earlier and was rebuilt by Sir Archibald Douglas, another of the bastard sons of the hero of Otterburn, brother, therefore, of his neighbour at Drumlanrig's Tower. It was burnt three times by the English, in 1523, 1542 and 1545, and its owners figured prominently in local affairs, often as justices. They tended towards the Covenanting end of the religious spectrum and, unlike most Douglases, fought against Montrose during the Civil War, resulting in many of the family being killed, particularly at Auldearn in 1645. There was the story of Lady Douglas, known as 'the gude leddie of Cavers', who refused to hand over the keys of the church to a High Church curate sent down to take it over in 1682 and encouraged the villagers to stone him instead. She was put in prison. The house remained in Douglas hands until 1878 and was finally abandoned in the 1950s. It produced two distinguished naval commanders, including Sir Charles Douglas, the admiral who saved Quebec.

Denholm, a further 3 miles away from Hawick, was the site of another Douglas sixteenth-century tower house south of the Teviot; it was destroyed by the English in 1545, like so many properties in this region, during the Rough Wooing, when the English sought to enforce a marriage between Mary Queen of Scots and Edward VI.

Two miles beyond Denholm we come to the minimal ruins of **Bedrule Castle** by the Rule Water. In the pre-Bannockburn period this was a strong Comyn castle of enclosure with five round towers and a gatehouse. It was handed over to Edward I in 1298, but after Bannockburn was one of the early properties awarded to the Good Lord James in the 1320s. After the fall of the Black Douglases it fell into the hands of the Turnbulls, who became notorious border brigands, 200 of whom James IV had rounded up for hanging in 1494.

Grey Peel is the site of another now vanished Douglas tower house just 2 miles short of Jedburgh, near Langlee.

Jedburgh lies on a main route up from England by the pass over the Cheviots at Carter Bar. To the south of the pass is the site of the **battle of Otterburn** in 1388, perhaps the most famous though probably not the most important border victory achieved by the Douglases. Beyond that are a number of other battle sites associated with raids southwards undertaken by the Good Lord James. These include **Myton-on-Swale**, near Boroughbridge, where he beat the Archbishop of Durham and his force in 1319, **Byland**, near **Rievaulx**, where he secured the vital pass for Bruce, and **Stanhope** or Haydon Bridge, near Hexham in Weardale, where he did his famous tent-cutting stunt in 1327 against young Edward III.

Jedburgh, commanding the central road northwards, was therefore one of the most fought-over towns in the Borders, being burnt in 1410, 1416, 1464, 1523 and 1544, as well as being captured and damaged several other times. Of the once important castle nothing remains, yet Malcolm IV died here, King Alexander III was married here – accompanied by a ghost which correctly foretold his early death – and the Good Lord James was given it by Bruce in 1324. The site is now mainly occupied by a nineteenth-century gaol, which has been converted into a museum.

One tower house does survive in Jedburgh, known as **Queen Mary's House**, as she stayed here recuperating from the nasty fever after her famous ride from Hermitage Castle, visiting the wounded Earl of Bothwell in 1566. It is now a museum.

Most impressive of all are the majestic ruins of **Jedburgh Abbey** (Historic Scotland L9001175), founded by David I for the Augustinian canons in 1138, with its arcade carried on high cylindrical piers. The design is similar to Romsey Nunnery, where King David's sister Matilda stayed.

Near Jedburgh there stands what is left of the ancient **Capon Tree**, its trunk 26 feet in circumference, survivor of the medieval forest which was such an excellent base for the cross-border raids of the Douglases:

> Old Capon Tree, cold Apon tree
> Thou student telling of the past,
> Old Jedworth's forest wild and free
> Thou art alone forsaken last.

To the north of Jedburgh are two Douglas tower houses. **Timpendean Tower** (L1719) is a ruined four-storey tower of the sixteenth century and was occupied by the Douglases for a considerable period. **Lanton Tower** was similar but has been incorporated into a more modern mansion and did not become Douglas property until 1687, when it was bought by the Cavers branch.

Lintalee (L2890) or Lynton-le was one of the Good Lord James's earliest properties and a base for many of his sorties into England via Carter Bar and Redesdale. We know that it was built by him as a 'fair manner' on a steep promontory above the Lintalee Burn, by the Jed Water, and was surrounded by parts of the Jed Forest. It was the scene in 1316 of a memorable English counter-attack against Douglas by the Earl of Arundel, which Douglas as usual outsmarted. Here Douglas could draw on the fighting skills and toughness of the local Jedart men with their heavy axes and long pikes. Later Lintalee was held for the Red Douglases by Kerr of Cessford, and a modern mansion was built beside it.

Nearby, 7 miles south of Jedburgh on the A68, was **Southdean** or Zedan Church, frequently chosen as a rendezvous for departing Scottish armies on their way south. The remains were excavated in 1910 and turned into a memorial to those who died at Otterburn.

TWEEDDALE

Kelso Abbey (Historic Scotland L900177) was founded by David I in 1128 close to the large royal castle of Roxburgh (L1718), which was expected to give protection as the foundation's previous location at Selkirk had proved unsafe. Not surprisingly, it became the richest and most powerful abbey in Scotland, and it was the abbot here who first employed the Freskins, so they took their new name of Douglas as protectors of the abbey's annexe at Lesmahagow. It belonged to the Tironensian branch of the Benedictine order which David I was the first to introduce anywhere in the British Isles. The abbey was severely damaged during the Bruce period and was burnt after the battle of Halidon Hill, in 1333. It was rebuilt during the reign of David II. Then after the battle of Flodden in 1513 it came into the hands of the Kerr family, who in due course became Dukes of Roxburgh. In 1545, when it was attacked by the English under Hertford, as part of the general destruction during the Rough Wooing, the monks barricaded themselves in the tower: when it was at last captured all were executed. In total Hertford, driven by hatred of Catholicism as well as of the Scots, destroyed 7 monasteries, 16 towers, 5 towns, 243 villages, 13 mills and 3 hospitals.

The **Butts of Kelso** mark an area set aside for archery practice, an important contributor to success in medieval border warfare.

Roxburgh Castle, a mile from Kelso, was once one of the four chief castles of royal Scotland, along with Edinburgh, Stirling and Berwick, but it was too close to the border to be easily held. It was handed over to the English as part of the price for releasing William the Lion from captivity in 1174 and was captured again by Edward I, who ordered Robert the Bruce's sister Mary to be suspended from its walls in a cage in 1306 as part of his intimidation strategy against the Scots. It was dramatically captured by the Good Lord James in 1314 with his men pretending to be cattle, retaken by the English after Halidon Hill, then again dramatically recaptured by Sir Alexander Ramsay, to the annoyance of his rival William Douglas of Liddesdale, who murdered him partly out of pique at his success. The castle was lost again and stayed in English hands until

1460, when it was retaken by the Scots for the last time and demolished. This was the siege that cost the life of James II because of an exploding cannon – the place is supposedly marked by a holly tree between the Tweed and **Floors Castle** – and where the Red Douglas Earl of Angus was badly wounded. Floors is the stately home of the Dukes of Roxburgh.

Ancrum, north of Jedburgh, was the site of a victory by a Scottish army under the 6th Red Douglas Earl over the English in 1545. The Scots were spurred on by a rumour, true or false, that the English had burnt a local woman to death. The best-known other combatant was a girl called Lilliard from Teviotdale who wanted to avenge the death of her lover, and according to legend carried on fighting even after she had lost both her legs:

> Fair maiden Lilliard lies under this stane
> Little was her stature but muckle was her fame
> Upon the English loons she laid many thumps
> And when her legs were cuttit off she fought upon her stumps.

Such is the epitaph on a small monument to her by the roadside on the A68 – the place is known as **Lilliard's Ledge. Ancrum Bridge** (L1720) is also of historic interest.

Coldstream, 10 miles east of Kelso, is most remembered for giving its name to a regiment of the Guards which followed General Monk from here to assist with the Restoration of King Charles II, the penultimate Stuart king, in 1660. Near it is **Scaithmoor**, site of a victory involving the Good Lord James over Gascon mercenaries sent in by Edward II. **Coldstream Bridge** (L2137) was an important access point to the south.

The battle site of **Flodden** is some 3 miles to the south-east of Coldstream, near Branxton, and provides a saddening diversion at this point, as it was an unnecessary attack made on the English by the Scots ordered by James IV, who up to that time had proved one of the most efficient and talented of the Stewart dynasty, but on this occasion indulged in an ill-advised war, supposedly to help the French. Having thus rashly started, he showed unfortunate lack of experience as a field general by poor handling of his army, which was defeated by a much smaller force. It has been subsequently sentimentalized but one person who was right about it was Archibald Douglas, 'Bell-the-Cat', who protested about both the war and the conduct of the battle, but was dismissed as a coward by the King. Two of his sons were left to die here with the Douglas contingent, along with Douglas of Glenbervie and Douglas of Drumlanrig, among the many others and of course the King himself.

Homildon or Humbledon Hill, site of the battle lost disastrously by Archibald Douglas, the Tyneman, along with Murdoch Stewart, Duke of

Albany, in 1402, is near Glendale, Wooler, east of Flodden, 10 miles south of the Tweed.

Just to the north of Coldstream is **The Hirsel**, a house originally first occupied by the Homes in the 1650s, then rebuilt several times as the Homes merged with the old Douglas line to become the Douglas-Homes. The Prime Minister Sir Alec Douglas-Home, who resigned his peerage as Earl of Home, was born and lived here.

Ladykirk Church, known as the Kirk o' Steil, stands on the north bank of the Tweed opposite Norham Castle and was supposedly dedicated by James IV to the Virgin Mary in gratitude for his being saved from drowning in the river. It was used as a convenient refuge by Archibald, 6th Earl of Angus, after his quarrel with James V.

Norham Castle, on the English side of the Tweed, figures significantly in the history of cross-border raids in both directions. It was captured along with nearby Wark by James IV in the brief euphoric period before Flodden.

EAST COAST

Berwick Castle was the scene of the desperate defence by William Douglas le Hardi in 1296 which ended with the massacre of the town's 16,000 inhabitants by Edward I, two years after which William died in the Tower of London. The castle and town, at one time among the most prosperous ports in Scotland, regularly changed hands between the Scots and the English until the issue was finally settled in 1482, when James III lost it to the English. Most of the castle was destroyed to make way for the railway station, but parts do survive. Berwick was the site of the amazing tournament between twenty Scottish knights and twenty English in 1342, with William Douglas of Liddesdale among the triumphant Scots.

South of Berwick are **Alnwick**, about 24 miles away, and a number of other towns regularly attacked by the Douglas raiding parties. So too is the site of **Neville's Cross**, just outside Durham on the road to Darlington, where David I suffered a disastrous defeat, lost an eye and was captured, William Douglas of Liddesdale was also captured and Robert Stewart, the future Robert II, made a somewhat early escape. To the north of Newcastle is **Fawdon**, the Douglas manor in Northumberland, where William le Hardi was almost killed in his youth. **Warndon** was another Northumberland manor held by the Douglases before the War of Independence.

Halidon Hill, site of the disastrous battle in which Archibald Douglas as Guardian led the Scots to defeat in 1333, lies just north of Berwick by the A6105.

Mordington, site of an early castle 3½ miles north of Berwick on the same road, was one of those properties acquired through marriage by the Douglases of Dalkeith and Morton. It was burnt down by the English under the future Richard III in 1482. After the Regent Morton's fall in 1581, the castle passed to the Red Douglases and a younger son of the Douglas Earl of Angus was made Lord Mordington by Charles I in 1634. His family and title died out in 1741. Even the modern mansion has now been demolished.

Seven miles further north on the B6355 is **Coldingham Priory** (L383), an important religious site, control of which was regarded as conferring considerable prestige. It is just inland from the awesome precipice of **St Abb's Head** (L385 and 2975), site of the martyrdom of the Princess Ebba during an attack by the Danes. The priory was rebuilt by the Benedictines in 1098 and associated with Durham Cathedral and its patron saint Cuthbert, as well as with St Ebba. This awkward situation of cross-border control from an English bishopric led to considerable friction, and it was Robert III who appointed Archibald, 3rd Earl of Douglas, to supervise it, with the Home family as his under-bailiffs. It was a row caused by James III trying to take over the revenues of the priory for his own use in 1485 which provoked the rebellion as a result of which he was dethroned and murdered. One of the most notorious incumbents as prior of Coldingham was William Douglas, a younger grandson of Bell-the-Cat, who despite his cloth led his troops into Edinburgh and created a minor massacre in 1520. The priory suffered regularly from English depredations, and the beautiful choir is now the only substantial part of this once fine monastery that still stands, with some superb internal carving.

The romantic ruins of **Fast Castle** (L4328), 4 miles to the north, inspired Sir Walter Scott to write the *Bride of Lammermoor* (taking his heroine from another castle connected with the Douglases at Baldoon). Reached by a bridge over a chasm across to its cliff-top promontory, this castle had a violent history and was owned by a number of families before it was finally bought by the Douglases in 1602.

Heading north-west another 7 miles brings us to **Cockburnspath Castle**, 1½ miles south of the village where the Southern Upland Way finally arrives at the North Sea. It is a ruined fifteenth-century keep beside the Heriot Water which was purchased by the Douglases from its previous owners the Sinclairs in 1545, presumably at a very low price since it was in an area at that time of huge destruction by the English as they tried to bully the Scots to get Mary to marry Edward VI. Early in the 1600s the family moved closer to the village to **Cockburnspath House** or Sparrow Castle, a newer property now restored for habitation.

Just over a mile to the north of the village are the limited ruins of **Dunglass Castle**, a stronghold of the Homes which later gave its name to the heir of the Douglas-Home earls. With the forfeiture of the Home family in 1516, it passed to the Douglases. It was burnt twice by the English in 1532 and 1547, then blown up during the Civil War in 1640 by an angry English serving-man who took a dislike to its Covenanter garrison. **Dunglass Collegiate Church** (Historic Scotland) was founded by the Homes in 1423, and though disused is in an excellent state of preservation.

Nearby is the site of the minor victory achieved by the Red Douglases over an English invading party in 1435 at **Piperdean**.

WHITEADDER AND BLACKADDER

We now need to zigzag again (unless in a hurry, in which case head straight for Tantallon by the A1) to take in a group of properties set slightly further back from the border, but roughly parallel to the line from Hawick to Berwick which we explored earlier. This area, known as the Merse, was one of the most fertile and fruitful in Scotland and therefore particularly vulnerable to raiding by the English at harvest time. With an initial detour heading inland via Abbey St Bathans, 7 miles to the south-east we can take in **Cranshaws Castle** on the upper Whiteadder near the B6355. This is a fifteenth-century rectangular tower house which was bought by the Douglases in 1702, still in private ownership and also inhabited by one of the customary brownies.

Bunkle Castle (L2407), now a very decrepit ruin 5 miles further south and 2 miles before Preston, was a large twelfth-century castle and from 1288 belonged to a junior branch of the main Stewart family, whose founder Sir John Stewart was killed fighting for Wallace at Falkirk in 1298. His descendants became Earls of Angus, so when the Douglases acquired that earldom through the tempestuous love affair of the last Stewart countess, mother of the 1st Black Douglas Earl's bastard, the property became part of the new Red Douglas patrimony. It was later held by the Regent Morton's devious father, George Douglas of Pittendreich, a useful starting point for his regular undercover visits to Henry VIII in London, but after the fall of Morton in 1581 it went to the Homes. It and two neighbouring castles were the subject of a rhyming prophecy which sadly came true:

> Bunkle, Billie and Blanerne
> Three castles strong as airn [iron]
> Built when Davy was a bairn

They'll all gang doon
Wi' Scotland's croon
And ilk ain [every one] shall be a cairn.

Of the three only Blanerne had no direct Douglas association.

The remains of the very early Norman church at **Bunkle** (L381) date from the period of Stewart ownership or earlier, and were quarried to build the newer parish church in 1820.

Heading south-east again for about 5 miles we come to **Billie Castle** (L4483), 3 miles north-west of Chirnside, and it is indeed now not much more than a cairn. It passed from the Dunbars to the Red Douglases in 1435 and was especially used by Archibald Douglas, 6th Earl of Angus, when James V was besieging his chief home at Tantallon. Billie, now very much ruined, had a very substantial keep on top of earthworks with a walled courtyard protected by a ditch. The Douglases forfeited it in 1540 and soon afterwards it was one of the many castles destroyed by the English during the Rough Wooing.

Heading east now past Duns and further up the Blackadder near Westruther is **Evelaw Tower** (L5654), yet another ruined sixteenth-century L-plan tower, bought by the Douglases in 1576 from the monks of Drylaw as part of the post-Reformation sales bargains.

When we join the main A68 from here near Thirlstane it is possible to take in **Lauder**, the site of the bridge where Archibald Douglas, 'Bell-the-Cat', made his name by defying James III, refusing to help lead the Scottish army against England and organizing the hanging from the bridge of James's unpopular royal favourites. This is on the main route south to Carter Bar, following the old Roman road, **Dere Street** (L4483), a regular route for Scottish armies heading southwards, as on this occasion James III had intended. Further north, on **Fala Muir**, was the mustering point where the Lauder debacle was repeated and the barons refused to follow James V when he too wanted to head southwards against the English. Nearby are the remains of the medieval hospital at **Soutra** (L3067), near which David II's mistress was murdered. This has been the scene in recent years of remarkable forensic archaeology which has provided increased knowledge of the considerable sophistication of medieval herbal medicines.

UPPER TWEED

Heading south again, 10 miles south of Lauder we come to **Melrose Abbey** (Historic Scotland L90214), which was not just the resting place for Robert the Bruce's heart, the enduring symbol of Douglas ambition, but also the burial place of the early heroes among the Douglases, particularly William of Liddesdale and the first two Black Douglas earls. This Cistercian abbey church was founded by David I around 1136 during the period when the Norman knights were first invited by him to settle in Scotland. The abbey was destroyed by English troops in 1385 to the intense disgust of the Black Douglases, who were angered at the desecration of the family tombs. In 1389 rebuilding commenced and Richard II of England actually contributed to the cost, so not surprisingly the architectural style followed the latest fashion from south of the border. As Richard Fawcett puts it: 'The magnificent east end with its vast window and array of niches across the gable and buttresses is related to English designs such as that of the earlier collegiate church of Howden in eastern Yorkshire. However, Melrose marks a positive advance in its design of a grid-like pattern of rectilinear tracery to the east window in the use of which it was in step with the latest English ideas.' We are certainly left with one of the most evocative and elegant ruined abbeys north of the border. **Dryburgh Abbey**, less than 5 miles away, is also superb, though it does not figure particularly in this narrative.

Melrose was the site of a factional battle fought and won in 1526 by the 6th Red Douglas Earl of Angus against a party led by Sir Walter Scott, who was trying to snatch control of the young King James V from Angus's clutches. Just south of Galashiels is **Abbotsford**, home of the other Sir Walter Scott, the hugely prolific writer, whom we have come upon on numerous occasions throughout our journey in connection with source material for his poems and novels.

At Galashiels **Old Gala House**, which itself has no Douglas connection, seems to have stood on the site of a fifteenth-century Douglas castle which was destroyed in the general culling by the English after 1544.

Heading west on the A72 we come to **Traquair House**, by Innerleithen, south of the Tweed, which has a notable reputation both as the oldest inhabited house in Scotland and for the quality of its home-brewed beer. It was a royal hunting lodge before the Bruces and seems to have gone to the Black Douglases in the 1320s though perhaps not for long, its main association being with the Stewarts, one of whose daughters was the mistress of the 6th Earl of Angus when he tired of his wife, the former Queen Margaret Tudor.

Mary Queen of Scots and Darnley were here in 1566. Montrose tried to shelter here in vain after the disaster at Philiphaugh; Bonnie Prince Charlie was slightly luckier on his way south in 1745, and the Bear Gates have been kept locked ever since his departure. The Douglas baronies of Cluny and Sunderland were associated with Traquair.

Castlehill Tower, 4 miles south-west of Peebles, is a ruined fifteenth-century tower house perched on solid rock which was acquired by William Douglas, Earl of March, in 1703 and sold again twenty-five years later. **Queensberry Hall** in Peebles was a residence here for the Douglases of Drumlanrig. Near Peebles was **Heppart**, where Sir James Douglas captured his future friend and rival Sir Thomas Randolph.

Neidpath Castle (L1496), just beyond Peebles to the east, is one of the most dramatic castles of the Borders, standing as it does on top of an impressive gorge above the River Tweed, a substantial fourteenth-century keep remodelled in later centuries. It was not a Douglas property until 1786, when it was bought by the Douglas Dukes of Queensberry, who held it until their demise in 1810. Sir Walter Scott, Wordsworth and Burns were all shocked by the insensitive deforestation policy conducted here by the reprobate 4th Duke, Old Q. It is reputedly haunted by the ghost of Jean Douglas, the Maid of Neidpath, a daughter of Sir William Douglas, Earl of March (b. 1705), another of the customary heartbroken Douglas women who were sacrificed to feed the Douglas need for dynastic marriages. Like several of the others, she apparently wears a long brown dress.

Drochil Castle (L1495), 6 miles north-westwards beyond Peebles off the B7059, is one of the most impressive castles built from scratch by the ambitious James Douglas, the Regent Morton, in the 1570s. It was a sixteenth-century Z-plan tower of four storeys built as a Renaissance country retreat, following the latest French fashion, for a very rich and powerful man. It is still a very elegant ruin and its style has been compared to Chenonceau. It has the then new feature of a central corridor, as did Morton's other new mansion at Aberdour. Comparing it with Tantallon, Charles McKean suggests: 'It is not entirely fanciful to suppose that Drochil was intended to stand out as a similar gesture of architectural magnificence in this fairly bleak upland position.' Its owner was executed, however, in 1581, and his castle was abandoned forty years later. It remains an impressive monument to the wayward ambition of an unprincipled man who had destroyed many other people's castles but nevertheless appreciated architectural style and did not skimp on detail.

Nearby Romanno and Cardrona were long-term components of the Douglas patrimony in the post-Bruce era, standing like so many Douglas properties on one of the main routes northwards, in this case that over the Tweed to Edinburgh. North beyond Romanno is **West Linton**, where the churchyard has a number of early Douglas graves mainly from the Morton side, one with the evocative message: 'Death is the end of a vain life and a beginning of the good one. All must die.'

MIDLOTHIAN

Travelling north-east on the A701 then the A6094, we head for Dalkeith, headquarters of the third of the great branches of the Douglas dynasty, the earls of Morton. Just south of it, however, a small diversion can take us to **Hawthornden Castle** (L1205), beside Rosslyn. This is a fifteenth-century keep with many later additions and stands above a gorge near the River North Esk. It belonged to the Abernethy family, so came to the Douglases when they acquired the earldom of Angus after the countess had become the mistress of the Black Douglas earl and mother of his bastard, the first of the Red Douglases. The castle has subterranean caves allegedly used by Robert the Bruce and later by Sir Alexander Ramsay, the murder victim of Hermitage. It was sacked by the English along with other Douglas properties in 1544 and 1547, but has been since refurbished for habitation.

Dalkeith Castle dates from the twelfth century and passed to a branch of the Lothian Douglases in the 1350s when William of Liddesdale was unofficial leader of the family and the finest guerrilla leader in Scotland for two decades. The town was besieged by the vengeful Black Douglas Earl in 1452, soon after his brother, the 8th Earl, had been murdered by King James II, and had then received the support of the Red Douglases. The castle survived and in 1454 its owner, Sir James Douglas, was promoted to the earldom of Morton for marrying the King's deaf and dumb sister Joan or Dumb Janet. It was here that James IV was first introduced to his bride, Margaret Tudor, sister of Henry VIII.

In the 1540s the 3rd Earl of Morton, a man of poor health and weak character, was being bullied by James V to hand over his wealth (newly amplified by the finding of rich seams of coal nearby) to the Crown, but he was rescued by a junior branch of the Red Douglases, who provided a young man of vigorous character to marry the Earl's feeble-minded daughter and save the earldom from extinction by taking it on for his own benefit. This was James Douglas, the future Regent Morton, who was besieged here by the English in 1547, captured and taken a prisoner to England. He pursued his ambitions doggedly, however, becoming senior adviser to Mary Queen of Scots when she returned from France, and a collaborator with John Knox. After participating in and probably orchestrating the murders of both Riccio and Darnley, he turned against Mary and contributed to her defeat at Carberry, her imprisonment at Lochleven, her second defeat at Langside and her final exile. Perhaps he would have liked to marry her like Bothwell, but his insane wife was still alive. He now had to wait patiently for the death of three other regents before five years later he reached that position himself.

After ten years of power he found, like other Douglas regents before him, that the boy king had grown up with a mind of his own. In this case the boy was James VI, son of Darnley, whom Morton had helped to murder. James was readily persuaded by Morton's enemies to have him arrested and tried for his crime. He was executed in 1581. Meanwhile, he had conducted an extensive building programme at Aberdour, Drochil and here at Dalkeith, but he left no legitimate heirs for any of them. In 1642 the property was sold to the Scott family, Earls and later Dukes of Buccleuch, who remodelled it with designs first by James Smith then Vanbrugh as a Georgian ducal palace. It is now part of a country park.

Dalkeith St Nicholas Collegiate Church (L1188) was erected by James Douglas, Lord of Dalkeith, between 1390 and 1420 on the site of an earlier church to St Nicholas, but has had many subsequent alterations as a post-Reformation parish church. It has some fine carving and at least one recognizable Douglas memorial, a recumbent knight with the Douglas markings beside a lady who is clearly of royal descent, so probably they are the 1st Earl of Morton and his wife, Princess Joan or Dumb Janet, who died in 1498. Sadly they lie moss-covered in the roofless chapel.

Lugton, just beyond Dalkeith, has the site of another castle belonging to the Lochleven branch of the Dalkeith Douglases. They produced Lady Elizabeth Douglas, who used her arm as a door-bolt trying to save James I, the tournament champion in the reign of James II and the gaoler of Mary Queen of Scots who had joined in the murder of Riccio; in his old age he succeeded to the earldom of Morton.

Two miles north is **Smeaton Castle**, a ruined fifteenth-century courtyard castle now incorporated in an inhabited farmhouse. At one time it belonged to Dunfermline Abbey but was used later by the Red Douglases, particularly the ill-fated Archibald Douglas, 8th Earl of Angus, who died here unexpectedly in 1588, giving rise to rumours that he had been murdered by one of the local North Berwick witches. In the end one of the well-meaning ladies was garrotted in Edinburgh after being found guilty by a credulous court.

Five miles south is **Crichton Castle** (Historic Scotland L90084), one of the largest and finest in Scotland, though never held by the Douglases. It was the scene of the softening-up process of the two young Black Douglas heirs in 1440 before they were lured to their deaths after the Black Dinner in Edinburgh Castle. Five years later it was attacked by William, 8th Black Douglas Earl, partly as retaliation, though his own father had almost certainly colluded in the murder.

Near here at **Boroughmuir** William Douglas of Liddesdale defeated an English force in 1338.

EAST LOTHIAN

Before heading into Edinburgh we divert eastwards to a series of sites associated with the Red Douglases.

Longniddry House, sited off the A198 east of the village, has no visible remains but was a seat of the Douglases of Kilspindie who played several exciting roles during the reign of James V and Mary Queen of Scots. One of them was Archibald Douglas, the famous Greysteel, favourite of James V until he was banished and died in France. Here very significantly Hugh Douglas in 1543 employed the Haddington notary John Knox to tutor his two sons and here he entertained the reformer George Wishart, so it was probably here that Knox took the final plunge towards active Protestantism, and probably from here that a number of Douglas families became supporters of the new religion.

Redhouse Castle (L775) is an impressive ruin just over a mile south of Aberlady and belonged to the same branch of the Red Douglases. It was a sixteenth-century courtyard castle with a four-storey tower house which had a Renaissance doorway and doocot (dovecote) added, presumably when Archibald Douglas of Kilspindie was Provost of Edinburgh. He was first attacked by the Crichtons in 1557, who sent 280 men to Aberlady to try to kill him. Then he was stabbed by a mob who disliked his support for the religious reforms of John Knox. He was reappointed provost in 1559 and sacked again because of his Protestantism by Mary Queen of Scots in 1561.

The modest remains of **Kilspindie Castle** (L5997) stand just north of Aberlady by the shore. It was formerly owned by the Bishops of Dunkeld, one of whom was Gavin Douglas, the poet, so it may be no coincidence that it came into Douglas ownership in 1561, forty years after his death, as the church was stripped of its assets by the powerful families. It was held by Archibald Douglas of Kilspindie, the favourite of James V, and rebuilt by Patrick Douglas, perhaps the father of the Swedish field marshal.

Herdmanston Castle, now demolished, was a sixteenth-century L-plan tower 4 miles south-west of Haddington, and is associated mainly with the Sinclair family, but this land was Douglas property from quite an early period, being held by an Archibald Douglas in 1240.

It was on the moor nearby that in 1406 James Douglas of Balvenie, the Gross, later 7th Earl of Douglas, ambushed a royal party and killed one of his own family's former allies, called Fleming. He was on his way back from escorting the young Prince James, who was being despatched to France for safety. The future James I was to be shipped out secretly from North Berwick to the Bass Rock ready for passage to France but was later waylaid by English privateers and made a prisoner in England. The killing of Fleming by James Douglas may have had nothing to do with his special mission, nor may the leak of the secret journey to the English, but it was a strange coincidence. James had just been involved in securing Tantallon Castle for the family, as both the Red and Black Douglas earls had been captured by the English after the battle of Homildon Hill.

Closer to Haddington is **Lennoxlove**, formerly known as Lethington, a property parts of which go back to the fourteenth century and were built by Maitland of Lethington. He shared with Morton in the plot to murder Darnley, but later fell out with him and died in suspicious circumstances after his capture during the siege of Edinburgh Castle. Lennoxlove was acquired by the Douglas Dukes of Hamilton in 1947 after Hamilton Palace had to be demolished. It contains many of the treasures from Hamilton and the famous casket which supposedly contained the casket letters used by Morton to discredit and destroy Mary Queen of Scots.

Hailes Castle (Historic Scotland L90160) is an imposing ruin standing on the Tyne just south of East Linton. The castle dates from the thirteenth century, with its curtain wall surrounding a fourteenth-century keep and later extensions. It was the scene of the defeat of Harry Hotspur Percy of Northumberland in 1400 by a Scottish army under Archibald Douglas the Tyneman, on this occasion not a loser, and was held by Hugh Douglas of Longniddry, the patron of John Knox, in 1548.

To the south is **Stoneypath Tower** (L777), a largely ruined fifteenth- or sixteenth-century tower house surrounded on three sides by a steep bank. It belonged in the Marian period to the Douglases of Whittinghame, who played a major role in the murder of Darnley and in the mixture of espionage and diplomacy which preceded the execution of Mary Queen of Scots. It is now being restored.

Whittinghame Castle, on the Stenton road, is a refurbished fifteenth-century L-plan tower which was acquired by the Douglases in the fourteenth century and held by James Douglas, the future Regent Morton. It was here that he met Maitland, Bothwell and others to plot the murder of Darnley. Archibald Douglas, the brother of the laird, despite being a church minister and a justice, was the chief coordinator of the murder and possibly the forger of the casket letters which were used to implicate Mary in her husband's murder. He was certainly present at the murder scene, probably lit the fuse and probably with his henchmen carried Darnley into his garden to strangle him when for some reason the explosion did not kill him. When he was later tried for the crime, his velvet slippers had allegedly been found there. After the murder he became a spy or secret agent shuttling between Queen Elizabeth and James VI. In 1581 he tried to save his master, Morton, from execution for the Darnley murder by forging some letters, hence the suspicion that he was also a forger in 1564. His brother William Douglas, laird of Whittinghame, was threatened with torture to betray Archibald, did so without much hesitation but then, as he too was a justice, sat as a judge at Archibald's trial which unsurprisingly let him off with very minor punishment. Two generations later this family produced a succession of brilliant soldiers who fought in the Swedish and Russian armies, one of them, Robert Douglas, rising to become a field marshal and a count in Sweden, where the family still survives. Many years later Whittinghame was the home of the future Prime Minister Arthur Balfour.

Tantallon Castle (Historic Scotland L90295) is still one of the most imposing of all Douglas Castles and seems to have been acquired by the Black Douglases under the 1st Earl in 1374, probably from King Robert II's son Robert, who had held it as Earl of Fife before becoming heir to the throne, or possibly from his son Murdoch Stewart. Having thus very briefly been a Black Douglas stronghold and rebuilt as an exceptionally fine one by the earl, it switched within a generation to being the centrepiece of the Red Douglases. It was given to the Earl's bastard son George, product of his love affair conducted in the castle with the Countess of Angus, hence George becoming the 1st Douglas Earl of Angus. As the Red Douglases supported the Crown against their Black cousins in the 1400s, its Douglas Tower, which has a pit prison, was sometimes used as a high-security gaol for important enemies of the state, including the widow of Murdoch Stewart, Duke of Albany, after James I had him executed, and later the Lord of the Isles. Tantallon was besieged several times, but proved very hard to capture, impossible 'to ding doon', as the old saying put it, surrounded as it was on three sides by high cliffs overlooking the North Sea. Most notably the siege by James V in 1529 failed ignominiously for the King, as his cannons could make no impression. It is probable that carponiers or reinforced musket points covered the angles of the landward ditch so that no cannon could be brought near enough to have any effect on its massive walls.

We have a hint of Tantallon's original appearance as a sketch of it appears in the corner of Arnold Bronkhorst's portrait of the Regent Morton (see plate). Charles McKean describes what it must have looked like before being battered by the troops of Oliver Cromwell: 'one of the most intimidating of the private seats . . . formidable three-towered facade closing off the promontory with a barbican whose ghostly appearance appears much to resemble the barbican of Saumur . . . Tantallon's skyline is a flamboyance of platforms, parapets and domes.'

The Red Douglases forfeited ownership of the castle after their fall from grace in 1528 but had it restored in 1543. Lord Archibald Douglas, its owner in 1651, was a Covenanter, so the castle was besieged by the English and severely damaged. The castle was later sold by the 2nd Marquis of Douglas when he was short of cash. Tantallon originally had a sea gate and small jetty – the 1st Earl mentioned several unpleasant trips across the Forth to Fife.

The Bass Rock which stands out in the Forth beneath Tantallon seems to have come under Douglas control and had cannon emplacements at **Bass Castle** (L765). The family also made an effort to fortify nearby Fidra Island to the west of Tantallon and it has some remains of **Tarbert Castle**, its name suggesting a place where boats could be dragged across.

Spott House is 2½ miles south of Dunbar and incorporates an earlier castle which was briefly held by the Douglases of Morton. One of the Regent's four bastard sons was based here. The **Spott Burn** was the scene of the ignominious defeat of the Scottish army under John Balliol by Edward I in 1296. Spott was later held by Robert Douglas, Earl of Belhaven.

EDINBURGH

Heading back towards Edinburgh we pass three important battle sites all close to Musselburgh. **Carberry Hill** was where Mary and her newly-wed third husband, the Earl of Bothwell, were defeated by a force led jointly by Morton and Moray in 1565. **Queen Mary's Mount** marks the spot where she was captured. She was escorted back to Edinburgh by a posse of Douglases, who handled her with little respect.

A mile to the north is **Pinkie Heugh**, where the Scots under the Red Douglas Earl of Angus and the Earl of Arran were badly defeated by the English under Hertford in 1547. The English had a slight advantage, as they had a fleet offshore which fired into the Scots, but the main reason for the defeat was the disastrous rift between Angus and Arran, who did not trust one another.

Pinkie House, now part of Loretto School, was held at that time by the devious Sir George Douglas of Pittendreich, brother of the Earl of Angus, a shady diplomat and double-dealer, who was extracting possession of it from the previous owner, the Abbey of Dunfermline.

The third battle site, 2 miles to the north-east of Pinkie, is **Prestonpans**, where Bonnie Prince Charlie's army scored a useful victory over the makeshift Hanoverian force led by Sir John Cope, caught unexpectedly early in the morning, hence the song 'Hey Johnnie Cope Are Ye Wauken [awake] Yet?'

Edinburgh Castle (Historic Scotland L901130) is self-evidently one of the most important sites in Scotland and this is not the place to try to elaborate on its history. It figures in our narrative mainly as the scene for its spectacular capture by William Douglas of Liddesdale when his soldiers got in dressed as beer delivery men (see p. 24). Thereafter Archibald Douglas the Grim was constable and responsible for the building of David's Tower. Its most regular Douglas occupant was his son Archibald, the 4th Earl, known as Tyneman, who was also made constable and used it as his official residence between his expeditions against the English. It was also the venue for the infamous Black Dinner in 1440 and the site of a long siege organized by the Regent Morton in 1571 when, with English help, he at last dislodged the garrison under Kirkcaldy. Mons Meg, the great cannon associated with the destruction of Black Douglas castles, particularly Threave in 1455, is also here.

St Giles's Cathedral had Gavin Douglas the poet as its provost before he became Bishop of Dunkeld, and was the scene of the stool-throwing incident by Jenny Geddes which sparked off the Civil War in Scotland and England. **Queensberry House** in the Canongate has had a chequered career in the last 100 years as a barracks and military hospital, but has recently been restored as an annexe to the new Scottish parliament building. It was originally built by Maitland of Lethington in 1681, but was acquired five years later by the first Douglas Duke of Queensberry, whose unfortunate wife, Isabel, was left here to drink the cellars dry. It was here that their even madder grandson, the Union Duke's heir, James, the Earl of Drumlanrig, escaped from his locked room, then proceeded to stab, roast and eat one of the family's cook boys. Surprisingly the resident ghost is not a cook boy but a maiden called Anne Douglas who carries her head in her hand. So many Douglas women were forced into loveless marriages that their one means of revenge seems to have been to come back to haunt the men.

Holyrood Palace (Historic Scotland L90132) features particularly in our narrative as the site of the murder of David Riccio by a group consisting mainly of the Douglas family, including especially George Douglas, the Postulate, and James, the future Regent Morton. The staircase up which the murderers probably came to the Queen's private apartments is still in existence. Holyrood was also over the years regularly the residence used in Edinburgh by Douglas Earls of Morton and Angus when in positions of power and by the Douglas Dukes of Queensberry. Since the reign of Charles I the Dukes of Hamilton, Douglases after 1660, have been hereditary Keepers of the Palace and have apartments here.

Holyrood Abbey (L90131) had at least one Douglas abbot, the dreaded part-time warrior William of Coldingham, hero of Cleanse the Causeway. Here are buried David II; James II and his queen, Mary of Guelders; James V and his first queen, Madeleine; and Lord Darnley, though the tombs have mostly been damaged. There is a monument dated 1639 to Robert Douglas, Viscount of Belhaven, one of the cluster of Douglases elevated by Charles I.

Some at least of the atmosphere of Marian Edinburgh can be gleaned from the **Cowgate**, where the poet–bishop Gavin Douglas had his Edinburgh lodgings as Bishop of Dunkeld on its south side. From here it was just a short distance to **Blackfriars Wynd**, where he tried to negotiate with the Regent Arran and the other Hamiltons in 1520. No grounds for a truce could be found, so Angus and the Douglases attacked the Hamiltons in a skirmish known as Cleanse the Causeway. The outcome was in doubt until William Douglas, Prior of Coldingham, brought reinforcements and turned it into a Hamilton rout. Cardinal Beaton fought on the losing side. Gavin Douglas noticed that he had armour on beneath his ecclesiastical robes, tapped his chest and quipped 'Your conscience clatters.' Afterwards Douglas saved his superior's life by dragging him into the Blackfriars monastery.

Nearby also was **Kirk o' Field** or St Mary-in-the-Fields, a church and mansion built into the city walls in an area now occupied by Roxburgh Place and part of Edinburgh University. Here Archibald Douglas, the double agent who had his own lodgings close by, organized with Bothwell's men the explosion meant to kill Darnley, dragged him into the garden and killed him, leaving behind, so it was alleged, his velvet slippers. The Regent Morton, who was later executed for his part in the crime, was buried in **Greyfriars Churchyard** with a stone marked J E M (James, Earl of Morton).

Back on the High Street a diversion down **Anchor Close** gives the atmosphere of a slightly later period. A stone lintel marked 'O Lord in Thee is all my Trust' stands over the doorway of what was once Douglas's Tavern, a famous eighteenth-century hostelry where Dawney Douglas, a little man with a very big wife, entertained notables such as Robert Burns, Adam Smith and other luminaries of the Scottish Enlightenment. He specialized in tripe and mince collops, with all meals at less than 6 *d*. Nearby was the Canongate Theatre where the first performance of John Home's *Douglas* was staged to great acclaim in 1756, followed by a move to London.

The **Museum of Scotland** contains many artefacts connected with our journey, including, for example, some fine pottery excavated from Bothwell Castle during its Black Douglas heyday, and the missing keys of Lochleven Castle.

To the west of Edinburgh is **Cramond Tower**, near where the River Almond flows into the Forth, a tall sixteenth-century tower house owned, like Kilspindie Castle, by the bishops of Dunkeld, one of whom was Gavin Douglas, the poet. Afterwards, the property, in the usual way, passed into the hands of his relations until 1622. It has now been restored for habitation.

WEST LOTHIAN

The Douglases held at least two sites in West Lothian, **Hailes** and **Strabrock** (later Houston or Uphall), from a very early period when the Friesians or Freskins first moved north, though no physical remains survive of their early occupation.

We can firstly take in some Douglas connection near points on the main Kilmarnock road. **Dalmahoy**, just off the A71, is a three-story Adam mansion which was bought by the Douglas Earls of Morton about 1750. It is now a hotel and country club, said to be haunted by one of the Morton daughters, Lady Mary Douglas, referred to as 'the white lady'. Nearby the site of **Hatton House** incorporates vestiges of a tower house occupied by the Lauders, who died fighting for the Black Douglases and were besieged by James II in 1453 when he began his assault on their power. Later, in 1870, it became part of the Morton establishment at Dalmahoy, but even the newer mansion was burnt and then demolished in the 1950s.

Calder House at Mid-Calder incorporates a sixteenth-century L-plan tower owned by the Douglases early on and passed to their supporters the Sandilands, one of whom was killed fighting for them in the 1450s. Near Calder was the other Morton from which the earls officially took their title. **Baads Castle**, near West Calder and now almost vanished, was a sixteenth-century Douglas tower house burnt down in 1736.

We can now double back on the M8/M9 to Queensferry and the coastline of the Firth of Forth. All that remains of 'many-towered' **Abercorn Castle**, 3 miles west of the Forth Railway Bridge in the gardens of Hopetoun House, is the tree-covered mound which hides its ruins, but from 1400 it belonged to the Black Douglases and was the main seat of James the Gross, who died here in 1443. In 1455, during the earldom of his son James, it was besieged and taken after a month by James II, after which he had it totally dismantled as he finally quashed the power of the Black Douglases. Three miles up the coast is **Blackness Castle** (Historic Scotland L90036), occasionally held by the Douglases but more often used to imprison them, as, for example, the young Regent Morton.

Kinneil House (Historic Scotland L90189), about 5 miles further west near Bo'ness and technically over the county border, close to where the Roman Wall met the Firth of Forth, was a Hamilton castle from the time of Bruce. In 1661 it came into the hands of the Douglas dukes of

Hamilton, who remodelled it in palatial style, but it was abandoned in 1828 and is now set in a public park. **Strathendry Castle**, 4 miles to the north, is a restored keep which was Douglas from 1700 to 1882, during which time the economist Adam Smith was kidnapped from it by gypsies.

Linlithgow Palace (Historic Scotland L90201) is again one of the great historical sites of Scotland but only marginally relevant to this particular narrative, except as the place where the 1st Black Douglas Earl made his abortive challenge to Robert II, and where Archibald Douglas played dice with James V. It was originally the Peel of Linlithgow, captured and refurbished by the English in 1301, destroyed by the Scots after its recapture and repaired much later by David II, then substantially extended by James I, James II and James IV, who turned it into a Renaissance palace fit for his Tudor queen; she reputedly haunts the tower room known as Queen Margaret's Bower, doubtless because she was irritated by her husband's infidelity. Mary Queen of Scots was born here in 1542. According to legend another ghostly apparition appeared in the nearby church of St Michael to warn James IV not to go to war with the English in 1513, but he ignored it and marched to his doom.

The same fate suffered by Abercorn applied to **Inveravon Castle**, about 6 miles further west, another important seat of the later Black Douglas earls on the River Avon, just 3 miles away from the royal palace at Linlithgow. After its battering by James II, only the base of one large round tower of this fifteenth-century castle and courtyard survives as part of a farm which sits on the site of the Roman Wall beside junction 4 of the M9.

Three miles to the south on the other side of the M9 is the site of **Manuel Convent**, also by the River Avon and near the Union Canal. It was here that Archibald, the Red Douglas Earl, defeated the Earl of Lennox in a battle for custody of James V in 1526, and George Douglas, his brother, earned the young king's undying enmity by threatening to kill him rather than lose custody. They lost it anyway soon afterwards.

FIFE

We now cross the Forth at the Kincardine Bridge and a short detour to the west takes in **Tulliallan Castle** (L736), near Kincardine, which was only Douglas for a short period between 1335 and 1390. It was strengthened by the English in 1304 and has a fourteenth-century keep surrounded by a ditch, its entrance protected by a drawbridge and portcullis. It later passed to the Bruce family, the non-royal branch of which settled in this area. Five miles to the east the remarkable Jacobean mini-palace of a sub-branch of the Bruces and evidence of their ingenious development of under-sea coal fields can be seen at **Culross**. This village was the scene of the meeting between Archibald Douglas the Tyneman and Robert Stewart, Duke of Albany, as they plotted the death of the wayward Prince David, Duke of Rothesay and heir to the throne, in 1400.

A dozen miles to the east, after crossing the A90, we come to **Aberdour Castle** (Historic Scotland L90002), which was given by Robert the Bruce to his nephew Thomas Randolph, associate of the Good Lord James, and, like many other Randolph properties, passed to the Douglases, this time the Lothian or Dalkeith branch, in 1342. In 1474 the 1st Earl of Morton built a hospital for the poor here, dedicating it to St Martin. His successor two generations later was the Regent Morton. He rebuilt the place to be his favourite seaside residence, with a number of new architectural features, like Drochil, particularly the corridor, also creating a delightful terrace garden in the new Anglo-French fashion. Aberdour Castle was abandoned as a residence in 1725 when the family moved into the more modern Aberdour House which they still held into the twentieth century when it was converted into flats.

Heading east again on the A921, we come near the Stenhouse Reservoir to the scanty remains of **Knockdavie Castle** (L5251), which was a Douglas tower house in the seventeenth century and associated with the persecution of the Covenanters during the Queensberry period.

A few miles further on a monument by the road at **Kinghorn** marks the spot where Alexander III rode his horse over the edge of the cliff in his haste to get back to his new young wife, Yolande, in 1286. It was this event which effectively sparked off the saga of the Balliols, the Bruces and the Stewarts in which the Douglases were to play such a prominent part.

Grange Castle, a mile north of Kinghorn, belonged to Sir William Kirkcaldy, one of those involved in the murder of Cardinal Beaton and himself the man who for so long frustrated the Regent Morton by his stubborn defence of Edinburgh Castle for the Marian party, and paid for it with his head after at last surrendering in 1573. Naturally the castle then came into the hands of the Douglases of Morton, who had already half-burnt it in a tit-for-tat raid after Kirkcaldy had stolen all the wedding goods intended for Morton's niece. The remnants of the sixteenth-century tower are incorporated in a newer mansion.

We can now head north again cross-country or by the motorway to **Lochleven Castle** (Historic Scotland L90204) on its island in the loch, reachable by a ferry in season from the B966. The island is larger now than it was because of a lowering of the level of the loch, so originally its fourteenth-century courtyard and fifteenth-century five-storey keep occupied nearly all of it. It had been a royal castle before the Bruces and was twice besieged by the English, in 1298 and 1301, retaken the first time by Wallace and saved the second by Sir John Comyn. It passed to a branch of the Red Douglases in about 1390. One of its early owners was killed in France; another was the second Scottish champion who took part with James Douglas in the famous royal tournament at Stirling in 1442. It was his sister, Elizabeth, who had earlier won fame for her courageous effort to save the life of James I in Perth by thrusting her arm into the monastery door. Robert Douglas of Lochleven was killed at Flodden and his grandson Robert at Pinkie; in the 1530s James V had an affair with the latter's wife which resulted in the birth of the future Regent Moray.

But Lochleven's best-known owner was Sir William Douglas who helped in the murder of Riccio and then became gaoler of Mary Queen of Scots. It was his brother, Pretty Geordie, and an orphaned nephew called Willie who plotted her escape and became her lifelong companions in exile. Sir William gained final infamy by his betrayal for money of the English asylum-seeker Percy, Earl of Northumberland, in what Sir Walter Scott called 'an eternal blight on the name of Douglas'. Having bargained up the ransom money with Percy's wife until it reached £2,000 Sir William then, with Morton's compliance, asked Queen Elizabeth to match it, and handed Percy over to her for execution. Meanwhile, Mary Queen of Scots had been accused, probably unfairly, of having an affair with Pretty Geordie. Sir William, who was nothing if not a survivor, outlived so many relations that in due course he became Earl of Morton in his old age, but his own eldest son was somehow captured by Moorish pirates in the Mediterranean and never seen again. Tired of their inaccessible island, the family built a new mansion near where Kinross House still stands. The old island fortress is still very impressive, and it was here that Morton spent some of his final months laying out the gardens.

A detour eastwards here can take in the delightful royal palace at **Falkland** (Historic Scotland L854), which features in this narrative as the place where David, Duke of Rothesay, died mysteriously while in the custody of his brother-in-law Archibald Douglas, the Tyneman, and his uncle the Duke of Albany. It also features in the escape of young King James V from Archibald Douglas, 6th Earl of Angus, and his minders, Douglas of Pittendreich and Douglas of Parkhead.

A detour even further eastwards takes us to **St Andrews**, where the main incidents in this narrative are connected with the use of the castle (Historic Scotland L900259) by the Red Douglases to hold James V captive, and later with the extraordinary career of the warrior–poet–bishop Gavin Douglas, who had the support of his family and Henry VIII in an effort to make himself Archbishop of St Andrews. To advance his case in 1515 he besieged and captured the archbishop's castle, only to be besieged and ejected by his rival, the Prior of St Andrews, John Hepburn. Gavin was later locked up in the castle again before in due course settling for the lesser appointment of Bishop of Dunkeld, and died of the plague as an exile in London seven years later.

In 1546 St Andrews was the scene of the murder of Cardinal Beaton, an enemy of the Douglases, but there is no evidence to connect any of them directly with the crime, though the lawyer James Balfour of Pittendreich, who was one of the team and also a major player in the murder of Darnley, was certainly later a close associate of the Douglases. John Knox came here for safety with his two Douglas pupils from Longniddrie the next year, and was captured by the French along with Balfour. The Rector of the University, John Douglas, became the first Protestant archbishop in 1571, persuaded by Morton, and a few years later he dropped dead in his own pulpit.

A detour westwards is possible, though not very rewarding, to **Glendevon**, north of Dollar, where a Z-plan tower house incorporates a fifteenth-century keep once owned by William, the last but one of the Black Douglas earls, who was murdered by James II in 1452.

Further north again on the M90, a brief diversion eastward reaches **Abernethy** in Perthshire, which was regarded as the spiritual home of the Red Douglases, several of their earls being buried there. It seems to have come into Douglas hands quite early, perhaps through the marriage of Hugh Douglas, uncle of the Good Lord James, to Marjorie of Abernethy in 1259, or perhaps at the same time as Tantallon in 1389. The town was an important religious centre, with its round tower (L836) – dedicated, like Douglas itself, to St Bride – which was restored as a collegiate church by Archibald, 'Bell-the-Cat', but demolished except for the round tower in 1802. The town had a useful little harbour at the mouth of the Earn where George Douglas the Postulate had his piratical fray, and near here was probably the original castle in the grounds of **Carpow**.

Three miles to the east are the crumbling but beautiful ruins of **Lindores Abbey** (L836), where James, the last Black Douglas earl, spent his final days. Even further east was **Tayport Castle**, now totally demolished, which was held by the Glenbervie Douglases in the seventeenth century.

PERTH AND ANGUS

Just south of Perth at Dupplin is the site of a thirteenth-century castle which was briefly acquired by the Douglases of Morton in 1623. This is near the scene of the disastrous defeat of the Scots under the Regent Mar by Edward Balliol and his Anglo-Scottish supporters in 1332.

We now head east towards Dundee, where there are three castles with Douglas connections. It is the natural heart of the earldom of Angus, which the Red Douglases held from 1384. **Mains Castle**, near Caird Park, is a fifteenth-century courtyard castle, rebuilt in 1562, which was held by the Red Douglases from 1384 until their fall in 1528. It has now been restored. **Dudhope Castle**, just south of Dundee Law, is most famous as the home of Bonnie Dundee or Bloody Clavers, but it had an earlier period of ownership by a branch of the Douglases. It has been restored as office accommodation. **Broughty Castle** (L90043), now a museum south of Broughty Ferry, was a significant site guarding the entrance to the Firth of Tay and an important crossing point. In 1544 Archibald, 6th Earl of Angus, obtained permission to build a tower here which would give him the same kind of control over the Tay as he had over the Forth from Tantallon and the Bass Rock.

Wedderburn Castle, 3½ miles north-east of Dundee, was a Red Douglas castle until 1528 but was totally demolished in the late nineteenth-century.

Ten miles to the north-east up the coast are the majestic red ruins of **Arbroath Abbey** (Historic Scotland L90018) and its **Abbot's House** (L90326). This has featured in our narrative mainly because of the extraordinary career of George Douglas the Postulate, the first man to stab Riccio, who despite official rejection for the post used armed bands of his Douglas relatives to help make himself abbot here by force in 1563, at a time when the monasteries were becoming a happy hunting ground for fortune seekers. He had been a priest at Douglas, where he organized a previous attempt to murder Riccio during a fishing trip, and he was a key player in the Holyrood murder plot which succeeded. He was, while abbot, found guilty of piratical raids on small boats across the Tay near Abernethy, and in his last years became a thoroughly incompetent Protestant Bishop of Moray.

Diverting westwards, if there is time, we can take in **Kirriemuir**, or that can be left to the return journey. Historically, though there is little to see, it fits in better alongside the other focal points of the Red Douglas earldom of Angus. A mile to the west on what remains of **Kinnordy Loch** after drainage, is the site of a crannog (artificial island) and ancient castle which was almost certainly once the seat of the Earls of Angus in this important part of their earldom. They dispensed justice from a mound, now half demolished, in Kirriemuir.

KINCARDINE AND ABERDEEN

Thirty miles north of Arbroath we come into the territory of the Douglases of Glenbervie, who took over the Red Douglas earldom in the seventeenth century.

Glenbervie House, 6 miles south-west of Stonehaven, is an eighteenth-century mansion built by the Douglases of Glenbervie, one of whom was killed at Flodden; another came to prominence at the battle of Corrichie, when he saved Morton from a humiliating defeat as he led the army of Mary Queen of Scots against the Catholic lords. It incorporates a much earlier castle visited by Edward I in 1296 and it became Douglas property by marriage around 1480. William, the second of the Glenbervie Earls of Angus, was the converted Catholic who was persecuted for his faith, nearly losing the earldom; he died in 1611 in Paris, where he was buried.

House of Mergie, 4 miles north of Stonehaven near the Slug Road to Deeside, was a tower house held by the Douglases until the time of the Civil War. It was later partially dismantled and is incorporated in a farmhouse.

Heading west from Crathes, near Banchory, are a further two Douglas castles. **Tilquhillie Castle** belonged originally to the Abbey of Arbroath but later passed by marriage to the Douglases of Lochleven, perhaps with the help of the reprobate abbot George Douglas, and they rebuilt it in the sixteenth century as a Z-plan tower house. Surprisingly, they seem to have been anti-Reformation and supported the Catholic side at the battle of Corrichie, where their near neighbours the Douglases of Glenbervie were successfully on the government side. It has been restored for habitation, and nearby was born Norman Douglas, the hedonist writer, in 1868. This same family of Douglases of Tilquhillie also later took over **Cluny Crichton Castle** to the north of Banchory, now a ruined seventeenth-century L-plan tower house.

Kildrummy Castle was briefly held by the first Black Douglas Earl.

Kemnay House, 5 miles south of Inverurie, was the second main seat of the Douglases of Glenbervie, a seventeenth-century L-plan tower house now incorporated in a more recent mansion.

Culblean Hill, near Ballater, was the scene of the victory by William Douglas, Flower of Chivalry, and an army of 800 Scots against the Anglo-Scottish supporters of Edward Balliol in 1335. There is a small memorial.

MORAY AND BANFF

Heading towards Fraserburgh from Peterhead we pass **Crimond** (famous for the psalm tune), a property held among others by the Guardian Archibald Douglas, brother of the Good Lord James, who died at Halidon Hill.

Near New Aberdour are the modest ruins of **Dundarg Castle** (L2450), once an important stronghold of the Comyn Earls of Buchan in Bruce's day, and destroyed by him for that reason in 1308. It was rebuilt by the

English in 1333, and captured a year later by the Regent Andrew Moray using cannon, the first recorded use of artillery in Scottish history. After this it came into the hands of the Black Douglases, perhaps when Archibald the Grim married Joanna of Moray. Archibald's younger grandson, Archibald, brother of the last Black Douglas earl, was Earl of Moray and was killed during their rebellion at Arkinholm, so Dundarg was destroyed by James II in his general culling of Douglas castles in 1455.

Heading west along the main coast road we come to **Spynie Palace** (Historic Scotland L90282), near Lossiemouth, which was the home of Brice Douglas, Bishop of Moray, until 1220. He started to rebuild a cathedral here but then changed his mind after a visit to the Pope in Rome, and organized the building of a bigger one at Elgin, closer to the main centre of population. The episcopal keep at Spynie was rebuilt and fortified, as was their harbour on Spynie Loch, at that time connected to the sea. Brice was canonized as a saint shortly after his death in 1222, and his day was fixed as 13 November.

The other famous Douglas resident here was George Douglas, the murderer of Riccio, who, despite a career involving violent seizure of Arbroath and piracy on the Tay, and despite having very modest knowledge of the scriptures, still managed to land the appointment as first Protestant Bishop of Moray. At least he was not canonized.

Elgin Cathedral (L900142) never fully recovered from its burning by the Stewart Wolf of Badenoch in 1490, though George Douglas made his feeble efforts at preaching in the remains; the roof was stripped of all its lead to help pay off the government troops in 1567.

Just outside Elgin is **Pittendreich**, from which George Douglas, the double-agent brother of the 6th Red Douglas Earl, took his title and perhaps where he fathered his famous son the Regent Morton. Nearby is the **Bog of Dunkinty**, site of the battle in which Archibald Douglas, Earl of Moray, beat Huntly in 1452.

> Where left thou thy men thou Gordon so gay?
> In the Bog of Dunkinty mowing the hay.

Pittendreich was also later the property of one of Morton's bastards, then of the devious lawyer James Balfour who took part in the murders of both Cardinal Beaton and Darnley, and perhaps received this property from the Douglases as his reward.

Heading south up the Spey towards Dufftown we come to **Balvenie Castle** (Historic Scotland L90028) on the famous River Fiddich. This is a large and spectacular thirteenth-century castle with numerous additions. Rebuilt by the Black Douglases around 1395 on the site of a former

Comyn castle used by the English and Edward I in 1304, then destroyed by Robert Bruce, it was held by the Black Douglases presumably after Archibald the Grim married Joanna of Moray. His younger son James the Gross held it as Lord of Balvenie before he was made an earl, passing it in turn to his youngest son, John of Balvenie, who fought at Arkinholm: he escaped but was later captured in Ewesdale and executed for his part in the Black Douglas rebellion of 1455. After that it passed to a branch of the Royal Stewarts, then other families.

Heading south-west and then turning north again at Grantown-on-Spey we come after 6 miles to **Lochindorb** (L1231), the Loch of Trouble. The thirteenth-century castle on its island here had a similar early history to Balvenie, built by the Comyns and captured by the English both in 1304 and 1333. It fell into the hands of Randolph, Earl of Moray, became a prison and a lair for the notorious Alexander Stewart, Wolf of Badenoch, then somehow became a property of the Black Douglas Earl of Moray, only to be dismantled after his defeat and death at Arkinholm in 1455. Granite balls presumably fired by a trebuchet during one of the many sieges were excavated here.

From here the A940 heading north towards Forres passes **Darnaway Castle**, just 4 miles before the town. Like Balvenie and Lochindorb it had belonged to the Earls of Moray from the Bruce era, then passed to Archibald the Grim and the Black Douglases by marriage during the reign of David II. In the following century it became the favourite home of Archibald Douglas, twin brother of the last Black Douglas earl, who extended it. It was he who won the little battle at Bog of Dunkinty in 1452 but rebelled with his brothers against James II, and lost the battle at Arkinholm and his life three years later. It is believed that the remarkable satirical poem 'The Buke of the Howl' was written here by Richard Holland, a Douglas retainer, to annoy the king and please Archibald and his wife. She showed true realism by remarrying nineteen days after her first husband's death. Darnaway was rebuilt as a classical mansion in 1810 by a subsequent Earl of Moray, incorporating a few remnants of the old one, and now has a visitor centre.

THE NORTH-EAST

Heading past Culloden – where Douglases fought on both sides – towards Inverness, we rejoin the A9 and cross Kessock Bridge to the Black Isle and another area which passed from the Randolph Earls of Moray to the Black Douglases. Just south of Avoch are the scanty remains of **Ormond Castle** set on its own mound, known as Lady Hill. Built originally in the reign of King William the Lion around 1210, it was held by the two Andrews, father and son Earls of Moray, both highly successful warriors, one alongside Wallace, the other during the minority of David II. Then, like other Moray properties, it passed to Archibald the Grim and his children, coming into prominence when Hugh, a younger brother of the last Black Douglas earl, was made Earl of Ormond by James II around 1445. Ten years later he was involved with his brothers in the ill-fated rebellion which ended Black Douglas power at Arkinholm. He was captured and executed.

At Muir of Ord, to the west back over the A9, is roofless **Red Castle**, also at one time owned by the Douglas Earl of Ormond. Built above a steep ravine, a sixteenth-century L-plan tower house incorporated an earlier twelfth-century castle, dating like Ormond Castle from the era of William the Lion. Naturally like Ormond it was forfeited in 1455 when the family was disgraced.

This is really as far north in practical terms as the Douglases stretched their tentacles, but for the purist it should be mentioned that the Douglas Earls of Morton were for a while custodians of the Orkney and Shetland Islands after 1615, when the piratical Stewart earls of Orkney were removed. The Douglases briefly used the former **Sinclair Castle** at Kirkwall, now long demolished, as their base here, and some of their support for Montrose during the Civil War was orchestrated from here. Several of them were buried in St Magnus Cathedral. However, ownership of the Northern Isles brought in very little revenue and the Morton earls unburdened themselves of this area soon afterwards. Douglas of Kilspindie also seems to have made enemies in Caithness, when he held a castle near **Latheron**.

PERTH, STIRLING AND ARGYLL

Heading south again down the A9 there are a few sites not taken in on the way north.

Dunkeld Cathedral (L90119) had its famous Douglas bishop, the poet Gavin. He does not seem to have spent much time here, but contributed to the ecclesiastical asset-stripping which greatly benefited the Douglas family in the declining years of the Catholic Church.

Nothing remains of **Blackfriars** in Perth where James I was murdered in the tennis court and nearly saved by the bravery of Lady Elizabeth Douglas, as he tried to escape through a blocked drain.

To the west of here is the route taken by Bruce and the Good Lord James after their defeat at Methven in 1306. The site of their further humiliation at the hands of the McDougalls at **Dalry** is close to Tyndrum, and beyond that on the road to Oban is the site of the great victory by Bruce and Douglas over the McDougalls when James made his famous flank attack above the ravine at the **Pass of Brander**.

Stirling Castle (Historic Scotland L90291) is the scene of numerous meetings and sieges in our story, but mainly figures as the site of the murder of the penultimate Black Douglas earl by King James II in 1452 and his ejection from an upstairs window. Just before that was the famous tournament in which two of the three knights representing Scotland in a tournament against Burgundian champions were Douglases: one of them was James, the 8th Earl's brother and subsequently himself last earl, who tried to avenge his brother by burning the town and dragging the dead man's safe conduct through the streets at the tail of a horse. The other was Douglas of Lochleven.

Cambuskenneth Abbey (L90055) is the burial place of King James III, who was murdered by Lord Gray in 1485 after his defeat at Sauchieburn, not far from here, by another Scottish army, led by his own son. James IV wore an iron belt in remorse for the rest of his life, except presumably when entertaining his numerous mistresses.

Bannockburn is a site extensively written about elsewhere, but should not escape mention if for no other reason than the presence of three of our original families – the Bruces, Stewarts and Douglases.

FRANCE

Normandy – Flanders

There are several places called **Bailleul**, but most probably the one near Argentan was the original home of the Balliol family, two of whose members, John and his son Edward, were briefly kings of Scotland.

The **Château Gaillard**, a magnificent ruined castle on the Seine, features in our narrative as the place where David II spent his youth along with for some time the first and third Black Douglas earls. Here ex-king John Balliol died, a blind old man.

Dun le Roi, now **Dun sur Auron**, was a castle and barony in Berry with the county of Longueville, previously held by Bertrand de Guesclin, given to Archibald, the Black Douglas Earl of Wigtown, son of Tyneman, for his part in winning the battle of Baugé against the English.

Rouen was the base for young James I when he was brought to France by Henry V to admire his fighting prowess.

Somewhere in Flanders was the original home of the Freskins, who in Scotland became known as Douglas, Moray and Sutherland.

Brittany

Brix, near Cherbourg, was the original home of the Bruces, two of whom, Robert and his son David, became kings of Scotland.

Dol, north-east of Saint-Malo, is a delightful small cathedral town which was the original home of the Stewards of Dol who became Stewards or Stewarts of Scotland. This family produced nine kings and one queen of Scotland, four kings and two queens of Great Britain and one queen of France.

Loire Valley

Tours is the capital of the Duchy of Touraine, which was presented to Archibald Douglas, 4th Earl, when he brought a division of Scottish troops to fight the English in 1424 as part of the Hundred Years War. Having landed at La Rochelle, he made a formal entrance to the city, then left his cousin Adam Douglas as constable when he went to war. After his death with many other Douglases at Verneuil, he and his second son were buried in the choir of the **Cathedral of St Gatien**. It was here a few years later that the Dauphin Louis, later King Louis XI, married Princess Margaret Stewart of Scotland, daughter of James I. It was not a very long or happy marriage.

Loches is an unspoilt medieval town in the Indre valley which has a large castle which was also given to Archibald Douglas, it having the deepest dungeons of any castle in the area. This was where just a few years later Joan of Arc begged the Dauphin to go to Rheims for his coronation.

Chinon, also on the Indre, had another castle occupied by Archibald Douglas, who lived luxuriously on credit, expecting good payment once he had beaten the English. It was here four years after his death that Joan of Arc picked out the Dauphin Charles from a crowd of lookalikes. Earlier this was where Richard the Lionheart died of a crossbow wound. At nearby Chatillon-sur-Indre Douglas did some useful fighting.

Verneuil was the town on the River Avre captured by Archibald Douglas using the trick of pretending that his Scottish soldiers were English, covering them with mud and blood, shouting that they had been beaten by the French and asking to be allowed into this pro-English town. It was his last success, for outside it he fought and lost against an English army under Bedford, who politely invited him to drinks beforehand but gave no quarter afterwards. A mass was said afterwards in the Abbey of Saint-Antoine de Viennois.

Aubigny, near Bourges, was the site of a colony of Scottish mercenaries during the Hundred Years War, including the Stuarts of Darnley and Aubigny, who returned to Scotland in the Marian period.

Two Douglas soldiers of fortune, both called William, survivors of Verneuil, helped Joan of Arc defend the city of **Orléans** against the

English. They were both killed and were buried in the Cathédrale Sainte-Croix.

Baugé was the site of the famous victory by the Scots under a Stewart and a Douglas against the troops of Henry V in 1418. Beforehand Sir William Douglas was based at **Le Puisset** in Beauce, north of the Château Gaillard, having landed with 450 foot soldiers and 300 archers. **Fresnay** near Le Mans, was the scene of a Scottish defeat which largely undid the work of Baugé.

Guillaume Douglaz was killed at the siege of **Cravant**.

Isabella Douglas, widow of Buchan, lived at **Saint-Saëns**, having inherited it from her ancestor, the 1st Earl, who had been given it after Poitiers. She died in 1418, leaving her statue in the priory.

Chatelherault was the centre of a duchy originally granted by Mary of Guise and her French relatives to the Hamilton Earl of Arran, but it passed theoretically to the Douglases when they took over the dukedom of Hamilton in 1660; this was confirmed by Napoleon III.

The 1st Earl of Douglas was a senior general with the French army at the battle of **Poitiers**, but his advice on tactics was ignored. He was captured in the defeat and ransomed. Archibald the Grim was also captured but pretended to be his own cook boy, and escaped with a very low ransom.

Auvergne

John Stewart, Duke of Albany, briefly Regent of Scotland after Flodden and rival of the Red Douglases, was the son of Alexander Stewart, Duke of Albany (d. 1484), also a would-be regent for his brother James III. Alexander married into the ownership of Auvergne and **Mirefleurs Castle**, south of Clermont-Ferrand in the Massif Central, so that for him life there was attractive enough to make even the regency of Scotland seem an unrewarding task. He was killed at a tournament in Paris and buried at the **Quai des Celestins** by the Seine. John married into the same family and was made governor of Bourbonnois d'Auvergne, and when he died in 1536 he was buried in the **Chapel of Vic-Le-Comte**.

Paris

William Douglas, 10th Earl of Angus, came in exile during the reign of Henri IV to **Saint-Germain-des-Prés.** He was buried there, many other Douglas exiles following his path, including the young soldier James Douglas who was killed leading Le Regiment Douglas for Louis XIII. The Douglas tombs of black marble lie in the abbey chancel.

The new château at **Saint-Germain-en-Laye** was the base not just for Mary Queen of Scots for ten years before she was married to the

Dauphin, but for Queen Henrietta, the wife of Charles I, and for James II, when he came here in exile after 1689.

ITALY

Vigoleno Castle, near Parma in the upper Po valley, was the home of the Counts Scoto d'Agazano, who claimed descent from the Black Douglases. They have a memorial in the **Church of Lorenzo** in Piacenza.

SPAIN

Teba de Andales in Andalucia is a small hilltop town 20 miles north-east of Ronda, where the Good Lord James Douglas was killed fighting for Spain against the Moors. A monument in the town centre commemorates the event. The Moorish Castle is in ruins.

SWEDEN

Linköping Castle was the home of Robert Douglas, field marshal in the Swedish army and Count Skenning and Baron of Skalby in Östergötland. The town is now better known for the production of SAAB aeroplanes.

CANADA

Fort Douglas is on the Red River, 2 miles south of the Assinboia.

Kildonan, Winnipeg, was the settlement founded by Thomas Douglas, 5th Earl of Selkirk, with many immigrants from the Kildonan area of Sutherland. **Fort Selkirk**, built by Robert Campbell on the Yukon, and the **Selkirk Range** in the Rockies recall the contribution of Thomas Douglas, who founded his colony on Prince Edward Island. **Baldoon**, on Lake Erie, was a marginally successful settlement founded by Thomas Douglas.

Douglastown, now in Gaspe County, at the railway terminus, was called after Vice-Admiral Sir Charles Douglas, who relieved Quebec in 1776.

USA

Fort Douglas, now a National Historic Landmark, was an army post established in Utah to protect the mail against Mormon raids. **Douglas**, Arizona, was a smelting town founded by James Douglas. Douglas, Wyoming, was a railway city founded in 1886 and called after Stephen Douglas.

Bibliography

Adams, Percy W.L., *A History of the Douglas Family of Morton*, Bedford, 1921

Andrew, Ken, *The Southern Upland Way*, Edinburgh, 1984

Auchinleck Chronicle, ed. T. Thomson, Edinburgh, 1819

Balfour, Paul J. ed., *The Scots Peerage*, Edinburgh, 1904–14

Barbour's Bruce, ed. M.P. McDiarmid and J.A.C. Stevenson, Edinburgh, 1980–4

Boece, Hector, *Scotorum Historiae*, Paris, 1527

Boswell, James, *In Search of a Wife*, ed. F. Brady and F. Pottle, Yale, 1957

Bower, Walter, *Scotichronicon*, ed. W. Goodall and D.E.R. Watt, Edinburgh, 1759, and Aberdeen, 1987

Brown, J., *History of Sanquhar*, Dumfries, 1891

Brown, M., *The Black Douglases*, East Linton, 1998

Buchan, John, *Montrose*, London, 1928

Buchanan, George, *History of Scotland*, ed. J. Aikman, Edinburgh, 1927

Burns, Robert, *Collected Poems*, Edinburgh, 1928

Burrow, G.W.S., *The Anglo-Norman Era in Scottish History*, Oxford, 1980

——, *Robert Bruce*, Edinburgh, 1976

Calderwood, David, *The History of the Kirk of Scotland*, Edinburgh, 1843

Chambers, Robin, *Traditions of Edinburgh*, Edinburgh, 1868

Coventry, Martin, *The Castles of Scotland*, Musselburgh, 2001

Cranstown, J. ed., *Satrical Poems of the Reformation*, Edinburgh, 1891

Davies, John, *Douglas of the Forests*, Edinburgh, 1980

Davis, I.M., *The Black Douglas*, London, 1974

Donaldson, Gordon, *Reformation*, Cambridge, 1979

Douglas, Alfred, *Complete Poems*, London, 1928

Douglas, Edgar L., *The John Douglas Family of Mississippi*, Jackson, Miss., 1962

Douglas, Gavin, *A Selection from his Poetry*, ed. S. Goodsir Smith, Edinburgh, 1959

Douglas, Keith, *Collected Poems*, ed. E. Blunden, London, 1966

Douglas, Norman, *The South Wind*, London, 1947

Douglas-Hamilton, James, *The Truth about Rudolf Hess*, Edinburgh, 2002

Duncan, A.A.M., *Scotland: The Making of the Kingdom*, Edinburgh, 1975

Fawcett, Richard, *Scottish Medieval Churches*, Edinburgh, 1985

Fischer, T.A., *The Scots in Germany*, Edinburgh, 1902

——, *The Scots in Sweden*, Edinburgh, 1907

Forbes Leith, W., *The Scots Men-at-Arms and Life-Guards in France*, Edinburgh, 1882

Fraser, Antonia, *Mary Queen of Scots*, London, 1994

Fraser, W., *The Douglas Book*, Edinburgh, 1885

Froissart, Jean, *Chronicles of England, France and Spain*, ed. and trans. T. Johnson, London, 1805–10

Gray, John M., *Lord Selkirk of Red River*, London, 1963

Henry, the Minstrel, *Harry's Wallace*, ed. M. McDiarmid, Edinburgh, 1969

Hewitt, George, *Scotland under Morton*, Edinburgh, 1982

Historic Scotland, Guidebooks for Bothwell Castle, Tantallon, Hermitage, Aberdour etc.

Holland, Richard, *The Buke of the Howlat*, ed. P. Barricutt and F. Riddy, Edinburgh, 1987

Hume, David, of Godscroft, *The History of the House of Douglas and Angus*, Edinburgh, 1996

Hunter, James, *A Dance called America*, Edinburgh, 1994

Johnson, Samuel, *The Letters*, ed. Redford, Oxford, 1992

Labanoff, A.I., *Lettres et mémoires de Marie Stuart*, 1844

Lang, Andrew, *The Myths of Mary Stuart*, Edinburgh, 1901

Leslie, John, *The Historie of Scotland*, trans. J. Dalrymple, Edinburgh, 1895

Lindsay, Robert, of Pitscottie, *The History and Chronicles of Scotland*, Edinburgh, 1899–1911

Lyle, E., ed., *Scottish Ballads*, Edinburgh, 1994

Macaulay, Thomas, *History of England from the Accession of James II*, London, 1889

Macdonald, Alastair, *Border Bloodshed*, Edinburgh, 2000

Macdougall, Norman, *James III*, Edinburgh, 1982

——, *Church, Politics and Society*, Edinburgh, 1983

——, *James IV*, East Linton, 1997

McGladdery, C.A., *James II*, Edinburgh, 1990

McHarg, J.F., 'Finding the lost *Lyon*', *History Scotland*, Mar. 2003

McKean, Charles, *Scottish Château: The Country House of Renaissance Scotland*, Stroud, 2000

Mahon, R.H., *The Tragedy of Kirk of Field*, Cambridge, 1930

Mary Queen of Scots, *Lettres . . . de Marie Stuart, Reine d'Écosse*, ed. A. Labanoff, London, 1844

Maxwell, Herbert, *A History of Dumfries and Galloway*, Edinburgh, 1896

——, *A History of the House of Douglas*, London, 1902

Nicholson, Ranald, *Scotland: The Later Middle Ages*, Edinburgh, 1978

Pennant, Thomas, *A Tour in Scotland*, Warrington, 1774

Ramage, C.T., *Drumlanrig Castle and the Douglases*, Edinburgh, 1876

Riach, C.C., *Douglas and the Douglas Family*, Hamilton, 1927

Royal Commission on the Ancient and Historical Monuments of Scotland, *Edinburgh*, 1914; *East Lothian*, 1924; *Roxburghshire*, 1956; *Selkirk*, 1957

Scott, R.M., *Robert the Bruce*, Edinburgh, 1993

Scott, Walter, *Poetical Works*, Edinburgh, 1869

Stringer, K.J., ed. *Essays on the Nobility of Medieval Scotland*, Edinburgh, 1985

Sumption, J., *The Hundred Years War*, London, 1990

Tancred, G., *The Annals of a Border Club*, Jedburgh, 1903

Tuck, Anthony, *Border Warfare*, London, 1979

Weir, Alison, *Mary Queen of Scots and the Murder of Lord Darnley*, London, 2003.

Wordsworth, William, *Collected Poems*, ed. J. Hayden, London, 1977

Wynton, Andrew of, *Orygenale Cronyklil*, ed. D. Laing, Edinburgh, 1879

Yeoman, P., *Medieval Scotland: An Archaeological Perspective*, Edinburgh, 1995

Index

208

Index